ROCK 'N' ROLL MONSTERS

THE • AMERICAN • INTERNATIONAL • STORY

Hemlock Books

England

PICTURE CREDITS: *Allied Artists, American International Pictures (AIP), American Releasing Corp, Anglo-Amalgamated Distributors Ltd, Anglo-EMI Film Distributors, Associated British Pathe, Border Films, Brent Walker Film Distributing, British Lion Film Corporation, Cannon Film Distributors Ltd, Cinecenta Film Distributors, Columbia Pictures, David Frankham, Denis Meikle, EMI Film Distributors, Film Traders Ltd, Filmways Pictures, Golden Era Film Distributors, Hemdale, Joseph Burstyn, Lippert Pictures, MGM-EMI, New Realm Entertainments, RKO Radio Pictures, The Film Group, Tigon Pictures, Transcontinental, Twentieth Century Fox Film Co, United Film Distribution Co, Warner-Pathe Distributors, Woolner Brothers Pictures. Any omissions will be corrected in future editions.*

Visit our website:
www.hemlockbooks.co.uk

First published in 2016 by
Hemlock Books Limited,
Maritime House,
Suite Oscar 3,
Basin Road North,
Hove
BN41 1WR

A CIP catalogue record for this book is available from the British Library.

ISBN 978-0-9933989-3-3

Design by Hemlock Books Limited.

Printed in Great Britain by Marston Book Services Ltd., Didcott, Oxon, OX11 7AW

ROCK 'N' ROLL MONSTERS

THE • AMERICAN • INTERNATIONAL • STORY

BRUCE G HALLENBECK

To the memory of my paternal grandmother, Martha Hallenbeck, who saw (and loved) many of these films with me; to my best critic and true love, Rosa Hallenbeck; and to the great David Frankham, an actor whom I've admired since I was seven years old.

Acknowledgements

The writing of this book would not have been possible without the invaluable assistance of the following: as always, my peerless publisher and extraordinary editor, Denis Meikle, the late Hazel Court, for her memories of *The Premature Burial*, *The Raven* and *Masque of the Red Death*, Tony Earnshaw, for providing me with an unpublished interview that he had conducted with Robert Fuest, Valli Kemp, for her memories of Vulnavia and *Dr Phibes Rises Again*, Jonathan David Dixon, for going above and beyond the call of duty and putting me in touch with David Frankham–and also my profound thanks to David himself, for providing the Foreword to the book and for his generosity and kindness in supplying some wonderful photographs from the filming of his two AIP classics, *Master of the World* and *Tales of Terror*. David's eloquence and prodigious memory have added tremendously to what I hope is a comprehensive work on a unique company in American cinema: American International Pictures.

CONTENTS

FOREWORD BY DAVID FRANKHAM

I am pleased and honoured to be asked to write a Foreword for Bruce Hallenbeck's history of AIP. In retrospect, working on my two AIP films really brought me the happiest memories of my career. They were a wonderfully creative group of people and it was a privilege to be part of their team. As a devoted movie fan myself, it also gave me the chance to work with some of my idols from the Golden Age of movies–Vincent Price, Basil Rathbone and Henry Hull.

I moved to the US in 1955 with no acting experience, but armed with a burning desire to be an actor. Thanks to an unexpected chain of events involving Alec Guinness and Angela Lansbury's agent husband Peter Shaw, I found myself debuting in front of NBC's live cameras on *Matinee Theatre* the following summer–petrified at the prospect of acting before a viewing audience of 25 million. But all went well and NBC gave me five more *Matinee Theatre*s to do by year's end. By then I had joined an acting group to learn my craft as quickly as possible!

Early in 1957, I got my Screen Actors Guild membership as a result of being cast in Disney's *Johnny Tremain.* That big-screen debut consisted of two words–'After them!'–spoken from behind a tree. But I was thrilled that I was in a real Hollywood movie!

I was totally in awe all over again in 1959 staring up at 6'4" Vincent Price on the first day's shooting of *Return of the Fly.* He had a huge appetite for life and acting and I was to learn much from him in our two subsequent films together. On our first meeting on the set, he snarled at me, 'I like a social set, kid. There's a chair with your name on it out there. Get your ass out here *now!'*–to break the ice and help me get over my awe of him. I remember his growling in my ear all during the shoot, 'I hope you know you have the best part in the movie, kid!' - just to bolster my confidence.

Return of the Fly was my favourite role because of the beautifully-written scene between me and Dan Seymour (the veteran of *Casablanca, To Have and Have Not, Key Largo* and *Johnny Belinda).* At the end of the master take, the crew broke into applause and I joined them. Dan acknowledged the tribute, beckoned me to join him and said, 'This is for you too, David.' Nothing in my 32 years out there has quite matched that moment of feeling I belonged.

I thoroughly enjoyed making horror and science fiction films. More than 'normal everyday life films,' they gave me the opportunity to really let loose at times.

I remember Vincent's wonderful surprise for me during the filming of my first AIP film, *Master of the World,* when he took me to an adjoining soundstage under the pretence of a publicity shoot–only to introduce me to one of my M-G-M idols, June Allyson, with the remark, 'Be back on the set in ten minutes, kid'–and then he walked away, leaving me speechless in front of her. And I recall another astonishing

surprise on *Master of the World*: after Vincent overheard me telling our co-star Mary Webster that I had just moved into an unfurnished house and had only a bed, I was surprised the next morning–a Saturday morning–by an out-of-the-blue phone call asking me if I could use any furniture.

Me: Gosh, yes.

Vincent: I live at (giving his address).

Me: But–I don't drive.'

Vincent: Christ, you mean I have to pick you up as well as furnish your house?

He then proceeded to drive back and forth in his station wagon all that morning, from my little house to his block-long mansion, transporting chairs, tables, lamps, even cutlery. And, as a reward, as he left and bent over to pet my Siamese cat Dara, she let rip on his right arm, drawing blood, while I frantically ran around looking for band-aids.

On *Tales of Terror,* the following year, I remember him breaking up with laughter, take after take, at my failure to lift petite little Debra Paget off the floor in the final scene: 'He can't even get her off the floor! Haw!'

Overall, my memories are of the laughter we shared on those three movies.

And yes, I really did climb down that rope at the end of *Master of the World.* I was scared to death... but Charles Bronson did it first–fearlessly, of course, and then I couldn't back out. It was a *long* drop to the sand below.

On *Tales of Terror,* I was nervous at first about working with Basil Rathbone because I had admired him so much in all his classic roles in *Robin Hood, Zorro, Sherlock Holmes*... Also, he scared me to death in *David Copperfield* when I was 10, as the evil Mr Murdstone, beating the tar out of Freddie Bartholomew. I had to ask my parents to keep a light on at night because I was terrified Mr Murdstone would come get me.

But at the read-through in Roger Corman's office before filming, I discovered that Basil had a wonderful sense of humour and no pretensions at all. For our week of filming I saw first-hand his legendary tremendous energy. His energy level was exactly the same after a full day of filming as it was in the morning - he was ramrod straight, never drooping. He and Vincent were obviously old friends and I was secretly envious when I would hear Vincent say at the end of a day, 'Come over to the house for supper tonight.' I wanted to go too, to spend more time with them and listen to their stories!

I thoroughly enjoyed working with Debra Paget and in 1961, she was as beautiful as in any movie I had seen her in previously. I didn't get to know her well because we were trying to film so much in such a short time, but she was super-professional and needed no direction from Roger Corman. She was focused and pleasant and seemed a bit shy.

I didn't meet Sam Arkoff, but James Nicholson was a daily visitor to the *Master of the World* set and occasionally joined us all for lunch. There was no question in my mind that he was the creative head of AIP. He was deeply involved in the day-to-day production. He was a very sophisticated, elegant man and I admired him.

I had such a good experience working with AIP that when I heard they were going to do future pictures in my home country of England for cost reasons, I asked for a meeting with Mr Nicholson. I offered to pay for my own transportation to the UK and to arrange my own lodgings with friends and family. He was very nice, but firm, and he said, 'Frankly, we can't afford you, David. American actors' salaries are beyond our budget in England.'

The last time I saw Vincent Price was in 1990, at a Weekend of Horror at the Los Angeles Hilton. We appeared on a panel with Roger Corman, interviewed by Tim Burton. At that point Vincent was very frail, needing to be helped up on the platform by two young men. He stumbled as he took a step up, but I knew better than to insult his pride by reaching out to help him.

After the event, as he was walking away, Vincent turned back to me and said his last words to me: 'Old age sucks, kid!'

As I wrote at the beginning of this Foreword, working on my two AIP films was the happiest experience of my career, because of the camaraderie on both sides of the camera. For those two movies, I felt I belonged to a family–seldom the case for a working actor–and it was a very creative family. I know Bruce's book will give you a deep sense of that family, from its beginning to its end.

All my best,
David Frankham

The terrifying story that COULD COME TRUE!
DAY THE WORLD ENDED
ATTACKED ...by a creature from hell!
starring RICHARD DENNING
LORI NELSON
ADELE JERGENS
CERT. X
SUPERSCOPE
ALL NEW! ALL TERROR!
SEE! THE WORLD ENDED BY ATOMIC FURY!
SEE! THE HORRIBLE "MUTANT" WHO SEEKS A MATE!
SEE! THE TERRIFYING "BEAST" ON THE OCEAN FLOOR!
SEE! FANTASTIC WORLD OF DEATH AND HORROR!
SEE! THE BATTLE FOR LIFE AT THE BOTTOM OF THE SEA!
THE SHOW THAT SHOCKED AMERICA!
FREEZING HORROR! ...A LIVING NIGHTMARE FROM THE DEPTHS OF THE SEA!
THE PHANTOM FROM 10,000 LEAGUES
starring
KENT TAYLOR · CATHY DOWNS
MICHAEL WHALEN
WIDE SCREEN
DISTRIBUTED BY
ANGLO AMALGAMATED FILM DISTRIBUTORS LTD.
Hammer House, 113-117, Wardour St., W.1.

1 FAST AND FURIOUS

NICHOLSON, ARKOFF AND AMERICAN RELEASING

In the early 1950s, the American film industry was in trouble. Threats to its dominance in the entertainment field were arriving on several different fronts. The Paramount Anti-Trust Consent Decree, which separated ownership of cinemas and production companies, had come into effect on January 1, 1950. More and more young couples were marrying and moving out to the suburbs, which was cutting into the profits of city-centre cinemas. International revenues were under attack from protectionism, including quota acts and import taxes. In the age of McCarthyism, the patriotism of the Hollywood product–and that of its producers, directors, writers and actors–was being questioned.

But the biggest threat was a four-syllable word: television. According to the US Census Bureau, weekly cinema attendance had dropped from an all-time high of 90 million in 1946 to 60 million by 1950. During and after the war, Americans had money to spend and only a few ways to spend it: petrol had been rationed, numerous consumer goods were limited because of the war effort, and the movies had enjoyed a virtual monopoly in mass entertainment; although radio thrived, it was no match for the motion picture screen. Television was another matter, however, and when sales of TV sets began to go through the roof, movie attendance decreased exponentially. In 1951, a poll conducted by Warner Bros noted that TV ownership was responsible, even at that early date, for a 3-4% drop in the audience. The omens were not good, as the take-up of television sets continued to grow year on year.

James H Nicholson

The Paramount anti-trust ruling did not directly hurt film attendance, but it ignited a firestorm between the studios and exhibitors. The idea behind the action was both that the break between studios and cinema owners would lead to greater competition throughout the industry and that it would bring about more product from independent producers who were not tied to major studios such as Warner Bros, Universal-International, 20th Century Fox, Paramount and M-G-M.

It was against this backdrop that two men from the Midwest–America's heartland–set out to change the film business. The first was James Harvey Nicholson, a lifelong movie buff who had transformed his parents' basement into a cinema whilst still in grade school. The films that he showed to his family were either rented from the local camera store or homemade. His sister Betty sold tickets for a penny and presided over the concession stand, where the goods consisted primarily of soda pop.

Born in 1916, James Nicholson was a teenager during the Depression years. Due to economic hardship, his parents, Percival and Esther, had been forced to split up and move in with *their* respective parents. Nicholson moved to Florida with his father, while Betty went with her mother to Washington.

Nicholson and his grandmother did not get along so when he was sixteen, he took a bus to San Francisco, where he had been promised a job as an usher at the El Ray Theatre. Nicholson gained valuable experience at his first job, and left his high school in Florida where he had been class president. At the El Ray, he worked the concession stand, tore tickets, ran the elevator and eventually became projectionist. He also helped to arrange special screenings to raise money for the Red Cross.

Nicholson had sinus problems which ultimately led to his decision to move to a warmer climate. Los Angeles, although not exactly known for its air quality, was his chosen destination, but he came down with scarlet fever and headed back to Omaha, where his parents had been reunited now that the Depression was over. They nursed him back to health, and he went to work for the Goldberg Theatre chain, managing two of their cinemas, the Avenue and the Arbor.

While collecting receipts from one of the theatres, Nicholson was shot by a thief who had climbed onto the running board of his car. The robber made off with a bag containing $1,500, but the bullet only grazed Nicholson's chest and he was quickly patched-up by a local doctor.

Nicholson met his future wife, Sylvia Svoboda, while working for the Goldbergs. She was an usherette with the chain. They were married after a whirlwind courtship–six weeks!–and then they decided to move back where the show business action was: Los Angeles. Nicholson picked up there where he had left off. He worked in several different branches of 'entertainment', including radio and burlesque houses, until a benefactor named Joseph Moritz helped him to purchase a small chain of cinemas. (Nicholson was one of the first theatre owners to show a closed-circuit television transmission on a cinema screen with the 1949 Rose Bowl game.) His mainstay, however, was in booking double-feature pairings of studio classics such as *The Maltese Falcon* and *Casablanca*, calling his cinemas The Academy of Proven Hits. When other exhibitors got wind of his success, they hit on the same idea and subsequently cornered the market, leaving Nicholson with nothing to show on his own screens. The business dwindled to the point where he and his wife were forced to live in one of their own theatres, the Market on Hollywood Boulevard. Nicholson doubled as the projectionist and Sylvia sold the tickets.

Samuel Z Arkoff

The stress caused Nicholson to fall ill and one of his lungs collapsed; Leon Blender, a friend and manager for Realart, a re-releasing company owned by Jack Broder and Joseph Harris, took up a collection so that he could get hospital care. When he recovered, Nicholson decided to leave the exhibition business and go into distribution. It was then that Nicholson's path crossed with that of Samuel Zachary Arkoff, a show business lawyer who was also from the Midwest (in his case, Iowa).

Arkoff's father Louis had immigrated to the

US from Russia. At the age of nineteen, Louis became an apprentice goldsmith, then worked for a jeweler in Chicago, before moving to Iowa where he met his future wife, Helen Lurie. There, he opened the Louis Clothing Company. His son Samuel, born in 1918, was, like Nicholson, a natural-born movie fan. When Sam was fifteen, he went to the Chicago World's Fair and saw his first copy of the trade magazine *Variety*, an event which changed the course of his life. He continued to read *Variety*, at 15 cents a week to the guy who ran the local pool hall, and dreamed of one day becoming a movie mogul.

In 1942, Arkoff entered the Air Force as a cryptographer. During this period, he met his wife-to-be, Hilda Rusoff, on a blind date. Arkoff kept his dreams of being a film producer to himself; instead, he hoped that becoming a lawyer might somehow lead to his goal of working in films.

After the war, Arkoff enrolled at Chicago's Loyola University, which hosted an accelerated course for veterans. On graduating, he headed for Hollywood and secured a post at the Lawyer's Building between Hollywood Boulevard and Sunset. Gradually, he built up a list of clients, most of whom were would-be film producers. One was a former Air Force buddy, Hank McCune and he and McCune formed a company called Video Associates to produce projects for television; together, they sold McCune's idea for a situation comedy, *The Hank McCune Show*, to the National Broadcasting Corporation (NBC). The series began as a local LA programme in 1949, but NBC put it on its national prime-time schedule during their 1950-1951 season. Filmed on 16mm without a studio audience, the show had the dubious distinction of being the first series to include a laugh-track, or 'canned laughter', as it came to be called. After its national premiere on September 9, 1950, *Variety* noted: 'Although the show is lensed on film without a studio audience, there are chuckles and yocks dubbed in. Whether this induces a jovial mood in viewers is yet to be determined, but the practice has unlimited opportunities if it's spread to include canned peals of hilarity, thunderous ovations and gasps of sympathy.'

At a time when most TV programming was live, Arkoff and McCune's innovation was short-lived and the series was cancelled after three months. Undeterred, Arkoff continued to nurture his relationship with the Hollywood fringe. One of his clients at the time was London-born Alex Gordon, who had served in the British Army from 1942 to 1946. At that point, he joined Renown Pictures, whose most famous release was the 1951 classic *Scrooge* (released in the same year as *A Christmas Carol* in the US), starring Alastair Sim in the title role.

Gordon had emigrated to America in 1948 to work at the Walter Reade Theatre Circuit. For a time, he was the public relations director for cowboy star Gene Autry. Gordon wanted to be a producer, however, and he had found a job on a low-budget western called *Outlaw Marshal*. The man behind this obscure opus was none other than Edward D Wood Jr, later notorious as the director of such Z-grade schlock as *Glen or Glenda* (1953) and *Plan 9 From Outer Space* (1959).

The production was so disorganised and poorly funded (part of it was financed by a Mormon bishop) that the film lab refused to release the print and Gordon was forced to find an attorney. As he later told Mark Thomas McGee for his book *Fast and Furious: The Story of American International Pictures*: 'It got to such a state that I needed a lawyer.. So that's how I first met Arkoff. I walked into his office and I told him what my problem was and that I had no money and he agreed to take the thing on, on a contingency basis. He wanted to get into production and he saw in me a way towards production and distribution because I'd been involved with my brother (Richard) in British productions and things like that.

'It took two years to get the picture out. The backers attached the picture so it couldn't leave the lab. Although Arkoff and I managed to get a release deal, first with Lippert, then Jack Broder, the backers would not lift the attachment. They insisted on being paid.. We were standing in a small room with all of these investors and Arkoff was talking to them and trying to explain to them that the only way they were going to get their money back was to let us release the picture.. Finally they agreed and United Artists took the picture on.'

Gordon had submitted an unsolicited script to Realart Pictures called *The Atomic Monster*. Realart then reissued the 1941 Universal horror film *Man Made Monster*, starring Lon Chaney Jr and Lionel Atwill, under the same title. Arkoff, who was a big, burly fellow and could appear intimidating, decided to pay Broder a visit; he left the meeting with a cash settlement of $500.

Having witnessed this incident, Nicholson asked Arkoff for his business card; he was amazed that anyone could get any money out of his notoriously tight-fisted boss. Nicholson and Arkoff got together and agreed to form a production company from Arkoff's office, and the American Releasing Corporation was established to produce and distribute independent (but highly exploitable) films. The question then became: what films, and where would they find them?

Fortuitously, they soon came across a fledgling producer-director named Roger Corman. Born in Detroit on April 5, 1926, Corman had ended up in California when his family moved there. His father had been an engineer and had retired to Beverly Hills. Corman had studied engineering himself at Stanford University but after receiving his degree, his 'career' at US Electrical Motors had lasted all of four days. He told his boss he had 'made a terrible mistake' and moved on.

Roger Corman

Corman had decided that his real interest was the film business and he got a job in the mail room at 20th Century Fox. Eventually, he worked his way up to the position of 'story reader', where he read a script for the film that would become *The Gunfighter* (1950), starring Gregory Peck. The script, by William Bowers and André De Toth, had been written with John Wayne in mind but the final draft (by Bowers and William Sellers) bore many changes, some of them suggested by Corman himself, along with writer Nunnally Johnson.

When Corman received no credit on the film, he became disenchanted with Fox and set out to work in the industry as an independent. He studied English at Oxford before returning to Los Angeles to look for ways to begin his film career in earnest.

Corman eventually sold a script that he had written called *The House By the Sea* to Allied Artists, for which he received the princely sum of $3,000. An additional incentive was a credit as associate producer, which he hoped would also make it easier for him to finance his own projects. *The House By the Sea* was released

Highway Dragnet

in 1954 as *Highway Dragnet* and starred Richard Conte and Joan Bennett. With his first film under his belt, Corman teamed up with a writer named Wyatt Ordung to make a science fiction film entitled *The Flaming Sea*. After raising $17,000 between them, they filmed the movie in six days, mostly at the beach near Santa Monica. By the time filming was completed, the title had been changed to *It Stalked the Ocean Floor*.

Ordung knew that James Nicholson, whom he had met at Realart, was looking for a film to start up his own distribution company and he organised a meeting between Nicholson, his wife Sylvia, and Corman. But they could not work out an agreement that satisfied all parties and Corman ended up selling the film to Lippert Pictures, which retitled it *Monster From the Ocean Floor,* for $110,000–quite a return on his paltry investment. When put into general release in May 1954, *Monster From the Ocean Floor* grossed an impressive $850,000. Corman was off and running as a film producer, having received a $60,000 advance from Lippert.

Corman used the money to produce his next picture, *The Fast and the Furious* (1954), originally known as *Crashout*. It was an early example of what would later be called a 'road movie', starring John Ireland and Dorothy Malone. Shot in ten days, with Corman producing and Ireland directing along with Edward Sampson,

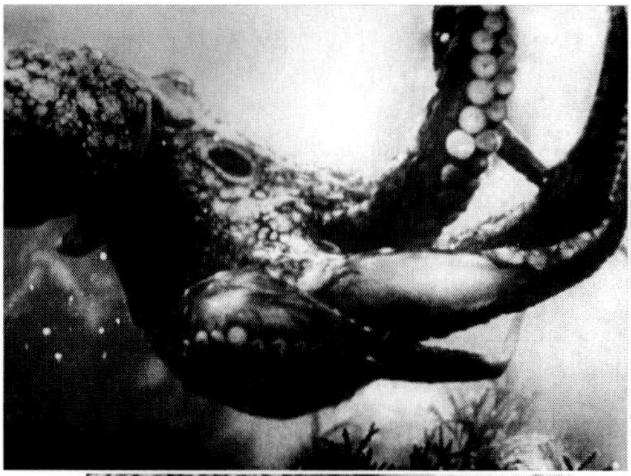

Monster From the Ocean Floor (Anne Kimbell)

the film included many exploitable elements in a plot dreamed up by Corman, Jean Howell and Jerome Odlum: a man on the run kidnaps a young woman as he escapes in her Jaguar. She tries to flee several times and their mutual antagonism eventually turns (rather improbably) to love. As they continue to elude capture, they slip into a cross-border road-race that will take them safely to Mexico.

When the film was completed, Corman took it first to Republic Pictures, who offered to distribute it. But ever canny about money, Corman was reluctant to accept the deal, which would have tied up his finances for several months. He was looking for a 'fast and furious' return on his $66,000 investment so that he could start work immediately on another project. Corman contacted Nicholson and gave him thirty days to come up with a better deal.

Nicholson borrowed money for travel expenses and took Corman's film around the country by bus. He secured deals with dozens of sub-distributors, everywhere from Buffalo to Los Angeles, and Corman was so impressed that he signed instead

The Fast and the Furious

The Fast and the Furious (John Ireland, Dorothy Malone)

with American Releasing. It was, to quote Humphrey Bogart's Rick in *Casablanca*, 'the beginning of a beautiful friendship'.

The Fast and the Furious is a tight, efficient little film. The two leads play well off each other and, considering the fact that it was shot in ten days, the production

values are solid and the monochrome cinematography very effective. For such a tiny film, it has left a lasting legacy: the plot was used again for a movie called *The Chase* (1994), starring Charlie Sheen and Kristy Swanson, and, of course, the rights to the title (though not the story) were purchased by the producers of 2001's *The Fast and the Furious* starring Vin Diesel and Paul Walker, which became a hugely successful franchise around the world.

In the beginning, American Releasing Corporation was a true family business. Nicholson's wife Sylvia was its secretary, while Alex Gordon wrote the copy for the company's press releases. Arkoff's brother-in-law, Lou Rusoff (a former social worker who had written for radio and TV), became the in-house scriptwriter. Bartlett A Carré, who had been a production manager on 'B' westerns in the 1930s before becoming production supervisor on the likes of W Lee Wilder's *Phantom from Space* (1953) was appointed to the same position at ARC.

Wages were low and Arkoff lived off his legal fees for the first eighteen months. After the release of *The Fast and the Furious,* Nicholson announced to the press that the newly-formed American Releasing had plans to make no less than eight features in 1955, four of them in colour. 'We are not interested in Academy Awards,' he said. 'Only in pictures which the exhibitor can play with the assurance that he will make a profit.'

Westerns were big business in the fifties, so ARC decided to make *Five Guns West*. It was to be directed by Corman, who cast John Lund, an actor who had made his film debut in *To Each His Own* (1946) with Olivia de Havilland for Paramount, as the male lead. Dorothy Malone was brought back to co-star, while others in the cast included Mike 'Touch' Connors and Corman's friend Jonathan Haze (who had appeared in the first two of Corman's films). The script was written by Haze's friend Robert Wright Campbell, for which he was paid a paltry $200.

Corman was so nervous about directing for the first time that on his way to the

***Five Guns West* (Dorothy Malone, John Lund)**

set, he pulled his car to the side of the road and threw up. During lunch, he sat apart from the cast and crew in an effort to compose himself. On the nine-day shoot, Corman went over his budget, which meant that money for the next production had to come out of his own pocket. Nevertheless, *Five Guns West* turned out to be a very serviceable mid-fifties oater. Filmed mostly at the Iverson Ranch near Chatsworth, LA, it was competently made, with colour cinematography by Floyd Crosby, who had shot *High Noon* (1952). Crosby would also become an important player in Nicholson and Arkoff's new company.

The plot of *Five Guns West* was relatively simple: the Malone character runs a stagecoach station with her father. Five outlaws who have just been pardoned by the Confederate Army arrive at the station to await the arrival of a gold shipment that they intend to steal. Malone becomes their hostage but the outlaws turn against one another. Lund is a Confederate officer who plays both ends against the middle and ultimately saves the woman–and the day. (Screenwriter R Wright Campbell, under the name of Bob Campbell, played one of the outlaws. Corman, Nicholson and Arkoff economised wherever they could; Corman had even driven one of the racing cars in *The Fast and the Furious*.)

As a result of his overspend on *Five Guns West*, Corman had only $33,000 to make his next film for ARC. This meant that he could not afford a union crew, nor could he direct it, as he was himself a union member. But he had in his possession a sci-fi script called *The Unseen,* written by Tom Filer, so he gave both the script and the budget to production assistant David Kramarsky. Meanwhile, Nicholson concocted an ad-campaign that became the first–and possibly the most extreme–example of the company's lurid ballyhoo. Nicholson thought that the original title was too bland

The Beast With a Million Eyes (Lorna Thayer, Dona Cole)

and he came up with a more sensational (and exploitable) alternative: *The Beast With a Million Eyes*. The new title was a reference to the notion in the script that its alien entity could 'enter' into the bodies of animals and humans, thereby providing it with a 'million' available eyes. Nicholson had an equally lurid poster created, showing a woman in a swimsuit menaced by a multi-eyed creature from space.

(ARC's style of exhibition was inspired by that used in the 1940s by such 'poverty row' studios as Producers Releasing Corporation, who ground out films with titles like *The Devil Bat* (1940), *The Mad Monster* (1942), *Hitler's Madman* (1943) and *Machine Gun Mama* (1944). The titles would come first and a plot would be cooked up around them.)

Nicholson loved science fiction. He had joined a sci-fi club while he was in high school which had been run by none other than Forrest J Ackerman, the super-fan who later became the editor of *Famous Monsters of Filmland*. (In fact, Nicholson and Ackerman published a short-lived fantasy fanzine together during their high school days.) He was far more enthused about producing a science fiction film than he had been about producing a western, but the question for Corman was: how to compete with current blockbusters like *This Island Earth* on a budget of $33,000?

A small but effective cast was assembled by Corman and his director Lou Place, previously Corman's assistant on *Five Guns West*, and the new film was to be shot in a desert location near Indio and the Coachella Valley in California. The cast included Paul Birch, an Alabama-born actor who had appeared as one of the outlaws in *Five Guns West*; also signed was Lorna Thayer, who would achieve her fifteen minutes of fame in 1970 in *Five Easy Pieces*, as the waitress who refuses to give Jack Nicholson a side order of wheat toast. Other roles were filled by Dona Cole, who would add the injection of sex-appeal, and silent screen comedian Chester Conklin.

Nine days into the filming, the union got wind of the production and threatened to shut it down. Corman called Kramarsky from the set and told him that he would have him join the union and they would finish the picture together. There were still forty-eight pages of interiors to be shot and only two days in which to complete them. Corman turned to Floyd Crosby to replace Everett Baker, a college professor, and he and Kramarsky took over the direction from Place. The film was brought in on time, but in something of a rush. Corman reportedly said to Crosby, 'I don't care whether the mike is in the shot or not.. Let's just finish this thing.'

The final result was shown to distributors at Pathe Labs in Hollywood. Most of those in the audience had seen the poster of the 'Beast' and were dismayed to find that there was no visible beast in the film. In fact, there were no effects at all, save for a spacecraft partly buried in the sand with a propeller spinning on top! According to Arkoff, the craft was actually a modified tea-kettle.

The screening was a disaster, but Nicholson and Corman determined to salvage the film. Corman contacted Forrest Ackerman, who was now a writers' agent as well as a collector of fantasy film memorabilia. Ackerman suggested to Corman that he get

hold of his friend Ray Harryhausen, who had just made *It Came From Beneath the Sea,* which featured a giant octopus terrorising San Francisco. Corman had heard, however, that Harryhausen had charged '$10,000 a tentacle' for the film and he had a paltry $200 to offer for the creation of a 'beast' that he said need just be 'a hand puppet or something'. Ackerman pointed out that $200 would barely cover the cost of materials but he knew a young artist named Paul Blaisdell, who currently worked for a sci-fi magazine.

Blaisdell hailed from Newport, Rhode Island, grew up in Quincy, Massachusetts, and attended the New England School of Art and Design in Boston. He had been drawing and building models since he was a child. After marrying and moving to California, he worked with Douglas Aircraft, but he had ended up illustrating sci-fi magazines with Ackerman as his agent. Years later, in his own magazine, *Fantastic Monsters of the Films*, Blaisdell 'explained' why the beast that he had created for the film was not a little underwhelming: 'The monster that appears with the hypnotic spiral superimposed over him is actually the slave of the beast with a million eyes. The true "beast" is never shown,'

Too little, too late, as things turned out. The Beast, dubbed 'Little Hercules' by Blaisdell, was not so much a disappointment as an unmitigated disaster, its brief appearance at the climax limited to a few barely-animated shots obscured by a cheap optical effect. Kramarsky was not pleased with the additional scenes and asked the lab to print the shots darker, to better disguise the poor effects. For whatever reason, this did not occur and the film went out with 'Little Hercules' clearly visible to viewers, who were uniformly unimpressed. At the preview, cards were given to the audience for them to critique the film. Responses included, 'Television is better' and, 'Fumigate the theatre.'

The film, which revolved around the exploits of a family operating an isolated farm in the California desert who are terrorised by the titular beast (or its slave), did not exactly set the world on fire, although there was one early example of Corman's ability to spot and discover talent hiding in the credits: the art director was Albert S Ruddy, who would later become the Academy Award-winning producer of such films as *The Godfather* (1972) and *Million Dollar Baby* (2004).

David Kramarsky was ultimately credited as director, with neither Corman nor Place receiving any credit for their contributions. *The Beast with a Million Eyes* was relegated to the bottom half of double bills, which meant that ARC's returns would be minimal. In the face of a word-of-mouth failure which even the usual exploitational advertising billboards could not compensate for, ARC needed a new strategy.

The rigid Motion Picture Production Code, which had been in force since 1934, was beginning to weaken in the face of foreign films such as Vittorio De Sica's *Bicycle Thieves* (1948), Giuseppe De Santis's *Bitter Rice* (1949) and Ingmar Bergman's *Summer With Monika* (1953), all of which dealt with more adult themes than American films of the time would dare to explore. The chink in the armour of the Code had come about in 1952, when the US Supreme Court overturned a 1915 decision which had held that films were a business to be regulated, and not an art form. The 1952 ruling accorded First Amendment protection to motion pictures, and the decision had come about because of a short film directed by Roberto Rosselini called *The Miracle,* which New York State had sought to ban because of its controversial subject-matter: it centered on a man (played by Italian director Federico Fellini) who deliberately impregnates a disturbed peasant woman (Anna Magnani) who believes herself to be the Virgin Mary. *The Miracle* was half of a portmanteau piece called *L'Amore*; the other half, also directed by Rossellini, was called *The Human Voice* and based on a play by Jean Cocteau. The Supreme Court realised that *The Miracle* was far from an exploitation film and the floodgates were opened to more adult fare on the American screen. In consequence, the fifties became the decade of Marilyn Monroe and Jayne Mansfield, of *Playboy* Magazine and imported 'shockers' like Roger Vadim's *And God Created Woman* (1956), starring wife Brigitte Bardot in various states of undress.

Nicholson and Arkoff were up to speed with the changing *mores* of the American public and the easing of the Production Code. They were aware that audiences desired to see things in films that they could not see on television, and sex was gradually added to the quota of required ingredients. Although tame by modern standards, there is a sequence in *The Beast With a Million Eyes* in which the daughter of the house (Cole)

L'Amore (Anna Magnani)

strips to a swimsuit and frolics in a pond, where she is spied upon by the family's dim-witted handyman (Leonard Tarver) who leers at her suggestively. The man then retires to the shed where he sleeps, surrounded by photos of half-naked women. He picks up a 'girlie' mag, leafs through its pages, and turns his back to camera...

Meanwhile, Alex Gordon wanted to put together a horror film called *King Robot* with friend and horror icon Bela Lugosi, who had now fallen on hard times. Gordon's brother Richard had produced a film called *Old Mother Riley Meets the Vampire* with Lugosi in Britain in 1952. It was the last of the long-running Old Mother Riley series starring Arthur Lucan. The two wanted to shoot additional scenes with Lugosi and cut out the scenes with Lucan (who meant nothing to American audiences), so that they could release it in the States. By 1955, however, Lugosi was bloated with the medication for his morphine addiction and his appearance had changed drastically; it was impossible to match his *Old Mother Riley* scenes with any new footage, so the project was scrapped. By way of consolation, ARC asked Gordon to produce another western to be directed by Corman, called *Apache Woman*. Gordon looked about for suitable 'names' to cast in the leads and he came up with Lloyd Bridges, Joan Taylor and Lance Fuller.

Lloyd Bridges had been in films since the thirties but had recently made a mark in both *High Noon* (1952) and Jacques Tourneur's *Wichita* (1955). Taylor, a Columbia contract player, had also appeared in a number of westerns, including *Fighting Man of the Plains* (1949) and *War Paint* (1953). Kentucky-born Fuller had appeared in *This Island Earth* but Gordon had been impressed by his performance in the Republic western *Cattle Queen of Montana* (1954). Other cast members included ARC regulars Jonathan Haze, Paul Birch, Lou Place, Chester Conklin and a friend of Haze's named Dick Miller, who was cast as an Indian called 'Tall Tree'. Miller was a native of the Bronx, New York, who had served in the US Navy and had earned a prize title as a middleweight boxer. He had moved to LA in the 1950s and *Apache Woman* would be his first film role. He would later become one of the most ubiquitous actors in the Nicholson-Arkoff repertoire.

Shot in ten days, *Apache Woman* was not a box office success either, even though it cost only $80,000 to make. Filmed at Ray 'Crash' Corrigan's Ranch in Simi Valley, California, it opened in LA as a second feature to the Audie Murphy war movie *To Hell and Back*. Arkoff said later that *Apache Woman* took ten years to turn a profit, and did so only when it was sold to television.

Apache Woman (Lloyd Bridges)

While Corman was directing *Apache Woman,* ARC picked up another western called *Outlaw Treasure* for distribution from Johnny Carpenter (with whom Arkoff had worked on *The Lawless Rider*; 1954). It was also at around this time that the company released a British quasi-documentary called *Operation Malaya,* for which writer-producer Herman Cohen put together the American version. Cohen would later become an important player in the story.

In September 1955, when *Apache Woman* went into general release, ARC issued a press release to trade paper *Film Daily* which read, in part: 'American Releasing Corp, by mid-1956, will increase its rate of release to one a month, according to James H Nicholson, president. ARC in its first year has delivered seven pictures, with the output to be nearly doubled next year.' It was an ambitious schedule, to say the least, especially in view of the fact that the company's films had yet to make a profit. As Mark Thomas McGee observed in *Fast and Furious:* 'Essentially ARC was a B-picture company but nobody could stay in business any longer making B pictures because B pictures got flat rentals. To stay alive, ARC needed to get a percentage of the box office.'

But Nicholson and Arkoff had a plan: if ARC could not make a profit producing second features, then they would make their own double-bills. And so was born the 'Top Shock Show of All Time' in the form of *Day the World Ended* and *The Phantom from 10,000 Leagues* (1956). Both were written by Lou Rusoff, Arkoff's brother-in-law, who would specialise in scripts which exploited the then-current fear of nuclear radiation. 'More than any other writer, Lou had a real appreciation for what we were trying to do,' Arkoff said later. 'He understood how to keep costs down by limiting the number of sets and locations. He framed his scripts beautifully into our titles and artwork. And he always kept a sense of humour, which was a real virtue under hectic circumstances.'

In the case of *Day the World Ended,* Nicholson had come up with the title and then commissioned Rusoff to do the script. Alex Gordon was the executive producer and casting director, and he wanted a couple of 'names' to top-line the picture. He

Day the World Ended

chose Richard Denning, who had previously appeared in Universal-International's *Creature from the Black Lagoon* (1954) to portray Rick, the heroic scientist of the piece. And he cast Lori Nelson, who had starred in *Revenge of the Creature* (1955) for the role of Louise Maddison, the put-upon heroine.

The plot of *Day the World Ended* involved an eclectic group of people, including a rancher, a gangster, his 'moll' and a geologist (Denning), holed up in a remote cabin after an atomic war, where they must battle a hideous mutant (Paul Blaisdell again) to survive. The geologist and the gangster also fight for the affections of the rancher's daughter (Nelson). After a reasonable amount of carnage, the film ends on a hopeful note with the cleansing rain washing away the radiation and Denning and Nelson walking into the sunset, hand-in-hand, as the words 'The Beginning' appear onscreen instead of end-titles.

Gordon cast some of the one-time B-movie stars that he so much admired in supporting roles. As Ruby the gangster's girlfriend, he went for Adele Jergens, who had played many a 'tough dame' in the likes of *Blonde Dynamite* (1950), *The Sound of Fury* (1950) and *Abbott and Costello Meet the Invisible Man* (1951). The buxom Brooklyn-born actress was perfect for the sassy but sad Ruby, whose boyfriend was played by Mike 'Touch' Connors. Gordon cast another favorite, Raymond Hatton, in the secondary role of Pete. Hatton was a veteran of silent films such as *The Hunchback of Notre Dame* (1923) with Lon Chaney, as well as many subsequent westerns like *Tall in the Saddle* (1945) with John Wayne. ARC regular Paul Birch returned to the fold as rancher Jim Maddison, and Jonathan Haze appeared in the small but memorable role of 'contaminated man'. Even Roger Corman got in on the act, appearing uncredited in a cabin photograph. The narrator–though he received no screen credit–was famed American news announcer Chet Huntley.

With Corman once again at the helm, *Day the World Ended* was filmed over a ten-day period, with three days of location work at Griffith Park, Bronson Canyon, and the Sportsman's Lodge in the San Fernando Valley. Made for a budget of just

***Day the World Ended* (Richard Denning, Paul Birch)**

over $96,000, some $7,500 (plus a percentage) was allotted to star Denning. ARC managed to keep its post-production costs to a minimum as Arkoff had an ongoing agreement with Pathé Labs in which it agreed to defer the payment for prints.

The shooting itself ran smoothly enough, although Blaisdell endured a couple of nasty falls in his 'mutant' costume because he could not see properly while he was wearing it. But the low budget also inspired moments of ingenuity: Bob Burns, who worked as an assistant on the film, recalled, 'In *Day the World Ended,* they stumbled upon this human skull that's been cannibalised. It had some skin left on it. That was the chicken left over from somebody's lunch!'

For the supporting feature, Nicholson and Arkoff worked out a deal with two film editors, Dan Milner and his brother Jack, to produce *The Phantom From 10,000 Leagues* for more or less the same price as *Day the World Ended.* Again based on a title that Nicholson had come up with, the script by Lou Rusoff starts out like a mystery, in the manner of Gordon Douglas's *Them!* (1954): charred, radioactive corpses start turning up on the Pacific coast. A government agent (Kent Taylor) attempts to get to the bottom of the deaths, while at the same time falling for an attractive young oceanographer (Cathy Downs) who lives near the beach. It transpires

The Phantom From 10,000 Leagues (Vivi Janiss, Michael Whalen)

Day the World Ended (Adele Jergens)

that the oceanographer's father (Michael Whalen), a local marine biology professor, has caused an ordinary sea turtle to mutate into a radioactive monster which has naturally gone on the rampage as a result.

Taylor was a popular B-movie actor who had appeared in modest programmers such as *Pirates of the Skies* (1939) and who had also starred as detective *Boston Blackie* on US television since 1951. Downs was a former Fox contract player who had once been groomed for major success by none other than director John Ford in *My Darling Clementine* (1940), but stardom had eluded her and she had ended up in a variety of minor westerns.

The sexpot role in *The Phantom of 10,000 Leagues* was taken by Helene Stanton, who had just appeared in Joseph H Lewis's *noir* thriller, *The Big Combo.* Stanton's role was far from the only sexy one in ARC's first double feature, however. Once again, Nicholson and Arkoff put all the exploitable elements into the production that the censors would allow. Both carnage and carnality were well represented. In *Day the World Ended,* Jergens performs a partial striptease and in *Phantom,* Downs has one of the first shower scenes in a genre film, during which she strips down to her bra before reappearing dressed only in a towel.

These elements worked wonders at the time, for despite the fact that both films are fairly indifferent in terms of overall production quality, the combination of *Day the World Ended* and *The Phantom from 10,000 Leagues* paid off handsomely for ARC: within two months of their release, the double bill had earned $400,000 and made a tidy profit for the company. It was not a moment too soon, as Arkoff noted: 'They had to make money. We literally could not afford failure.'

Putting out two films at a time instead of the usual one had shown the way to the future for ARC, and its next duo was the pairing of *Female Jungle* and *The Oklahoma Woman. Female Jungle* was a 'pick-up'–an independent film picked up for distribution after completion. It was directed by Bruno VeSota and written by him and Burt Kaiser.

Bruno VeSota was an interesting character–an actor-director who was the son of Lithuanian immigrants. He had worked in radio, film and TV and his first credit had been in a television production of Poe's *The Tell-Tale Heart* in 1947. He had also directed several episodes of a series

Female Jungle (Jayne Mansfield)

Female Jungle (Jayne Mansfield, Burt Keiser)

called *They Stand Accused* (1949). *Female Jungle,* which was shot in late 1954, was his first feature as director, and he scored something of a coup by persuading Jayne Mansfield to star.

Born Vera Jayne Palmer, Mansfield was famed for her self-proclaimed 41" bust. While attending the University of Texas in Austin, she had won several beauty contests and in 1950 had accepted a bit part in a movie called *Prehistoric Women.* Her first real acting job was a small role on the *Lux Video Theatre* television series in 1954, but her most prominent appearance came when she posed nude for the February 1955 issue of *Playboy.* Her statuesque figure made a memorable impression on regular readers of Hugh Hefner's 'adult' mag and her career was off and running. She soon signed on with 20th Century Fox for Frank Tashlin's *The Girl Can't Help It* (1956), a follow-up of sorts to Billy Wilder's *The Seven Year Itch* (1955), which had starred Marilyn Monroe. *The Girl Can't Help It,* which co-starred Tom Ewell from the previous film, featured Mansfield in the type of blonde bombshell part that Monroe had made famous and it catapulted her to stardom.

VeSota's film had actually been produced before the *Playboy* shoot and he and Kaiser had tried (and failed) to sell the distribution rights to both Paramount and Allied Artists. Now that Mansfield was famous, however, ARC jumped at the chance to distribute *Female Jungle,* and it became the company's one and only venture into film *noir.*

Female Jungle had a troubled production history. Its original star was Kathleen Crowley, an actress who specialised in seductive roles in both television and films; she had recently appeared in the sci-fi thriller *Target Earth* (1954), acting opposite Richard Denning. But during the shooting of *Female Jungle*–which was filmed in a mere six days–Crowley alleged that she had been raped by two men in downtown Los Angeles. Consequently, she felt unable to continue on with the production and it was decided to beef up the secondary role that was being played by Mansfield. Additional scenes were shot using a double for Crowley, and the film was completed on schedule.

The singular cast included Lawrence Tierney, who had specialised in gangster

The Oklahoma Woman (Richard Denning, Peggie Castle)

movies after playing the title role in *Dillinger* (1945), and second billing went to none other than John Carradine, veteran of many a Universal horror film, including *The Mummy's Ghost* and *House of Frankenstein* (both 1944). Prior to his typecasting in horror, Carradine had proved himself to be a fine actor in such as Edgar G Ulmer's *Bluebeard* (1944). Both VeSota and producer Kaiser also took roles in the film.

Production values on the film may have been low–it was rumoured that Mansfield was paid a mere $150 for her role–but it was made with enough style to garner a good reception, helped enormously by Mansfield's Amazonian presence. *Female Jungle* was also notable for representing Tierney's return to the screen after a prolonged absence, during which time his off-screen bar-brawls and arrests had kept him out of the Hollywood spotlight for several years.

The co-feature, *The Oklahoma Woman*, marked Corman's return to the western, and also the return of Richard Denning and Cathy Downs. The film co-starred yet another blonde bombshell, Peggie Castle, who had appeared in several of the same, including *Wagons West* and *Jesse James's Women* (both 1954). 'Touch' Connors was back as well, as were Jonathan Haze and Dick Miller in character roles. Bruno VeSota joined them on the cast-roster.

Written by Lou Rusoff, *The Oklahoma Woman* treads familiar territory: after six years in gaol, Steve (Denning) arrives to claim a ranch that has been left to him

Gunslinger (John Ireland)

in a will. His home town is in the midst of a corrupt election that is being presided over by saloon owner Marie (Castle). Steve finds himself on the side of the opposing candidate, in part because of the man's attractive daughter (Downs). But the town's sheriff (Martin Kingsley) seeks to gain by setting each side against the other, and thereby hangs the tale.

Corman directed with his usual efficiency, and Ronald Stein, who would score many of Corman's horror films, provided the music. With the marketing for ARC's latest double bill emphasising the sex angle–the tagline for *The Oklahoma Woman* was 'Queen of the Outlaws, Queen of Sin!', while that of *Female Jungle* was, 'As the night grows dark, the women turn deadly'–Nicholson and Arkoff found themselves with another successful dual-release to crow about.

Corman directed one more western in 1956–*Gunslinger,* this time penned by Charles B Griffith and Mark Hanna. Griffith, who was born in Chicago, would quickly become a member of ARC's 'family'. Born into a family of actors and performers, he broke into show business by writing scripts for the radio serial *Myrt and Marge,* in which his mother and grandmother acted. Griffith was recommended to Corman by Jonathan Haze, and the canny director hired him to write *Gunslinger*. It became his first motion picture credit.

Gunslinger can claim a number of 'firsts' for ARC. It was the first film to star Beverly Garland, who had appeared in the *noir* classic *DOA (*1950*)*, in which she was credited as Beverly Campbell. (She was also in the sci-fi film *The Neanderthal Man* [1953], in which she was raped by the title character!) *Gunslinger* was the first of many appearances for Nicholson, Arkoff and Corman.

The same was true of the voluptuous Allison Hayes, who had made her debut in *Francis Joins the WACS* (1954). In her second film, *Sign of the Pagan* (1954), she played opposite Jack Palance. Stunningly beautiful, and with acting talent to spare, Hayes would go on to become a B-movie icon in the likes of *Attack of the*

50 Foot Woman (1958) for Allied Artists, which is now considered to be a camp classic.

In the lead on this occasion was John Ireland, returning to the ARC fold, and the single-sentence plot had Garland as an unlikely female sheriff who finds herself at odds with a saloon owner (Hayes) who hires a 'gunslinger' (Ireland) to murder her. As an early example of female emancipation, both in story-terms and in front of the camera, Corman's film was something of a groundbreaker–albeit for exploitation reasons rather than the advancement of womanhood!

Corman's brother Gene, who was also starting out as a producer, had warned him against making another western because of problems with exterior shooting, trouble with horses and so forth. Corman had ignored his brother's advice and begun filming *Gunslinger* in February 1958, attempting to shoot it in six days before a change in union contracts came about which would limit actors to working only five days a week instead of six. He later described the experience as 'one of the worst' of his life.

Gene Corman, despite his own misgivings, had provided half the financing for the film and it was shot at the Jack Ingram Western Movie Ranch in Topanga, California, where it rained for five out of the scheduled six shooting days. Corman had to go

over–something he rarely did–and it took seven days to complete. The rain turned the whole location into one gigantic mud-puddle, causing trucks, cameras and just about everything else to sink into the ground. The weather forced several rewrites, and many exteriors were switched to interiors to keep things moving.

Both Hayes and Garland sustained injuries during production. Hayes's horse slipped in the mud and threw her, breaking her arm. While the crew waited for an ambulance to arrive, the ever-improvisational Corman shot a number of close-ups of Hayes looking left and right, in the hope of cutting them in to the film while using a double for long-shots of the hapless actress. Garland, for her part, twisted her ankle running down stairs in the saloon. The next day, despite the fact that her ankle had swollen to almost twice its normal size, Corman insisted on continuing to shoot with her also. The crew had to cut out the back of her boot and tape it to her foot in order to make it fit. In *Fast and Furious,* Garland was quoted as saying, 'With Roger you always worked.. I mean, you could have one eye hanging and he'd just shoot you from another angle. You really had to be a trouper. But he was a brilliant man.'

***Gunslinger* (Beverly Garland)**

Despite the various problems, the character that Garland played in *Gunslinger* became one of her own personal favorites. In the biography *Beverly Garland: Her Life and Career,* she told Deborah Del Vecchio, 'I think I was the first woman to play a marshal in a movie western. Roger would often cast against type in those days. I could never resist a plum role like a lady marshal in a genre that would never have considered such a gender reversal like that before.'

Gunslinger was Roger Corman's fourth and final western. It was also the last film for ARC. The company was growing and westerns were no longer engendering the kind of cash that Nicholson and Arkoff desired to make. There was a new audience in town, one which did not want to stay home in the evening to watch TV: an audience for whom no one was catering–that was almost completely untapped...

A *teenage* audience.

2 AMAZING! COLOSSAL!

JUVENILE DELINQUENTS AND GIANT MONSTERS

Roger Corman had proven himself to be a fast and efficient filmmaker, but Nicholson and Arkoff realised that if they needed to churn out several films a year, they could hardly rely on only one director, *wunderkind* or not. So it was that James Nicholson introduced Alex Gordon to director Edward L Cahn.

Cahn had been making films since the thirties and his 1932 feature, *Law and Order*, starring Walter Huston, Harry Carey and Andy Devine, had greatly impressed Nicholson when he had seen it in his youth. Since then, Cahn had made a number of *Our Gang* shorts interspersed with occasional second features such as *The Great Plane Robbery* (1950) with Tom Conway and Margaret Hamilton. More to the point for Nicholson and Arkoff was that Cahn had just directed the sci-fi/horror *Creature With the Atom Brain* for Columbia's 'B' unit, penned by *Wolf Man* scriptwriter Curt Siodmak and starring Richard Denning.

Gordon liked Cahn from the outset and it was decided that he would produce and Cahn would direct a film called *Girls in Prison*, written by Lou Rusoff. Shortly after that decision was made, Nicholson and Arkoff changed the name of American Releasing Corporation to American International Pictures; they felt that the company was growing and it needed to go 'international' in scope in order to keep generating business. Besides, the new name sounded more impressive.

Girls in Prison was calculated to turn a profit; it was AIP's first real 'sexploitation' picture–an erotic tease with implicit lesbian undertones, starring Richard Denning, Joan Taylor and Mae Marsh. During the filming, an official from the Production Code

warned Gordon that even a hint of lesbianism, whether in dialogue or action, would have to be struck from the screenplay. Gordon ignored the edict and went ahead with the script as written.

The plot for the film became the basis for every 'woman in prison' film thereafter: Anne (Taylor) is sent to a penal institution after being found guilty of participating in a bank robbery. She finds herself incarcerated with three beautiful cellmates in tight-fitting uniforms, Jenny (Adele Jergens), Dorothy (Phyllis Coates) and Melanee (Gilbert). The latter makes a play for Anne, but the kindly prison chaplain (Denning) has taken an interest in both her and her predicament.

The implied lesbianism and the film's generally rough tone, along with its stylish opening in which a torch singer in a low-cut cocktail dress warbles a siren song while the main characters are introduced *sans* dialogue, helped to make *Girls in Prison* a hit, alongside co-feature *Hot Rod Girl,* directed by Leslie H Martinson. The latter was not a Golden State Production (Gordon's company) but was produced for AIP by Norman T Herman, the company's accountant, in a deliberate attempt to grab the attention of the so-called 'teenage' audience; the ploy worked, thanks to the catchpenny title and the presence in the cast of Lori Nelson, Chuck Connors and Frank Gorshin. The story, written by John McGreevy, is a trifle about illegal street racing but its atmosphere of 'wild' teenagers, burger-joints, dragstrips and hot rods proved an intoxicating brew. The score by Alexander Courage (who would later compose the theme for television's *Star Trek*) included a song called 'Hot Rod Rock', which completed the package.

Part of AIP's new approach was to make its advertising campaigns even more blatantly exploitative than those for *The Beast with a Million Eyes* and *Day the World Ended*. The poster for *Girls in Prison* highlighted the 'cat fight' between Taylor and

Alex Gordon, Mari Finley, Richard Denning, Helen Gilbert

Hot Rod Girl / LEFT: Girls in Prison

Helen Gilbert, and has since become a collector's item. (All of AIP's posters would prove ultimately to be of more enduring quality than the films themselves!)

The very word 'teenager' first came into accepted use in the 1950s, primarily as a result of the 'Be-bop' groove in hit parade records, such a those by Frankie Lymon and the *Teenagers*. Teens were a post-WW2 phenomenon; a new generation which was wealthier and had therefore become more independent and free-thinking than that of its parents. Because of the growing prosperity of the postwar era, it was also able to buy more goods, such as clothes, records and movie tickets.

Teenagers arrived at the same time that rock 'n' roll exploded as a new musical form, thanks to the likes of Bill Haley and the Comets and Elvis Presley. Rock 'n' roll had its roots in rhythm and blues, gospel music and country and western. Disc jockey Alan Freed is credited with being the first person to have coined the term to describe the music that he was playing on a Cleveland, Ohio, radio station in 1951.

By 1955, rock 'n' roll was a musical sensation, with singers such as Carl Perkins, Jerry Lee Lewis and Buddy Holly joining Elvis in the charts. It was inevitable that this phenomenon would spread to the cinema, and Bill Haley's 'Rock Around the Clock' was employed in the opening credits of Richard Brooks's seminal 'juvenile delinquent' drama *Blackboard Jungle*, starring Glenn Ford, Anne Francis and Sidney Poitier. The song–and the film–became instant classics. The record had been released the previous year but had only sold moderately well; after its appearance in the film, 'Rock Around the Clock' reached number one on the US Billboard charts and the rest is rock history.

AIP wanted in on the trend, but Nicholson and Arkoff had to do so on a budget. *Hot Rod Girl,* in particular, had been aimed at that new youthful audience and when released together with *Girls in Prison* in July 1956, it had paid off.

The trend was still in its infancy, however, and making films for a specifically teenage audience was something of an experiment on the part of AIP. Realising that science fiction films, especially those featuring 'monsters', were a sound investment, Nicholson and Arkoff commissioned Alex Gordon to produce a movie called *The She-Creature*. The title had actually been suggested by one of AIP's exhibitors, Jerry Zigmond, who said he did not have a story to go along with it but thought it was 'a great title'. Always eager to please their customers, AIP had agreed.

Nicholson asked Gordon to come up with $40,000 of the film's proposed $104,000 budget. Israel Berman, a friend of Gordon's brother Richard, knew a financier named Jack Doppelt, who agreed to stump up the $40,000.

The She-Creature was ultimately scripted by Rusoff. The story was inspired by the popularity of a non-fiction work called *The Search for Bridey Murphy* by Morey Bernstein, a Colorado businessman and amateur hypnotist. In the book, he claimed to have used a technique called hypnotic regression to put housewife Virginia Tighe into a trance in which she was able to recall her 'past life' as a nineteenth-century Irishwoman. The book became a sensation–despite its dubious claims–and Rusoff

decided to base his story for *The She-Creature* on a similar case of reincarnation, combining it with overt elements of the 'monster movie'.

Cahn was brought back to direct and wanted his old friend, distinguished actor Edward Arnold *(The Devil and Daniel Webster*; 1941), to star as the hypnotist. Cahn also notionally cast Peter Lorre in a supporting role. But Arnold died two days before production began and when Lorre read the script, he promptly turned it down. Cahn then asked John Carradine to play the hypnotist, but he turned it down also.

Ultimately, Chester Morris, an actor who had been in Hollywood movies since 1917, agreed to take on the role of Dr Carlo Lombardi. It was not his first flirtation with the genre; he had played the title role in *The Bat Whispers* in 1930! Tom Conway, the younger brother of perennial star George Sanders, agreed to essay the role that had been destined for Lorre. Conway had carved out his own niche in Hollywood as 'The Falcon' in a series of 'B' mysteries, and he had also given fine performances in two of Val Lewton's best horror films, Jacques Tourneur's *Cat People* (1942) and *I Walked with a Zombie* (1943).

Cathy Downs returned to the fold to play Dorothy Chappel, Conway's daughter in the film. Andrea Talbott, the subject of the regression in the story, was played by Marla English, a former model who had signed a contract with Paramount Pictures in 1952. English had played a bit part in Hitchcock's *Rear Window* (1954), but her Paramount contract had led nowhere and she had found herself working in B-movies such as *Desert Sands* (1955) and *Three Bad Sisters* (1956)–which meant that she was now within AIP's price range.

Rusoff's outlandish script took the concept of hypnotic regression to its ultimate extreme: Talbott is unwittingly regressed to a past life as a prehistoric sea creature, half human-half crustacean. Lombardi discovers a way to introduce the creature into the present as a physical entity and he uses it to commit murder. One weakness of Rusoff's script is that Lombardi's motives are never clearly delineated, but AIP had a commercial-sounding screenplay that combined a monster–a 'female' with enormous breasts, no less!–with the currently fashionable subject of reincarnation. Who would

The She Creature

The She Creature (RIGHT): Marla English / INSET: Chester Morris)

be concerned with a few implausibilities in the plot when the promise of mayhem and Marla English in skimpy attire were there to offset them?

Once again, Paul Blaisdell designed, built and played the monster. He was given a month to build it from scratch and could not afford foam rubber on the meagre budget that he had to work with, so he created his She-Creature out of cheaper 'black foam' and assembled it piece by piece. Bizarrely, he included six 'teeth' on the creature's abdomen. When he saw the finished result, Cahn asked what they were. 'I call them lunch hooks,' Blaisdell said. He then demonstrated that they actually worked by clenching his own stomach muscles and the jaw-like appendage closed. As Mark McGee put it in *Fast and Furious,* 'The horrific possibilities were immediately apparent. The monster could puncture someone to death during an embrace.'

One thing Blaisdell had not thought about was the fact that the She-Creature was supposed to be at home in the water. When it came to a scene with the creature actually in the sea, and shot at Paradise Cove in Malibu, Cahn instructed Blaisdell to walk into the surf. As the costume got soaked, it became heavier, and the waterlogged creature had trouble standing up in water, much less wading through it.

Blaisdell also had trouble with a scene in which he was required to break down a door to reach one of his victims. On the first take, he tripped over a piece of balsa wood that had splintered off the prop door and fell flat on his face. Not only was it embarrassing, the door had then to be replaced at additional cost. On the second take, he bounced off the new door and landed on his back; no one told him that the props department had run out of balsa and the replacement was made of pine!

Gordon had deferred his $2,500 producer's fee until the film returned its cost,

The She Creature (Chester Morris / INSET: Tom Conway)

which would take some eighteen months. *The She-Creature* is torpid and talky, but it has its merits. The black and white cinematography by Frederick West is often moody and evocative, and Ronald Stein's score is eerily effective, with striking cues which would turn up again in Roger Corman's *The Terror* (1963).

As usual, the most was made of Marla English's sex-appeal, and she is regularly in and out of a variety of revealing costumes. Some have called her AIP's Elizabeth Taylor, and her screen presence is certainly memorable. Old warhorses Conway and Morris chew the scenery, and the creature itself makes some effective appearances, despite Blaisdell's problems with the costume.

At script stage, the US censors were concerned that not too much of the creature's 'cleavage' should be displayed. Cahn and Blaisdell made sure that an appropriate amount of seaweed covered its size DD breasts. It is an original and novel creation–a buxom beast with whiskers, horns, armour-plating, ears that resemble corn stalks, lobster-like claws and what appears to be hair or seaweed flowing down the back of its misshapen head. Altogether, something from a drug-induced fever dream.

The obvious inspiration for the design would have been *The Creature from the Black Lagoon* (1954) and its two sequels, *Revenge of the Creature* (1955) and *The Creature Walks Among Us* (1956). Universal-International's creature was designed by Millicent Patrick, though her role in its creation was downplayed by the make-up artist on the film, Bud Westmore, who for fifty years received the sole credit.

The few newspapers which bothered to review *The She-Creature* were generally unkind to the film. *Motion Picture Herald* found it 'awkward' and 'pedestrian', but it did eventually turn a profit on a double bill with a second AIP 'monster movie', Roger Corman's *It Conquered the World.*

Corman produced and directed *It Conquered the World* from another Lou Rusoff script, but with Charles B Griffith doing some uncredited rewrites. The film featured an interesting cast: Peter Graves, who played Paul Nelson, had appeared in several sci-fi films, including *Red Planet Mars* (1952) and *Killers from Space* (1954)–the latter directed by W Lee Wilder, the brother of famed director Billy. Graves himself was the brother of James Arness, who had starred in both *The Thing From Another World* (1951) and *Them! (*1954). The third lead was Lee Van Cleef as Tom Anderson, a well-intentioned scientist who has made contact with an inhabitant from the planet Venus. Van Cleef also possessed monster-movie credentials, having appeared in *The Beast from 20,000 Fathoms* (1953) as the marksman who shoots the beast dead at the climax; Van Cleef would, of course, go on to international stardom in 'spaghetti' westerns in the 1960s, including Sergio Leone's *The Good, the Bad and the Ugly*, in which he would co-star with Clint Eastwood and Eli Wallach.

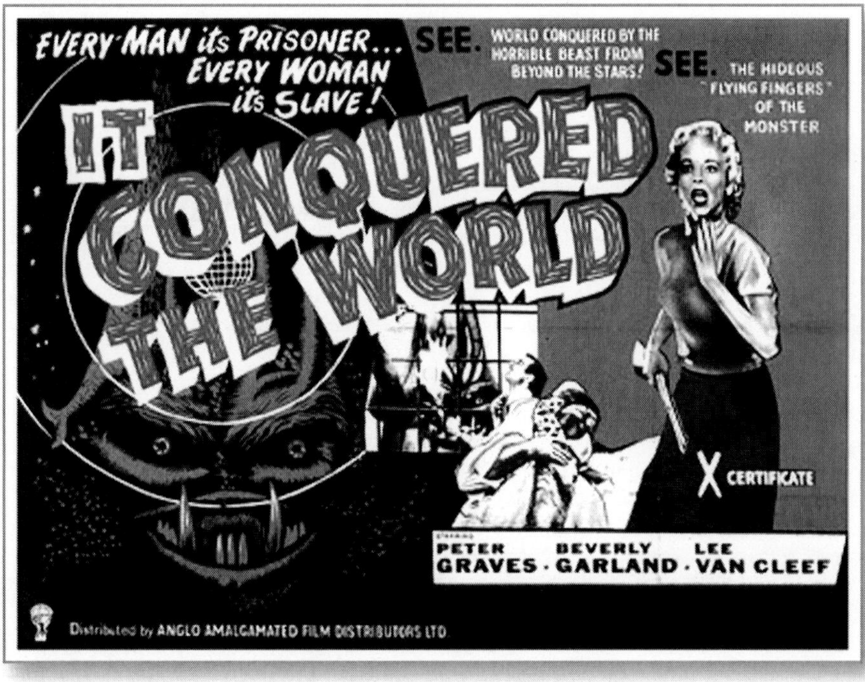

It Conquered the World (Beverly Garland, Lee Van Cleef)

The female lead in *It Conquered* was Beverly Garland, back for AIP and Corman in another tough, sassy role–that of Anderson's wife, Claire.

Before Rusoff had time to complete the script, his brother became seriously ill and he was called away to Canada, where the brother died soon after. Corman called Griffith in to finish things off a mere two days before the start of shooting, but 'Chuck' chose to take no credit for his contribution.

It was Corman who came up with the idea for the alien's design, thinking that as it was supposed to come from one of the larger planets, it would have had to evolve under a more oppressive gravity and would therefore have been low to the ground. When Garland first saw the short, squat costume, again built by Blaisdell, she asked sarcastically, '*That* conquered the world?' and promptly kicked it over.

In a 2005 *Senses of Cinema* article entitled, 'Little Shop of Genres: An Interview with Charles B Griffith', Griffith recalled, 'I called it Denny Dimwit and somebody else called it an ice-cream cone. I was around when Paul Blaisdell was building it, and he thought the camera would make it look bigger.'

The first day of filming took place in Bronson Canyon, one of the most familiar locations in Hollywood. Used as a background in countless B movies, the canyon is located above Hollywood Boulevard, off Franklin Avenue. Once a mineral quarry, it has four tunnels carved into it, the entrance to which can be used for a cave due to its unique aspect and the fact that it can be photographed from any angle without revealing a single sign of civilisation. It has been seen in everything from westerns to high-profile films like *Lost Horizon* (1937).

In the script, the Venusian–whom Blaisdell affectionately referred to as 'Beulah'–spends most of its time inside said cave, plotting world domination. Blaisdell built the creature to Corman's instructions but added his own concepts: he had read that Venus was more likely to harbour plant life than animal, so Beulah came to look like a squat, crab-clawed cucumber. He also thought that Corman would only film the creature in the semi-darkness of its cavern; in that, he was wrong.

It Conquered the World (Russ Bender)

Rounding out the cast were Corman regulars Dick Miller and Jonathan Haze as two of the GIs who battle the beast. But it is Van Cleef who despatches the Venusian with the help of a blowtorch to one of its eyes. An insert was shot of the eye-socket squirting blood (Hershey's chocolate syrup, in reality), to which the British censor initially objected but which was ultimately passed for exhibition.

Released theatrically with *The She-Creature, It Conquered the World* did good business and even garnered some favourable reviews: *Variety* called it 'a cut above' the usual B-movie fare.

The film is a calculated cross between such sci-fi classics as *The Day the Earth Stood Still* (1951), *Invaders from Mars* (1953) and Don Siegel's *Invasion of the Body Snatchers* (1956). Embittered scientist Anderson has guided the Venusian, one of the few remaining members of its race, to Earth. He believes that the creature has great wisdom and can save mankind from itself by using mind control to make humanity less emotional and therefore less prone to violence. The Venusian employs bat-like 'helpers' which attach themselves to the cortices of their victims. Eventually, Nelson convinces Anderson that he has been misguided and that the Venusian is bent on world conquest so that its own race might populate the Earth, and the two join forces to vanquish 'It'.

The film's low budget meant that 'conquering' the world consisted only of causing all forms of transport to stop working, a device pinched from *The Day the Earth Stood Still.* The marks on the necks of victims who are under the creature's control came from *Invaders from Mars,* while the idea of emotionless humans in thrall to aliens was an idea straight out of *Invasion of the Body Snatchers.* Nevertheless, *It Conquered the World* has a charm all of its own, in spite of its cheesy effects.

The screenplay is surprisingly adult. When Anderson assures his wife, 'I'll still need you when there are no emotions,' she retorts bitterly, 'For a few dollars you can hire a woman who'll fulfill all your fetishes. And when you get tired of her, you can run down to the employment agency and hire another.' When she then faces the

It Conquered the World (Beverly Garland)

monster down in its cave–which does not end well for her–she admonishes it: 'You think you're gonna make a slave of the world?–I'll see you in Hell first!'

Anderson's speech in sacrifice is equally strong, no doubt due to Griffith: 'I made it possible for you to come here.. I made you welcome to this Earth.. You made it a charnel-house!'

At the end of the film, after a reasonable amount of carnage in which many of the soldiers (a small contingent, of course, on a small budget) have been killed in their attempt to save the planet, Nelson waxes philosophical in voice-over as the camera draws far away from the Earth: 'He [Anderson] learned almost too late that man is a feeling creature–and because of it, the greatest in the universe. He learned too late for himself that men have to find their own way, to make their own mistakes. There can't be any gift of perfection from outside ourselves. And when men seek such perfection, they find only death.. fire.. loss.. disillusionment. The end of everything that's gone forward. Men have always sought an end to the toil and misery, but it can't be given; it has to be achieved. There is hope, but it has to come from inside–from Man himself.'

It was not Corman's first attempt at social commentary, which was almost par-for-the-course in the anti-bomb messages of most fifties' sci-fi movies, but it helped to raise the film 'a cut above', as *Variety* had indicated.

Cahn's next assignment after *The She-Creature* was a change of pace: a western. *Flesh and the Spur,* written by Charles B Griffith and Mark Hanna (with additional dialogue by Rusoff and Cahn) was originally entitled *Dead Man's Gun*. The film was produced by Alex Gordon and executive produced by star Mike 'Touch' Connors, who raised the $117,000 budget with the help of some Armenian friends (Connors was an Armenian-American, whose real name was Krekor Ohanion).

Connors was called to a meeting by Nicholson and Arkoff, whereupon he was shown a poster for the film featuring leading lady Marla English tied to a stake with fire-ants crawling over her half-naked body. When Connors pointed out there was no such scene in the script, the pair told him that the film had been pre-sold on the basis of the poster art (by Albert Kallis) and that the scene of English on the ant-hill would be written in later!

English, playing a Native American named Wild Willow, has several provocative scenes in the film, including the nude swim that marks her initial appearance. The storyline is basic: Luke Random (sci-fi icon John Agar of *Tarantula* and *Revenge of the Creature* fame) is searching for the man who murdered his twin brother. and Connors cast himself as villain Stacy Doggett, who has his eye on Willow. The torture of English on the ant-hill could have been more vivid but the ants would not co-operate; in Tom Weaver's *Science Fiction Confidential,* Gordon recalled that the ants (harmless ones, not fire ants) were dropped on the bound and gagged actress but, for whatever reason, they did not take to her and promptly disappeared to parts unknown. Freeing herself from her gag, English asked producer Gordon in exasperation, 'Look, you've got six ants there–isn't that enough?'

The ever-busy Cahn also directed *Runaway Daughters* that same year (1956), allegedly based on an incident from screenwriter Rusoff's time in social work. With a catchpenny title reminiscent of exploitation king Kroger Babb, *Runaway Daughters* is actually a sober and well-acted tale of teenage angst. László Benedek's *The Wild One* (1953) and Nicholas Ray's *Rebel Without a Cause* (1955) had explored teenage rebellion from the male point of view but AIP was the first studio to portray 'delinquent' females, and *Runaway Daughters,* while slow-paced, is one of Cahn's better efforts.

The film came about from AIP's research into audience viewing habits and the finding that 70% of filmgoers were now between the ages of 12 and 20. The company had already tapped into that viewership with its sci-fi films, but it wanted to exploit the drive-in audience more directly, in movies about teenagers themselves.

Flesh and the Spur thus became AIP's final western. Although modestly successful, Nicholson and Arkoff decided to concentrate on movies that would be aimed squarely

***Flesh and the Spur* (John Agar, Raymond Hatton)**

Flesh and the Spur (Mike Connors, Marla English)

at that 12-to-20-year-old audience. And *Runaway Daughters* did that in spades.

Marla English was the natural first choice for Audrey, one of the titular daughters. She was 23, but she had both a timeless beauty *and* the acting chops to pull off the role of a high school girl who falls for an older man. Another daughter was played by Mary Ellen Kay, who had appeared in a number of Republic westerns.

Gordon was less than thrilled to be making a movie about juvenile delinquents; he preferred working with old-style actors whom he knew, and he tried to shoehorn them into his films whenever he could. For *Runaway Daughters,* he cast Anna Sten as Audrey's mother. Sten had been discovered by M-G-M head Sam Goldwyn, who had brought her over from Russia to appear

Runaway Daughters (Marla English, Adele Jergens, Anna Sten)

Shake, Rattle & Rock! (Fats Domino)

in films such as *Nana* (1934). Her American career never really took off, however, and she was looking for work. Tom Conway was signed again to play her husband but, just before the shooting began, he was taken ill (Conway suffered bouts of alcoholism). Gordon contacted John Litel, another veteran who had lent his no-nonsense presence to the likes of *Jezebel* (1938); Litel was available and readily accepted Gordon's offer to replace Conway.

Runaway Daughters hit home with its intended audience. The plot concerned three troubled 'teenagers' with the usual family issues–parents and boyfriends–who find themselves unable to adjust, both at home and at school. They are tempted into a life of crime, with the predictable result. Although marred by a 'happy' ending that is all too abruptly tacked on, *Runaway Daughters* benefits from a thoughtful script and solid playing, especially from English and Kay.

The film's low budget is in some ways its greatest virtue. Whereas *The Wild One et al* had been produced by major studios, AIP's film exhibited a gritty realism that its bigger-budgeted counterparts lacked. It was also more sexually frank.

The companion feature to *Runaway Daughters* was even more blatantly aimed at the teen audience: *Shake, Rattle & Rock!* was a musical comedy and the title was a take-off of 'Shake, Rattle and Roll', a hit song made popular by Big Joe Turner, a blues singer from Kansas City, Missouri. Turner had been singing the blues since the '30s but in 1954, he had huge success with this rock 'n' roll number, which also helped to transform popular music. He had already sung the song on film for 1955's concert compilation *Rhythm and Blues Revue,* and he was invited by AIP to do the same in *Shake, Rattle & Rock!*

Once again, the ubiquitous Cahn directed under the supervision of Alex Gordon as producer. The duo also wanted Fats Domino in the film, playing himself as Turner would do; Domino, who hailed from New Orleans, Louisiana, had reached number two in the hit parade in 1956 with his rock 'n' roll version of 'Blueberry Hill'. Cahn and Gordon were so eager to sign Domino that they drove all the way to Ontario to watch him perform in a nightclub. Meeting him after the show, Gordon pointed out to Domino that his scenes for the film could be shot in a single afternoon. The singer told them that he had a free day in two weeks time and could work in his appearance then. At the time, Domino was under contract to Imperial Records, which was owned by Lou Chud. Chud agreed for Domino to receive only a modest sum for his one-day shoot–a mere $1,500–because he wanted him to have the exposure.

Five days before Domino was scheduled to appear in the film, Chud called Sam Arkoff to say that the deal was off, as Domino had been offered $25,000 to sing one song in the Fox movie *The Girl Can't Help It,* with Tom Ewell and Jayne Mansfield. Arkoff pointed out that he had Chud's letter of agreement and that he would use it to get an injunction to prevent Domino from working with Fox. Chud relented and the deal was on again. On the morning of the shoot, Gordon drove to the Roosevelt Hotel in downtown Los Angeles to pick up Domino and drive him to the set. At first, the hotel clerk told him that no one was registered in that name, then suggested that he might be staying at the *other* Roosevelt Hotel. When Gordon asked him where that was, the clerk replied, 'In the negro section.'

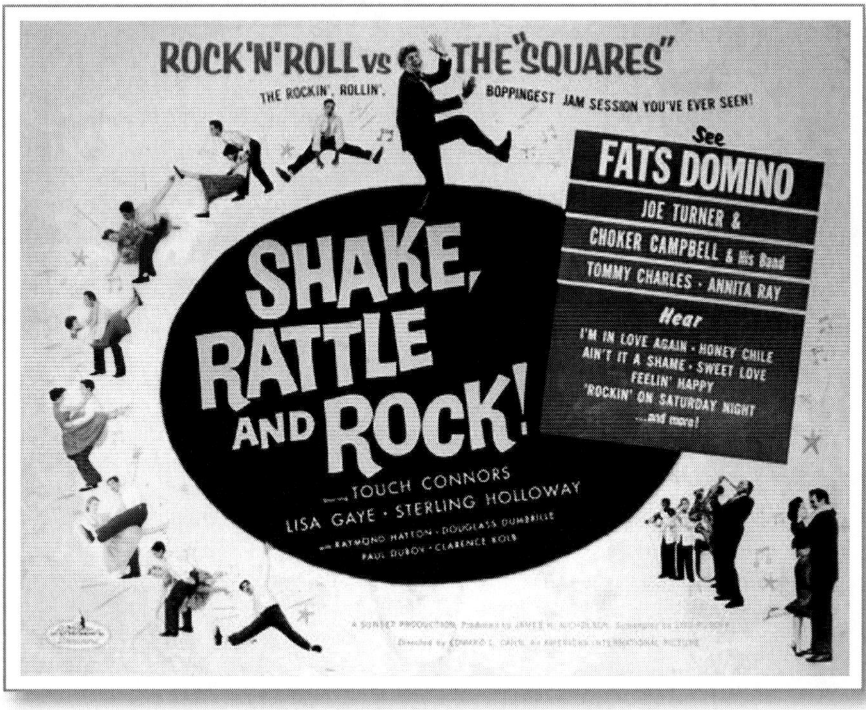

Gordon eventually found Domino and took him to the set, where he performed all three of his numbers–'I'm in Love Again', 'Honey Chile' and 'Ain't That a Shame'–in one take. The remainder of the movie was shot a few weeks later.

The plot of *Shake, Rattle & Rock!* is merely trifle on which were hung the musical numbers, and ultimately it became something of a cliché in rock 'n' roll movies: a group of 'square' adults try to ban popular music in their town because they think it is 'the devil's' work and encourages delinquency. But thanks to the local deejay, the teenagers manage to save their beloved rock 'n' roll.

Starring Mike Connors, the film also featured a number of Gordon's old chums–this, despite the accent on youth: distinctive character actor Sterling Holloway, who had voiced many a Disney cartoon character, veteran actor Douglass Dumbrille, who had been a pompous foil for the Marx Brothers in several films, Margaret Dumont, ditto, and Percy Helton, who had appeared in numerous B westerns such as Fred F Sears's *Fury at Gunsight Pass* (1956).

Shake, Rattle & Rock! (Big Joe Turner)

In the film, Big Joe Turner performed 'Feelin' Happy', 'Lipstick, Powder & Paint', 'The Choker' and 'Rock, Rock, Rock', while Tommy Charles–later a radio talk show host who would lead the boycott of the Beatles after John Lennon made his notorious 'more popular than Jesus' remark–sang 'Sweet Love on My Mind' and Annitta Ray warbled 'Rockin' on Saturday Night'. It was a substantial line-up for the likes of AIP, and the double feature of *Shake, Rattle & Rock!* and *Runaway Daughters* made a bundle for the company.

Viewed today with nearly sixty years of hindsight, *Shake, Rattle & Rock!* seems rather sweet and naïve–which it probably always was. The acting is mostly over the top, with Holloway especially egregious in that department, spouting 'hipsterisms' fast and furiously and sounding like his later characterisation of Winnie the Pooh, but on acid. There are some cringeworthy scenes, like the presentation that compares rock 'n' roll to African 'native' dancing, with the implication that the music is somehow 'sub-human'. For the most part, however, *Shake, Rattle & Rock!* is a time-capsule of late fifties musical trends and the film's greatest asset is its capture on celluloid of the performances of Domino, Turner and the rest.

Not that AIP had forgotten its sci-fi roots, as witnessed by its simultaneous pick-up for distribution of an ultra- low-budget indie production called *The Astounding She-Monster* (UK: *Mysterious Invader*), a dreadful, blissfully brief (62 minutes) clunker about a scientist (Robert Clarke) who finds himself trapped in a remote cabin with a gang of thugs who have kidnapped a rich heiress (Marilyn Harvey). The reason that they are trapped: a 'flying saucer' has crashed nearby and an alien (Shirley Kilpatrick) has emerged who can kill with a radioactive touch. In true AIP fashion, the alien is a sexpot in a skin-tight body suit; the only thing especially odd about her appearance is the fact that her eyebrows look like they are about to blast off a launching pad at any moment.

Flying saucers or 'UFOs' (Unidentified Flying Objects) were all the rage in the early 1950s, ever since a civilian pilot named Kenneth Arnold had reported seeing disc-like objects zipping through the sky as he flew over Mount Rainier, Washington, in 1947; Arnold noted that the objects moved as a saucer might when it 'skimmed across water', and so the popular concept of alien craft was born. In another incident that same year, an unknown object was alleged to have crashed in Roswell, New Mexico. The following day, newspaper headlines screamed, 'Air Force Captures Flying Saucer!' The Air Force later claimed that the downed object was merely a weather balloon, but conspiracy theorists thought otherwise and the notion of government cover-up also took hold. The *Astounding She-Monster* was only one of a raft of exploitation movies born out of the American public's fascination with this new 'threat' from outer space, and it was largely responsible for the whole 'sci-fi boom' in 1950s cinema.

The infamous Edward D Wood Jr was unofficial 'consultant' on *The Astounding She-Monster,* which gives an indication of the film's quality. It was released on the lower half of a double bill with Corman's spoofy *The Saga of the Viking Women and Their Voyage to the Waters of the Great Sea Serpent,* starring Abby Dalton and Susan Cabot, in which Jonathan Haze, as a Viking, had the immortal line, 'Get your filthy hands off her, you big slobbering dog!'

***The Astounding She-Monster* (Shirley Kilpatrick)**

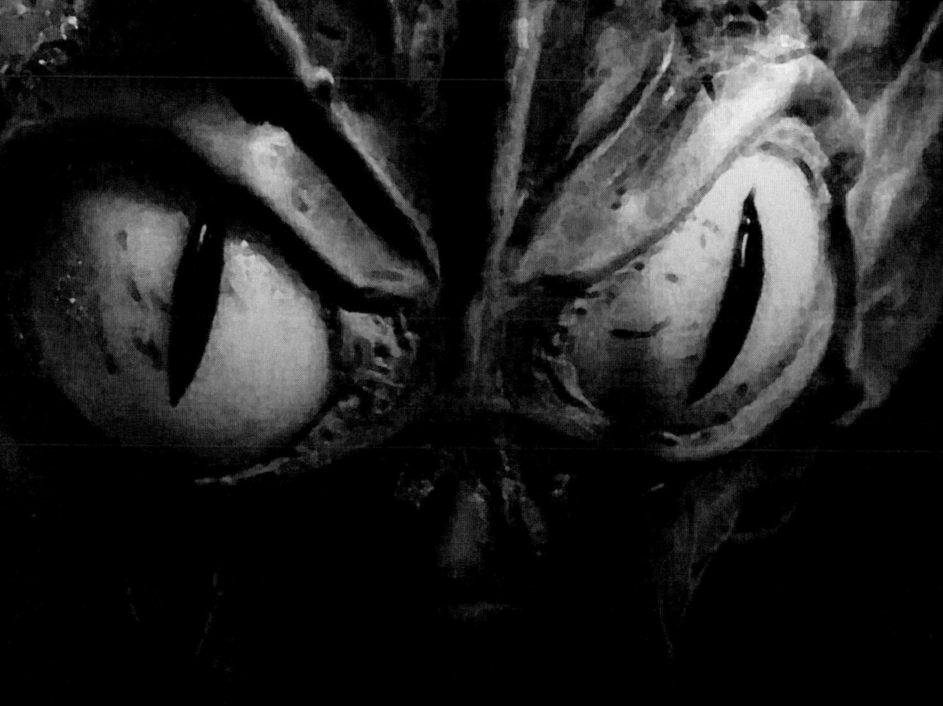

More sci-fi came in the form of *Invasion of the Saucer Men* (UK: *Invasion of the Hell Creatures*, 1957), which was personally produced by James Nicholson and was another attempt to combine the topic of UFOs with teenagers and rock 'n' roll. For the most part, it worked under Cahn's direction. The screenplay by Robert J Gurney Jr and Al Martin was based on the 1955 short story 'The Cosmic Frame' by Paul W Fairman, the rights to which were handled by Forrest J Ackerman's Science Fiction Agency. Nicholson's friendship with Ackerman assured that AIP would obtain the necessary clearance and the film went into production with the working title of 'Spacemen Saturday Night'.

Invasion of the Saucer Men was loosely based on an incident which is alleged to have occurred in 1955, when a bizarre encounter between humans and aliens was said to have taken place between the Kentucky towns of Kelly and Hopkinsville. A family in a rural farmhouse reported seeing unidentified creatures, later referred to as 'goblins' or 'little green men.' Witnesses also reported strange lights in the sky and weird sounds, and the August 22 edition of *Kentucky New Era* claimed that 'twelve to fifteen little men' had been spotted near the farmhouse. Although public opinion tends to view the story as a prank, it has become one of the most celebrated cases of alien encounters over the years, and the family have stuck firmly to their story in the interim.

Whether or not Fairman's story was based on this case, *Invasion of the Saucer Men* bears much resemblance to the Kelly-Hopkinsville sightings. According to Paul Blaisdell, who designed and built the creatures for the film, they had been in production for two days before they decided to turn the movie into an out-and-out comedy. Gurney made script changes and ordered Blaisdell to alter the appearance of the 'Martians,' and the bug-eyed aliens were changed to 'cabbage heads,' with small heads and gigantic brains. Composer Ronald Stein was asked to write a humourous score and the film became a comedy-sci-fi/teenage/rock 'n' roll movie, in which the Saucer Men were vanquished by a gang of heroic teenagers. Steven Terrell and Gloria

Invasion of the Saucer Men

Castillo starred, along with Frank Gorshin and Lyn Osborn. Castillo had appeared in Charles Laughton's classic thriller *The Night of the Hunter* (1955), but she had also played one of the runaways in *Runaway Daughters*.

In the film, a teenage couple (Terrell and Castillo) who are 'making out' in their car in a wooded area accidentally run over an alien being. The creature's hand falls off but comes to life again, complete with its own independent eye, and begins to stalk the teenagers. Meanwhile, the town drunk (Gorshin) wants to store the alien body in his refrigerator, but the creature's companions inject him with a fatal amount of alcohol and he dies. Many other mishaps occur until the military becomes involved and an end is brought about to the modest 'invasion'. As Castillo's character remarks, with an innuendo that dates the film to the fifties, 'I expected to be frightened on my wedding night, but nothing like this!' Meanwhile, the Colonel (Sam Buffington) topically declares, 'Our job is to prevent a possible nationwide panic by keeping the information from the public.'

Invasion of the Saucer Men is one of Cahn's best movies, second only to his later classic *It! The Terror From Beyond Space* (1958), a United Artists release that was one of the many inspirations for Ridley Scott's *Alien* (1979). It whizzes by at a breezy 69 minutes, the acting is uniformly good and the characters are likeable and upbeat. At the climax, it is the teenagers and not the military who defeat the invaders when

Invasion of the Saucer Men (Steven Terrell, Gloria Castillo)

they inadvertently discover that the Saucer Men cannot stand the glare from the headlights of their hot rods. It is certainly the only movie (except for its remake) in which teenagers making out in a 'lover's lane' rescue mankind from aliens. Comedy it may have been in intent, but gore-scenes (albeit using chocolate syrup) of the 'Hell Creatures' in the British print getting their various come-uppances were cut by the censor, even with his 'X' certificate applied.

As Mark Thomas McGee put it, 'It has the distinction of actually bringing to life one of the most popular clichéd phrases of the fifties: 'little green men from Mars.' Although the film itself is rarely seen these days (thanks to a rights issue involving Nicholson's widow), Blaisdell's make-up effects have become iconic, with photos of

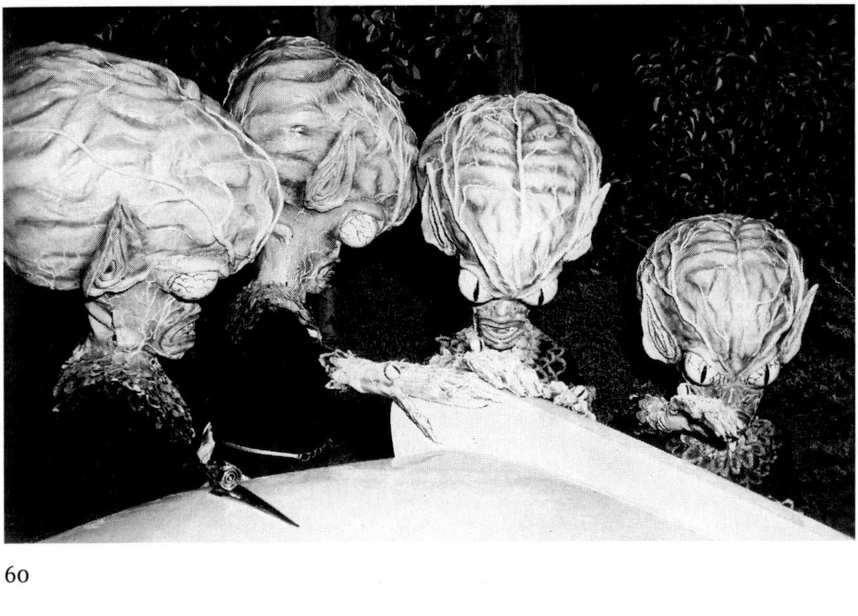

them having been published in dozens, if not hundreds of 'monster magazines' over the years.

(In 1965, AIP produced a remake of *Invasion of the Saucer Men* directed by Larry Buchanan, a Texas-based filmmaker known for his exploitation cheapies. Buchanan's version, *The Eye Creatures*, was intended to fill out a package of AIP films released to US television. In the mid-1960s, AIP decided to remake some of their early films in colour, which made it easier to sell them to TV at a time when the sales of colour TVs were booming. *The Eye Creatures*, starring John Ashley and Cynthia Hull, was shot in 16mm in Dallas on a paltry budget of $40,000. Ashley stated in later interviews that his salary took up half of this; he went on to say that the film ranks 'with some of the worst all-time horror films ever made.' Buchanan also remade *It Conquered the World* (as *Zontar, the Thing From Venus*; 1966), *The She Creature* (as *Creature of Destruction*; 1967), *Day the World Ended* (as *In the Year 2889*; 1967) and *Voodoo Woman* (as *Curse of the Swamp Creature*; 1966), all in colour and released directly to TV, although some were shown at drive-ins in the American South. Each film is distinguished by its sheer ineptitude.)

Cahn returned to horror (and to some of his *She-Creature* cast) with *Voodoo Woman* (1957). Tom Conway, Lance Fuller and Marla English were back from the previous film, along with the actual She-Creature costume, this time topped off by an anachronistic blonde wig. The original make-up design for the so-called 'voodoo woman' was found to be unsuitable at the last minute, and so the She-Creature was trotted out again, *sans* tail, fins and claws, and with the addition of the wig. Paul Blaisdell wore the costume once more, this time swathed in a sarong and topped off with a customised skull mask.

Conway was Dr Roland Gerard (but only after other actors had turned the role down), a mad scientist holed up in an unspecified jungle who dreams of creating a

Voodoo Woman (Mike Connors, Marla English)

powerful superbeing out of a compliant female; a native girl proves too good at heart to provide him with a reliable victim but but when the avaricious Marylin Blanchard (English) appears, along with a band of ne'er-do-wells hunting for gold, he finds the perfect subject. The resultant film was tedious in the extreme, with little action and even less monster, and even Gordon's then-fiancee (and later wife) Ruth thought it 'trash' when she attended the opening night screening.

Dragstrip Girl, also directed by Cahn, starred Fay Spain, a voluptuous blonde who had appeared in several TV shows such as *Cheyenne* and *Dragnet* and would go on to make more of a mark in Italian *pepla* of the 1960s. In *Dragstrip Girl,* she

Voodoo Woman (Mary Ellen Kay, Tom Conway)

Dragstrip Girl (Fay Spain, Steven Terrell / Frank Gorshin, Fay Spain)

was cast as Louise Blake, a teenager who loved dragsters and the men who drove them. One such man was played by John Ashley in his first leading role. Ashley had turned up on set in support of his then-girlfriend, who was auditioning for a role in the film; she did not get the part, but screenwriter Lou Rusoff asked Ashley to audition instead and he won the lead–thanks to an Elvis Presley impersonation. He would become a mainstay at AIP for many years.

The film was the usual mixture of rock 'n' roll, teenage rebellion, mild sex and violence, but it should be noted that AIP was ahead of its time in portraying 'strong' women on the screen. Its heroines tended to be hard-driving, tough-talking, feisty 'chicks' who test their men's mettle at every turn. Spain's character drag-races with the male characters (just as Lori Nelson did in *Hot Rod Girl*), giving them a real run for their money in the process.

Corman's contribution to the rock 'n' roll genre was *Rock All Night,* written by Charles Griffith, based on an episode of TV's *The Jane Wyman Theatre* entitled 'Little Guy'. The film starred Dick Miller, Russell Johnson and Abby Dalton. AIP decided to pair it with *Dragstrip Girl* in release, and Corman persuaded The Platters to contribute to the movie, thanks to the intervention of manager/songwriter Buck Ram. Corman filmed the group lip-synching their songs on a separate set in scenes which would be inserted later. The whole movie was shot in five days.

At one stage during pre-production, the film was known as *Rock 'n' Roll Girl* and Dane Clark was sought to play the lead role of Shorty. When Corman bought the rights to the story from Wyman, he gave it to Chuck Griffith to redraft and expand into a feature. According to Griffith, he wrote the script over the course of a weekend.

Corman assembled an interesting cast, with Dick Miller in the role destined for Clark–one of Miller's few lead performances in a film. Former teenage model Abby Dalton made her film debut in *Rock All Night* as the female lead, and Russell Johnson, who had appeared in both *It Came From Outer Space* (1953) and *This Island Earth* (1955) was cast in the key role of Jigger.

A character called Sir Bop was originally to have been played by hip poet and stage comic Lord Buckley, but Griffith recalled years later for the magazine *Senses of Cinema:* 'Mel Welles ended up playing it because Buckley was out of town. Mel wrote his own "hiptionary" for sale in the theatre to go with it.' Welles was quite a character; he had been a clinical psychologist, a writer and a radio disc jockey before entering the film business, and he made his debut in Jacques Tourneur's *Appointment in Honduras* (1953), starring Glenn Ford. Once he met Corman, however, there was no turning back, and he quickly became part of the director's stock company.

Essentially, *Rock All Night* grafts together the genres of crime thriller and rock 'n' roll musical. The first half of the film includes The Platters performing such songs as 'I'm Sorry', 'He's Mine' and, of course, 'Rock All Night'. Between the music tracks,

***Rock All Night* (The Platters)**

we are introduced to the main characters, with Miller–the 'Little Guy' of the story's original title, but a tough youth who is afraid of no one. Welles's hipster character is attempting to promote a young *chanteuse* played by Dalton.

Three reels of *Rock All Night* are mainly one rock 'n' roll number after another, punctuated by some expository dialogue. The crime portion cuts in when two hoods decide to hide out from the police in the Cloud Nine nightclub and end up holding the customers hostage to stave off the cops. A typically brisk Corman production (it runs a mere 62 minutes), *Rock All Night* was again aimed at the drive-in audience and along with *Dragstrip Girl,* it also turned a tidy profit.

Although their rock 'n' roll films were doing good business, Nicholson and Arkoff did not want to keep all their eggs in only one basket. Their first real success had come with sci-fi and 'monster' movies and as Nicholson in particular loved that genre, he was not about to turn his back on it.

As fast and cheaply as Corman worked, he could not possibly direct everything for the ever-ambitious Nicholson and Arkoff. They had to bring in some new blood, and they found it in another 'Gordon', producer-director Bert Ira Gordon–or 'Mr BIG', to his fans. Born in Wisconsin, Gordon had begun making home movies in 16mm when his aunt bought him a cine camera for his thirteenth birthday. During the war, he dropped out of college to join the Air Force and when he returned to civilian life, he married and made television commercials with his wife. He became a production assistant on a crime series called *Racket Squad* in 1951 and in 1954, he was given the job of lighting cameraman on the adventure film *Serpent Island,* directed by Tom Gries and starring Sonny Tufts.

Gordon's first film as a director was *King Dinosaur* (1955), a sci-fi thriller made over a seven-day period. The film included stock footage from the 1940 Hal Roach production *One Million BC*, as well as new footage using live lizards as stand-ins for dinosaurs. Despite its many shortcomings, it made money for its distributor, Lippert Pictures, and Gordon was up and running in Hollywood. His next production was *The Cyclops* (1957), another sci-fi yarn, this time starring James Craig, Gloria Talbot and Lon Chaney Jr, rather than *King Dinosaur*'s cast of unknowns, in a wild story about gigantic mutated animals (and one mutated human) lurking in the wilds of Mexico. Gordon refined his special effects techniques from *King Dinosaur* by using

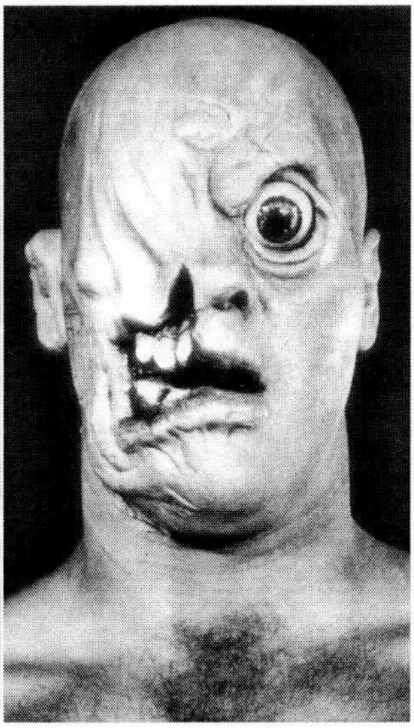

King Dinosaur / RIGHT: *The Cyclops* (Dean Parkin)

The Amazing Colossal Man (Glenn Langan)

rear screen projection, through which the supposedly enlarged human and animal monsters appear to be in the same frame as normal-sized characters. Released by Allied Artists on a double bill with Edgar G Ulmer's *Daughter of Dr Jekyll* (also starring Gloria Talbot), *The Cyclops* cashed in on the sci-fi boom for giant monsters, which had begun in 1953 with Ray Harryhausen's Warner Bros spectacular *The Beast From 20,000 Fathoms*, and became another oversized step on the way to fantasy fame for Gordon.

Gordon's next film was *The Beginning of the End* , for a new company clumsily called AB-PT (American Broadcasting-Paramount Theatres). On this occasion, he 'giantised' grasshoppers to terrify Peter Graves, Peggie Castle and that ubiquitous character actor from dozens of American sci-fi movies of the era, Morris Ankrum. By then, Gordon was making enough noise in low budget production to attract the attention of Nicholson and Arkoff, and they met with him in 1957.

Nicholson had read a short sci-fi novel called *The Nth Man*, which was written in 1926 by Homer Eon Flint and featured a man who was ten miles tall. He had bought the film rights to the story and felt that it could be adapted to cash in on the excitement generated by Jack Arnold's hugely successful *The Incredible Shrinking Man,* which had been released only six months earlier. Roger Corman was announced as director and Charles Griffith adapted the story, but Griffith had turned it into a comedy. Corman subsequently dropped out and Bert Gordon was hired to direct instead.

Gordon collaborated on the script with Griffith, but 'creative differences' ensued and Griffith quit the project after working with Gordon for only a day. Griffith's usual writing partner, Mark Hanna–who had co-written *Flesh and the Spur* and *Gunslinger*, among others–was quickly brought

Cathy Downs

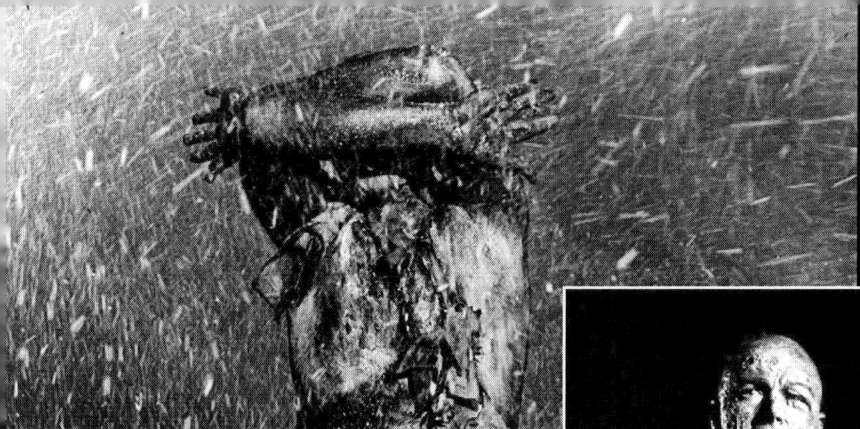

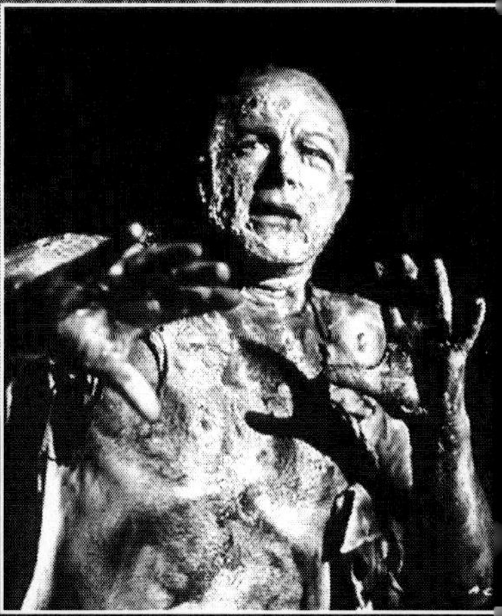

n to pick up on the rewriting duties with Gordon in Griffith's place.

The two threw out Griffith's script completely; originally, Dick Miller had been tapped to play the lead, as a malcontent who stumbled into a lab and ended up growing to gigantic proportions. The satirical script had Miller's character travelling to the United Nations to make demands, playing 'Navy' by sinking real ships, and getting revenge on the Russians for dropping a bomb on him. Hanna and Gordon took out the comedy and turned it into a tragedy, which would eventually be called *The Amazing Colossal Man*.

The new version of the script owed as much to Richard Matheson's novel *The Shrinking Man* and Arnold's film adaptation as it did to *The Nth Man*. The title character was now the victim of an atomic test of a plutonium bomb. The protagonist, Lieutenant Colonel Glenn Manning, is inadvertently exposed to the blast in the desert and though burned over 90% of his body, he somehow survives. However, he begins to grow in size and as he grows, his heart and circulatory system fail to keep pace. He gradually loses his mind as a result of the reduced blood supply to his brain. When he finally reaches a height of fifty feet, the growth stops, but by now, he has become quite mad. He escapes into the desert and destroys part of the city of Las Vegas before finally meeting his end at Hoover Dam.

For the lead role of Glenn Manning, Gordon chose Denver-born Glenn Langan, an actor who had made his film debut as a North Carolina congressman in a short feature called *The Bill of Rights* (1939). He played an intern in Humphrey Bogart's only horror film, *The Return of Dr X* that same year. Tall and muscular, Langan was soon given a contract by 20th Century Fox, for whom he appeared in John Brahm's thriller *Hangover Square* (1945) and Joseph L Mankiewicz's *Dragonwyck* (1946), in which he co-starred with Vincent Price.

But Fox never quite knew what to do with Langan and he usually found himself in stalwart supporting roles. By the early 1950s, he could only find work in television and when Gordon came calling to ask him to make another feature, he jumped at

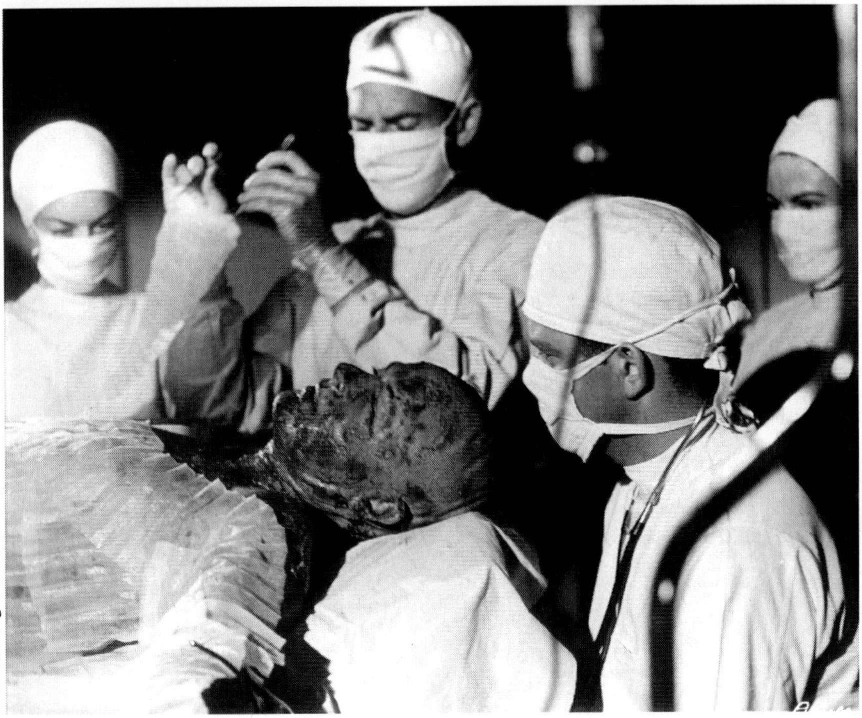

The Amazing Colossal Man

chance. His wife was Adele Jergens, who had already worked for ARC/AIP, so he had few qualms about working for the company. Cathy Downs, who had starred in *The Phantom From 10,000 Leagues*, was brought back to play Manning's long-suffering girlfriend, and William Hudson, who had appeared in *The She-Creature*, was cast as the resident scientist, Dr Paul Linstrom.

The Amazing Colossal Man required a lot of location work and it ranged over a fairly wide area. Locations included Boulder City, Nevada, the Colorado River, the Hoover Dam on the Arizona-Nevada border, Lake Mead, Arizona, and Las Vegas, Nevada. The biggest challenge for Gordon was in filming the movie's climax, when the Colossal Man rampages through the streets of Las Vegas. AIP could never have come up with a budget big enough for Gordon to rope off the streets or pay hundreds of extras to run screaming through them, so he ended up taking transparencies of Vegas and its many famous landmarks during the early hours, when the place was quiet. These slides were then projected onto a screen and handfuls of extras were hired to stand in front and react accordingly. The Colossal Man was then superimposed onto the images and *voila!* - An instant rampage through the streets of the city.

Most of the film's cheesy effects do not really hold up today. As Gordon only used a positive 'matte', the Colossal Man is frequently transparent as he stomps through the desert and his fall from Hoover Dam at the climax is risible; it appears as though Langan was leaning over a chair to obtain the shot, his arms and legs dangling as he falls into the river.

Nevertheless, *The Amazing Colossal Man* was a stupendous moneymaker for AIP on its release in October 1957 on a bill with *Cat Girl,* AIP's first Anglo-American production and the first film to star future Hammer Horror icon Barbara Shelley. The film also received some of the best reviews of any AIP release up to then, with *Variety*, at least, feigning blindness to the film's many and various optical deficiencies

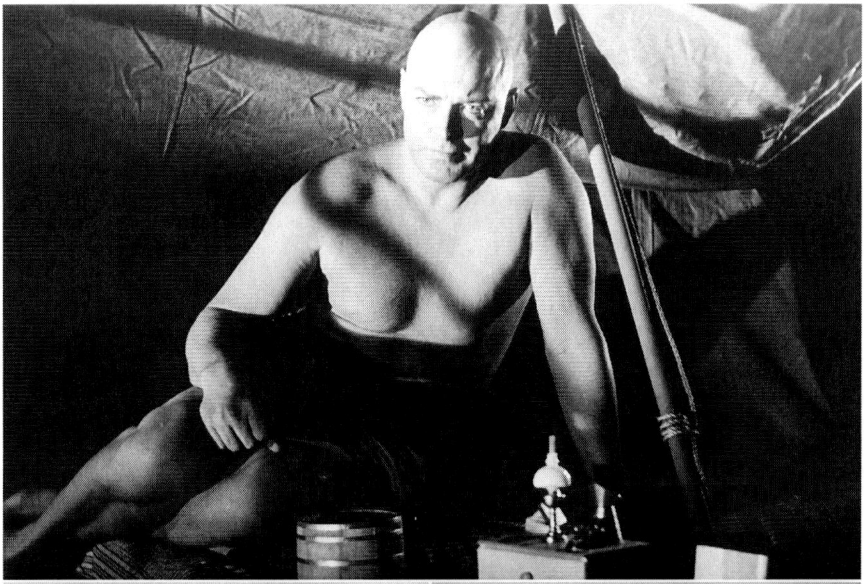

DANNY THOMAS

Attack of the Puppet People (John Hoyt, John Agar)

and oddly observing, 'Glenn Langan delivers persuasively.. Technical departments are *well handled.*'

The film's success led to AIP calling for a sequel but first, Gordon wanted to try something different–though still, to large degree, derived from the premise of *The Incredible Shrinking Man*. The working title for the new screenplay was *I Was a Teenage Doll*–a nod to the contemporaneous success of Herman Cohen's 'Teenage' monster thrillers for AIP (see Chapter 3), but it went onto the floor under the title of *The Fantastic Puppet People* and was ultimately released as *Attack of the Puppet People* (UK: *Six Inches Tall*). It was one of the most remarkable of Bert I Gordon's fantasies, and those of AIP.

In the story, deranged doll-maker Mr Franz (John Hoyt) creates a machine that can shrink human beings to a mere six inches tall. He keeps them in glass tubes in a kind of suspended animation and makes dolls based on their features, which he sells to children. Before long, he has acquired an entire troupe of tiny prisoners whom he forces to perform for him in puppet shows. He even shrinks his secretary, Sally (June Kenney), and her fiancée, Bob (John Agar), which turns out to be the beginning of the end of his little kingdom. They rebel against the idea of being Franz's diminutive playthings and eventually transform themselves back to normal size.

An outrageous plot, to be sure, but so over the top that it almost becomes a study in surrealism. Paul Blaisdell and his wife Jackie were credited as 'special designers' on *Attack of the Puppet People*, which meant that they created the oversized props for the 'tiny' people to interact with, although the film's 'giant' telephone was actually an advertising gimmick and supplied by the phone company.

Beyond the unique designs, however, what shines most brightly about the film is John Hoyt's performance. Born in Bronxville, New York, Hoyt was a veteran actor and writer who had appeared in many sci-fi features, including *Lost Continent* (1950) and Universal-International's *The Black Castle* (1952). His performance in *Attack of the Puppet People* is multi-faceted; he appears to be a lonely, tortured, gentle soul,

Attack of the Puppet People (June Kenny)

yet he commits the monstrous, grotesque crime of shrinking his fellow humans and turning them into toys to combat his isolation.

Shrinking John Agar turns out, of course, to be a big mistake. Agar was already well known in the field of sci-fi, having starred in such iconic examples of the genre as Jack Arnold's back-to-back 1955 monster epics, *Revenge of the Creature* and *Tarantula*. He had also appeared in *The Mole People* (1956) for U-I, *Daughter of Dr Jekyll* for Allied Artists–and he was in *Flesh and the Spur* for AIP. Agar is athletically heroic in his

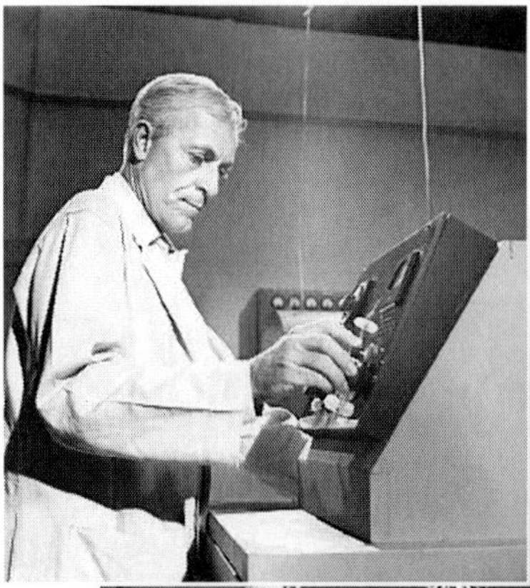

shrunken plight and it is fun to watch him clamber over the oversized sets in his valiant attempts to save the day. (An amusing scene, early on in the film, sees him and Kenney attending a drive-in that happens to be showing *The Amazing Colossal Man*–one of AIP's typically self-serving in-jokes.)

Attack of the Puppet People also benefited from a clever and unusually thoughtful and mature screenplay by George Worthing Yates, who had come up with the story for Gordon Douglas's seminal 'giant bug' movie *Them!* (1954) and had written the screenplays for Ray Harryhausen's *It Came From Beneath the Sea* (1955) and *Earth vs the Flying Saucers* (1956). Yates had also done uncredited work on the script for *The Amazing Colossal Man*.

The concept is as much about loneliness as it is about shrinking people, and the theme hits home at the close of the film, when all of Franz's 'puppets' have escaped and he is once again alone. The scene is beautifully acted by Hoyt, who was rarely given a leading role in Hollywood and clearly relished this one.

The effects in the film are simple, yet they work on an almost dream-like level. The shrunken people are more believably rendered than had been the Colossal Man, and the special props are nicely designed and effectively used. *Attack of the Puppet People* owes a considerable debt of gratitude to Ernest B Schoedsack's 1940 fantasy of miniaturisation *Dr Cyclops*, but it still represents a high-water mark in the early days of AIP and perfectly demonstrated what the company could do when firing on all cylinders.

After this 'small' gem of a film, it is depressing to contemplate the mediocrity of Gordon's next effort, *War of the Colossal Beast* (UK: *The Terror Strikes*), which shared the other half of the bill with *Puppet People* in the US. The inevitable sequel to *The Amazing Colossal Man*, the film is padded with footage from the original, yet *War of the Colossal Beast* still manages only a 69-minute running time. The effects are distinctly average, with the now-disfigured Manning (played here by Dean Parkin) picking up what are obviously 'toy' trucks and stomping about (in poor matte shots)

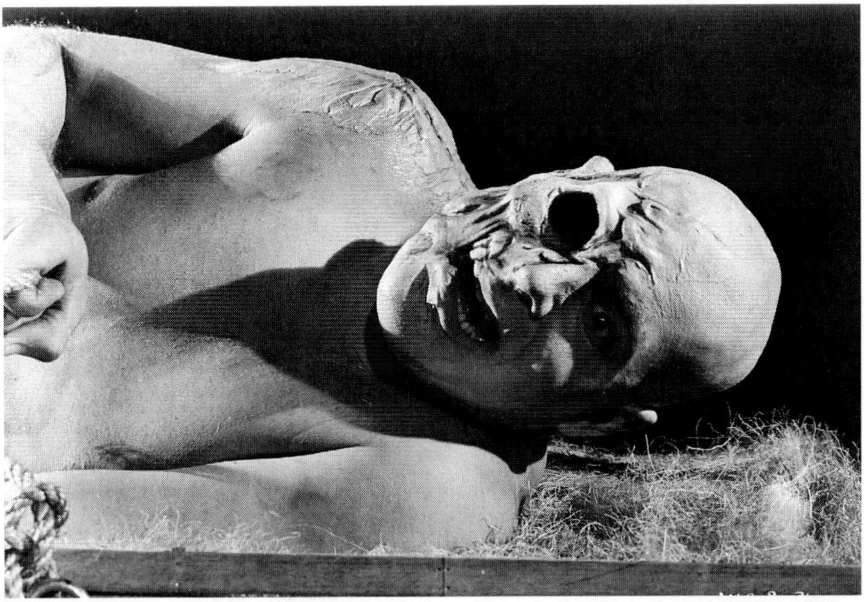

War of the Colossal Beast (Dean Parkin)

in Mexico and southern California. The plot has Manning, who was believed dead after falling from the dam in *Colossal Man*, found alive but facially mutilated in the Mexican desert. He is also quite insane and takes to robbing food trucks to keep his strength up. The military is once more called into action; the soldiers drug him and take him back to California, where, King Kong-style, he escapes and wreaks havoc in Los Angeles (specifically, Griffith Park).

War of the Colossal Beast is strictly a by-the-numbers sequel, its one startling scene being the final one in the film, which was shot in colour in the manner of the

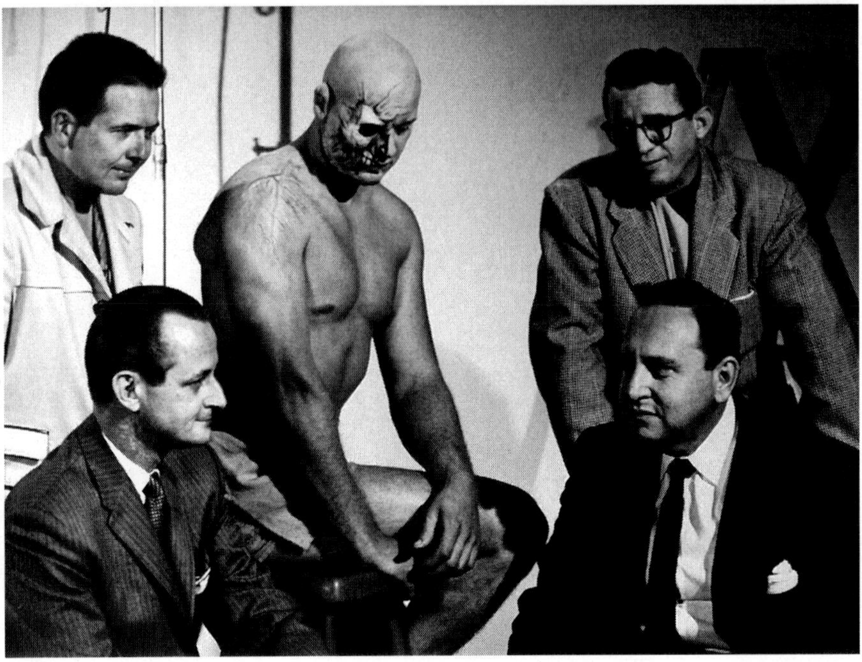

Bert Gordon and AIP sales manager Leon Blender with Nicholson and Arkoff

climaxes to both *I Was a Teenage Frankenstein* and the upcoming *How to Make a Monster* (see Chapter 3): Manning effectively commits suicide by grabbing hold of power lines and electrocuting himself. Parkin's make-up is suitably grotesque, but it was also devised to disguise the fact that he is not Glenn Langan, the actor who originated the role.

War of the Colossal Beast is directed in lackadaisical, almost careless fashion by Bert Gordon, with the actors–including Sally Fraser, Roger Pace and Russ Bender–

merely going through the motions and reciting too much expository dialogue until the brief, spectacular finale. Again, the screenplay was by Yates, but it has none of the depth or sub-text of his script for *Puppet People*. Despite having the expertise of AIP behind it, *War of the Colossal Beast* was little advance on Gordon's independent effort *The Cyclops* of the year before and looked far too much like the cheap cash-in which it was obviously designed to be.

Yates and a screenwriter named László Görög, who was born in Austria-Hungary but who had immigrated to the US in 1939, wrote the script for Gordon's next opus, *Earth vs the Spider*. Görög had penned one of the segments of Julien Duvivier's *Tales of Manhattan* (1942) and had been nominated for an Academy Award for co-writing *The Affairs of Susan* (1945). More recently, he had written the scripts for U-I's *The Mole People* and *The Land Unknown* (1957).

Impressive pedigree notwithstanding, the script for *Earth vs the Spider* was not especially original, mixing elements from Jack Arnold's *Tarantula* with the spider scene from—yet again—*The Incredible Shrinking Man*: a teenage couple (June Kenney and Gene Persson) go in search of the girl's father, who has failed to return home. Near the wreckage of his pickup truck, they find a cave in which they encounter a gigantic spider. They have trouble convincing the town sheriff that there is a giant arachnid nearby, but he eventually accompanies them to the site and the spider is 'killed' by a huge dose of DDT. The creature is put on show in the local high school, where it is suddenly revived by loud music when a rock 'n' roll band shows up for the school dance. The spider, which was only stunned by the DDT, rampages through the town until it is finally electrocuted when it eventually returns to its cave.

The story is absurd on virtually every level, but it could have worked as a spoof of the teen genre. Alas, the film contains little *intentional* humour. The effects are good, though nowhere near the level of Clifford Stine's excellent optical work on *Tarantula*. Paul Blaisdell had created a tiny make-up appliance 'about the size and weight of a postage stamp' which was intended for the spider's back to make it look as though it

had 'eerie, catlike eyes', but the device was never used. The tarantula still managed to give the most effective performance in the film, however.

Earth vs the Spider–the title was a take-off of Harryhausen's *Earth vs the Flying Saucers*–was the film's original title but when it was released late in 1958, shortly after the blockbuster success of Kurt Neumann's sci-fi thriller *The Fly,* Nicholson and Arkoff decided, in their usual expedient fashion, to cash in on the success of the Fox film by releasing Gordon's movie simply as *The Spider*.

The Spider (Gene Persson, June Kenny)

AIP's latest thriller was barely in the same ball-park as Fox's Cinemascope and DeLuxe colour offering, but the in-jokes which were fast becoming something of an AIP trademark were at least in plentiful supply. In the foyer of the cinema at which Persson's character works is a poster advertising *The Amazing Colossal Man,* while the marquee display is for *Attack of the Puppet People*, which also featured Kenney. At another juncture, a teenager is shown reading the first issue of *Famous Monsters of Filmland*, the new 'monsterzine' edited by agent and superfan Forrest J Ackerman. (Ackerman's cult fanzine would help to promote many of AIP's monster movies in the coming years.)

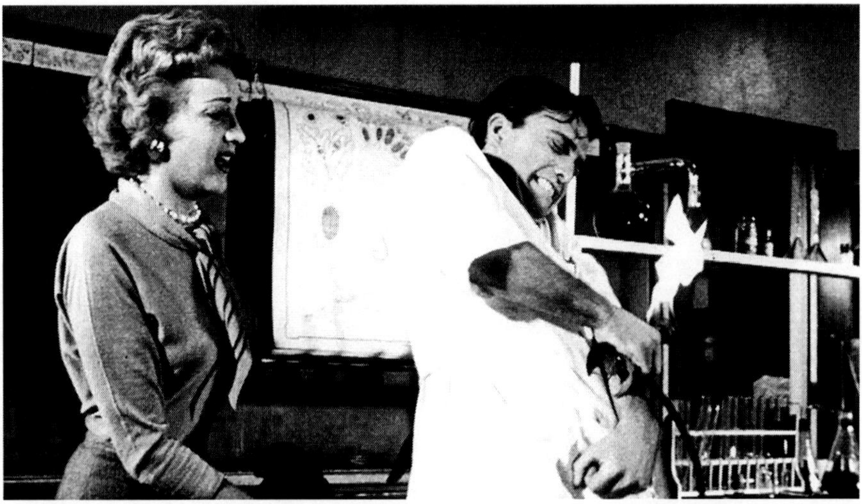

The Brain Eaters (Joanna Lee, Ed Nelson)

Released in the US in September 1958 on a double-bill with *The Brain Eaters,* an adaptation of Robert A Heinlein's science fiction novel *The Puppet Masters* directed by Bruno VeSota, *Earth vs the Spider* did excellent business. But whenever there is money involved, there are bound to be disagreements and, sure enough, Bert Gordon sued Nicholson and Arkoff in the wake of *Earth vs the Spider*, claiming that they had diverted profits from the four films that he had made for them into their other companies, like Alta Vista Productions, and had siphoned off his $15,000 executive producer's fee for themselves.

In consequence of his legal action, Gordon terminated his relationship with AIP and made his next film, *Tormented* (1960) for Allied Artists. He would not return to AIP for nearly twenty years.

3 TEENAGE TERRORS
FOWLER, STROCK, COHEN AND CO

Producer Herman Cohen had begun his career in show business as a cinema usher at the Dexter Theatre in Detroit, Michigan. He was only twelve years old, and he was arrested twice by the Labour Board for working underage. By the age of eighteen, he was the theatre's manager. From there, he became assistant manager at the Fox Theatre, also in Detroit, until he was drafted into the Marines and stationed at Camp Pendleton in Oceanside, California, which was only a few hours from Hollywood.

After serving his time in the Marines, Cohen became a sales manager for Columbia Pictures, first in Michigan, and then in Hollywood working in the publicity department. In the 1950s, he began producing films for Realart with titles such as *Bride of the Gorilla* (1951) and *Battles of Chief Pontiac* (1952), both of which starred Universal regular Lon Chaney Jr.

While he was at Realart, Cohen met James Nicholson, who gave him a copy of a short story called 'Deadly City' by Paul W Fairman. The story became the basis for Cohen's first science fiction film, *Target Earth* (1954), which he produced for Allied Artists. Starring Richard Denning and Kathleen Crowley and directed by Sherman Rose, *Target Earth* was made to cash in on the current sci-fi trend; the killer robot featured prominently may have looked cheap and corny, but it did no harm to the film at the box office.

Cohen went on to make a bigger-budgeted production for United Artists. *Crime of Passion* (1957) was directed by Gerd Oswald and the *film noir* featured a name cast, including Barbara Stanwyck, Sterling Hayden and Raymond Burr. Although the movie received positive reviews, it died commercially, leaving Cohen to scratch

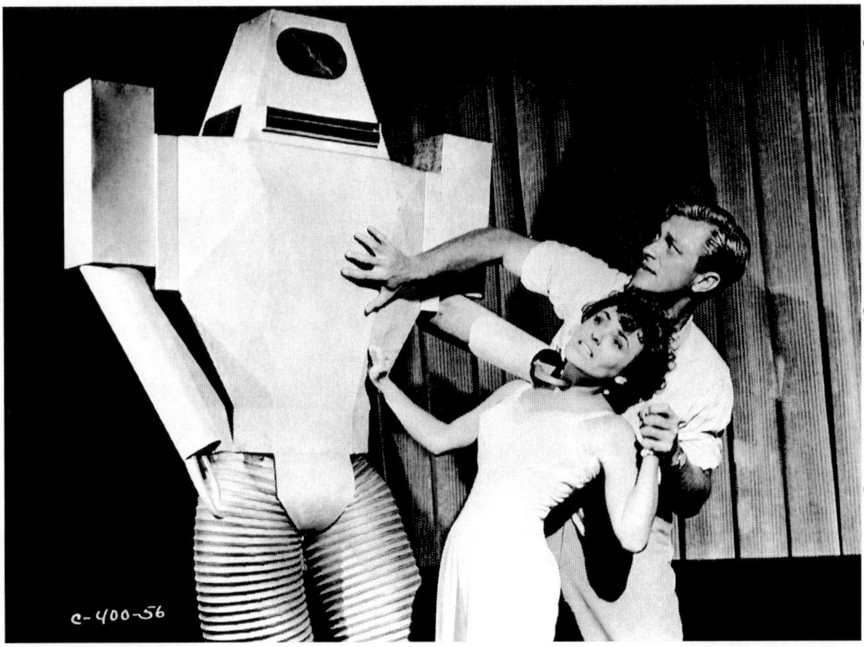

Target Earth (Kathleen Crowley, Richard Denning)

I Was a Teenage Werewolf (Whit Bissell, Michael Landon)

his head about what to do next. He eventually decided to do some travelling around the country to see if he could discover what it was that audiences wanted to see in the rapidly-changing cultural landscape of postwar America. What he found was that his old acquaintance, Nicholson, was making movies for a new 'teenage' audience–and making a bundle. Cohen made up his mind to team up with Nicholson and his partner Arkoff. But what exactly could they make together?

No one seems to know who came up with the title *I Was a Teenage Werewolf,* one of the most famous in genre film history. In a newspaper article written shortly after the film's release, the moniker was credited to Nicholson's daughter, who was just repeating something that one of her classmates had said. Alex Gordon, on the other hand, claimed that the title arose from a meeting between Nicholson, Arkoff and himself. At that meeting, they had idly been chattering about who could think of the longest film title in history. *I Am a Fugitive from a Chain Gang* (1932), *I Was a Prisoner on Devil's Island* (1941) and *I Was a Communist for the FBI* (1951) were all contenders. (One wonders why no one mentioned Corman's *The Saga of the Viking Women and Their Voyage to the Waters of the Great Sea Serpent,* which Corman had just directed for AIP!) In later years, Cohen regarded the title as just an example of 'little minds at work', although he claimed that Nicholson only came up with the first half of it; as McGee opined in *Fast and Furious:* 'Whatever, it's a great title, a beautiful blend of monsters and teenagers, sounding as if it were ripped from the pages of *True Confessions* magazine.'

Now that they had their title, the three needed a script, which Cohen co-wrote with Aben Kandel. In the story, a troubled high school student seeks help through hypnotherapy, but his therapist uses the boy for regression experiments (à la *The She-Creature*) and transforms him into a murderous werewolf.

Cohen was a producer, not a director, so he also needed someone to helm the film. That someone turned out to be Gene Fowler Jr, a first-rate Hollywood film

Herman Cohen

editor who had worked with the likes of Fritz Lang (*While the City Sleeps*; 1956) and Samuel Fuller *(China Gate*; 1957) before embarking on a career as a director.

While working on the screenplay, Cohen had been hesitant about attaching his name to it; he was far from certain that he wanted to be associated with such a project–that is, not until journalists from magazines such as *Time, Life* and *Newsweek* began to call his office to ask who the producer of this new novelty horror movie was! He quickly revised his thinking and took producer credit, using the *nom de plume* of Ralph Thornton for his contribution as co-screenwriter.

Although John Ashley would claim in later years that he had been considered for the lead role of Tony Rivers in the film, Cohen always stated that only two actors were ever in the running: Scott Marlowe and Michael Landon. Ultimately, Landon, a young actor who had appeared in several television series (including an episode of *The Loretta Young Show)* and a short film called *Fight for the Title* (1957), was chosen. *I Was a Teenage Werewolf* would be his feature film debut.

Landon's leading lady in the film was to be Yvonne Lime, who had just played an uncredited role in the Elvis Presley musical *Loving You* (1957). The AIP formula was to cast relative unknowns in the 'teenage' roles, while older and more recognisable

I Was a Teenage Werewolf (Michael Landon)

performers were cast in the conventional parts. The requisite 'mad doctor' role in *I Was a Teenage Werewolf* went to character actor Whit Bissell, who had appeared in everything from Jack Arnold's *Creature from the Black Lagoon* (1954) to Don Siegel's *Invasion of the Body Snatchers* (1956). As Dr Alfred Brandon, Bissell gave *I Was a Teenage Werewolf* the gravitas it demanded.

Some of the smaller roles were also of interest. Dawn Richard, who appeared in a memorable scene in the film as a teenage gymnast, was actually a 22-year old who had appeared as a centerfold in *Playboy* in May 1957, about a month before the film was released (AIP always kept publicity firmly in mind!), while Pepe, a Romanian janitor (with a Spanish name?) in a police station, was portrayed by Russian-born Vladimir Sokoloff, a veteran of the Moscow Art Theatre and prolific character actor, who had appeared in dozens of Broadway plays and films, including Edward Dmytryk's *Back to Bataan* (1945).

Production on *I Was a Teenage Werewolf* began on February 13, 1957. It was Fowler's debut as director and he proved his worth by bringing the picture in for $150,000 on a meagre seven-day shooting schedule. On its release in July, as one half of a double bill with Cahn's teenage sci-fi movie *Invasion of the Saucer Men* (which featured some of Paul Blaisdell's best make-up effects), *I Was a Teenage Werewolf* was an instant smash for AIP, ultimately grossing $2 million. The usual AIP ballyhoo certainly helped: 'The most amazing picture of our time!' screamed one ad. 'Explosive! Amazing! Terrifying! You won't believe your eyes!' declared another. The film even received some favourable reviews. *Variety* noted that it was 'handled well enough to meet the requirements of this type of film.. Michael Landon delivers a first-class characterisation as the high school boy constantly in trouble...' The *Los Angeles Times* opined poetically, 'The title is a magnificent piece of composition. It has a haunting quality about it, and I ought to caution you that if you let it pierce your consciousness it will echo in your brain in a constant refrain.'

The title alone was enough to bring in curious patrons, and *I Was a Teenage Werewolf* quickly became one of the most profitable films in AIP's history. It also launched the career of Michael Landon, who became a regular in the popular, long-running Western television series *Bonanza* just two years later.

Period horror films were making a dramatic resurgence in the UK at around the same time, thanks to Terence Fisher's Hammer Gothic *The Curse of Frankenstein*, which had been released in America by Warner Brothers that summer to similar smash business. *I Was a Teenage Werewolf* was something of a modern-day US equivalent - at

least enough to inspire the prestigious *Time* magazine to run a feature headlined 'Shock Around the Clock', which began: 'Far below the dizzying spires of cinematic art (musicals, adult westerns), lower even than the swarming, unswept streets of cinematic commerce (cops-and-robbers film, childish westerns), lies a dank catacomb, for years the lair of wound-up scientists, unwound mummies, vampires, hyper-pituitary apes, cat men, spacemen and skirt-chasing dinosaurs. Here, budgets are low, actors obscure...' The article went on to single out AIP's unique contribution to the genre: the 'teenage' horror film.

Many parents were outraged, however. *I Was a Teenage Werewolf* became a source of controversy, which, of course, only increased its box office receipts. Senator Estes Kefauver, a Tennessee politician who had previously investigated organised crime, was put in charge of a Senate sub-committee to investigate the causes of juvenile delinquency. He was convinced that there was a link between fictional cinematic violence and real-life violence, but his eventual 123-page report was inconclusive in its findings.

When AIP held a luncheon in Miami for cinema exhibitors, Fox producer Jerry Wald, who also attended, insulted his hosts by claiming that they were producing 'irresponsible motion pictures'. He went on to declare, 'These are not the sort of pictures on which we can build a market for the future. While they may make a few dollars today, they will destroy us tomorrow.' Nicholson's retort pointed out that Wald had just produced *Peyton Place*, which featured elements of rape, murder and incest. He went on to remark, 'I'd rather my own children see one of our pictures than something like, say, *God's Little Acre*. Our monsters don't drink, smoke or lust.' The last was not quite true in the case of Landon's werewolf, the metaphor in whose behaviour was plain for all to see, but most of the exhibitors at the luncheon were more than happy with Nicholson's comeback. The owner of a San Fernando drive-in remarked of AIP, 'Before they came along, we were thinking of shutting down to three nights a week. They saved us.'

Viewed today, *I Was a Teenage Werewolf* is an unremarkable film, but it is better directed than one might have expected. The script is perfunctory; as previously stated, it has elements of both *The She-Creature* and *The Undead*, but the notion of subconscious regression into a past life is carried here to its ultimate extreme. As *Variety* put it: 'Another in the cycle of regression themes is a combo teenager and science-fiction yarn. Only new thing about this Herman Cohen production is a psychiatrist's use of a problem teenager...' In the film, Bissell's Dr Alfred Brandon states this now-familiar mantra to his assistant: 'I'm going to *transform* him and unleash the savage instincts that lie hidden within.. and then I'll be judged the benefactor. Mankind is on the verge of destroying itself. The only hope for the human race is to hurl it back into its primitive form - to start all over again. What's one life compared to such a triumph?'

The movie opens on Tony Rivers (Landon) engaged in a furious fistfight with fellow high-schooler Jimmy (Tony Marshall) that is shot mostly in a series of bone-

Herman Cohen, Dawn Richard

crushing close-ups. If this opening had been directed by, say, Edward L Cahn, it would probably have been filmed in routine medium shots but Fowler's experience as an editor served him well and the sequence is assembled through a series of quick cuts, rather than long, uninterrupted takes. Later on, we see Jimmy pursued by an unseen creature in the woods. Eventually, it catches up to him and kills him, but we still do not see what it is; all we see is Jimmy's screaming face as the camera tracks in.

The first time that Rivers is shown transforming into a werewolf is perhaps the most memorable in the movie. We first see the voluptuous Theresa (Dawn Richard) working out on the parallel bars in the school's gymnasium. Rivers walks in on her and watches her, unseen, from near the school bell. Suddenly, the bell rings as she hangs upside down on the bars. Alarmed by the bell, Rivers turns into the slavering 'teenage werewolf' and approaches the girl. We see, from her point of view, a close-up of the werewolf's face *upside down*; she screams, leaps from the bars and runs for the door. It is too late, however, and the beast is upon her. It is one of the most dynamic scenes in the entire AIP pantheon.

The scene also incorporates a significant sub-text: in watching the girl, Rivers has obviously become sexually aroused. The school bell interrupts his reverie and he

is turned into a frustrated beast. Disaffected teenage boys everywhere could relate to that scene in more ways than one. With this single sequence, AIP had found its cultural touchstone–and it would be made of gold.

The ending of the film is somewhat disappointing. After turning on Dr Brandon and killing him (another example of a lazy script defaulting to horror clichés), Rivers/ the werewolf is simply shot to death by the police. (One of the officers is played by Guy Williams, who would soon rocket to fame as television's *Zorro* for Walt Disney Pictures.)

The flat ending notwithstanding, *I Was a Teenage Werewolf* remains one of the strongest of the early AIP offerings. Michael Landon is consistently good throughout, and there are numerous directorial touches that go beyond what audiences were then used to seeing from AIP. A Halloween party sequence, for instance, is especially well staged, culminating in Rivers suddenly losing his temper and attacking one of the revellers. As they both recover themselves, the camera pans across the faces of their shocked companions, settling on the face of a girl (Cynthia Chenault) made up as a harlequin.

Paul Dunlap's musical score is effective and Joseph LaShelle's black and white cinematography is crisp and evocative. The most telling line in the film, and the one most likely to push the right buttons in the movie's target audience, is when Arlene's father (S John Launer) tells Rivers, 'You've got to bow to authority!' In the world of AIP, authority figures are almost always evil adults like Dr Brandon, whose main goal is to exploit the young and dash their hopes for the future.

The huge success of *I Was a Teenage Werewolf* led AIP to travel down that path again, not with a direct sequel, but with other 'teenage' monsters. It may even have inspired Walt Disney to adapt a novel called *The Hound of Florence* into a comedy-horror film called *The Shaggy Dog* (1959). In many ways, the plot was quite similar to that of AIP's movie, with teenager Tommy Kirk transformed into a shape-shifting canine courtesy of Fred MacMurray–in more or less the Whit Bissell role–in one of

Disney's more successful live-action efforts of the fifties. MacMurray even refers to werewolves in the line, 'Don't be ridiculous! My son isn't any werewolf! He's just a big, baggy, stupid-looking shaggy dog!'

Back at AIP, its next two teenage monster movies came about as a result of a conversation that Nicholson and Arkoff had with RJ O'Donnell, a Texas exhibitor. During lunch, the three men discussed business when O'Donnell started complaining about the amount of money the major studios were asking for their films. 'I hate to give those bastards Thanksgiving week,' he said to the AIP heads, referring to one of the most profitable weeks in the American movie business. Arkoff did not miss a beat. He said, 'What if we could make *two* pictures?'

It was the proverbial offer that could not be refused. O'Donnell was looking at two films for a fraction of the price of one major studio release and he agreed to book AIP's 'teenage monster' double bill into his chain of cinemas.

AIP asked Herman Cohen to produce *I Was a Teenage Frankenstein* and *Blood of Dracula* back to back. According to Cohen, the two films were written and shot in a mere four weeks, '...So I had to really, really cut down,' he said, in respect of their production quality. The reason for the rush: the films had been promised to O'Donnell for Thanksgiving, the fourth Thursday in November.

I Was a Teenage Frankenstein was shot at Ziv Studios, a television outfit which produced more than 250 half-hour episodes of various syndicated series per year. Written by Aben Kandel again, under the alias of Kenneth Langtry, the story followed AIP's newly-established horror formula: Professor Frankenstein, a 'mad scientist'

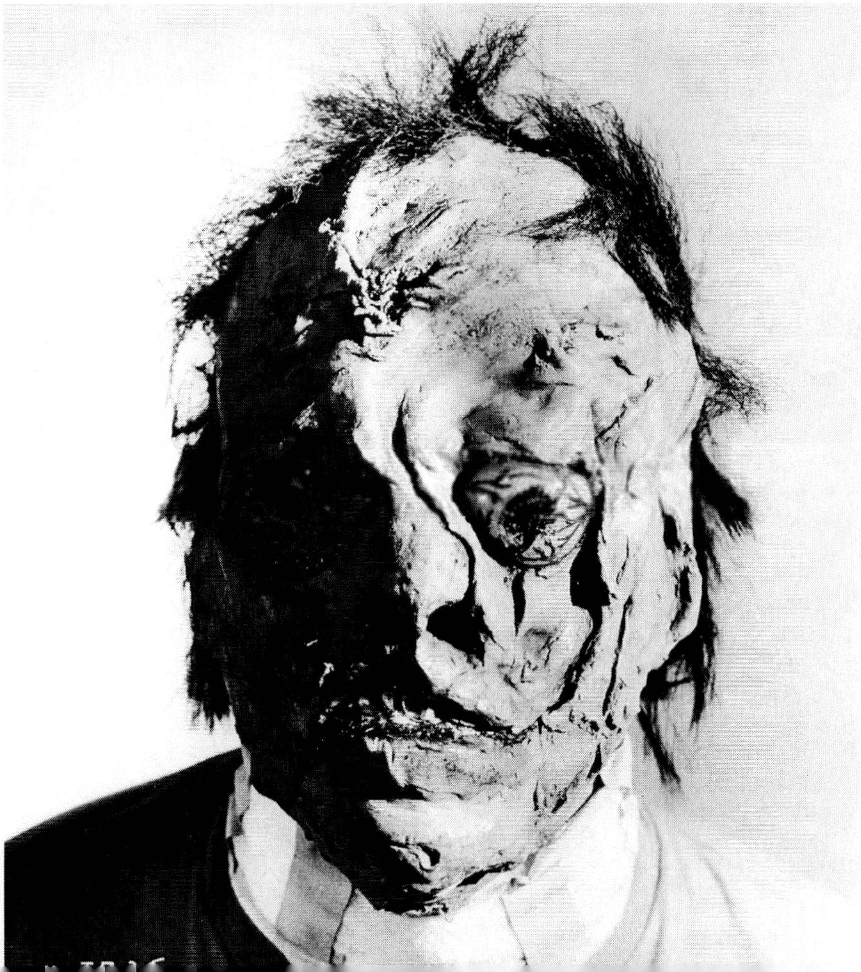

***I Was a Teenage Frankenstein* (Gary Conway)**

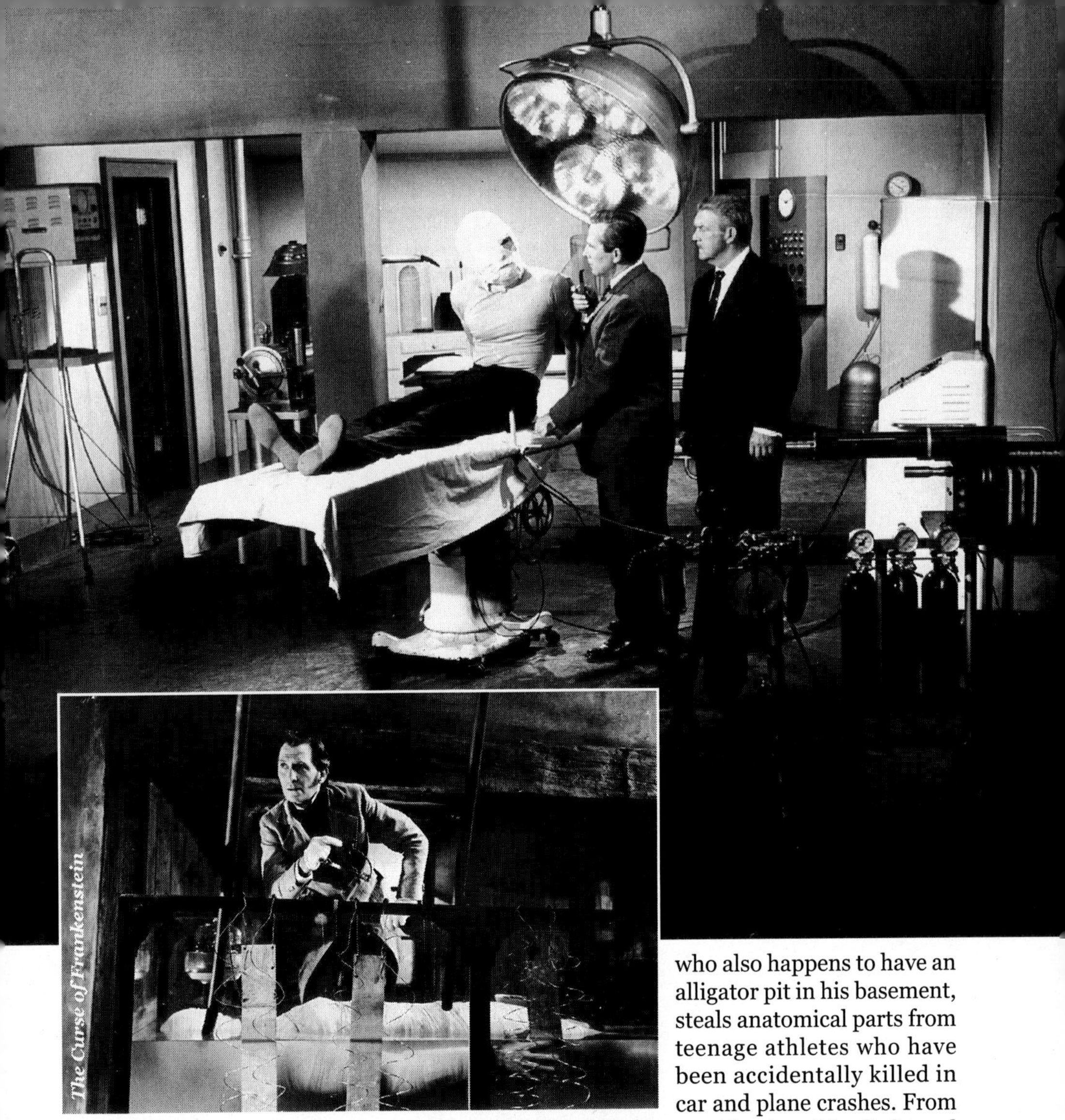

The Curse of Frankenstein

who also happens to have an alligator pit in his basement, steals anatomical parts from teenage athletes who have been accidentally killed in car and plane crashes. From this assemblage, he constructs a muscular male monster with a horribly-disfigured face. Needless to say, the creature embarks upon a reign of terror.

Unfortunately, Gene Fowler Jr was not brought back to direct; his success with *Werewolf* had led directly to an offer from Paramount Pictures to helm *I Married a Monster From Outer Space* (1958), a sci-fi/horror starring Tom Tryon and Gloria Talbott. *I Was a Teenage Frankenstein* ended up being directed by Herbert L Strock, a journeyman producer/director who had been involved with many of the television series filmed at Ziv, including *Highway Patrol* and *Sea Hunt*. Boston-born, Strock had entered the film business as a director of Fox Newsreel productions, visiting Hollywood stars in their homes. He had later worked as an editor at M-G-M and had then moved into the burgeoning world of television.

Strock's entry into the genre had been as an uncredited director of *The Magnetic Monster* (1953), which was nominally directed by Universal veteran Curt Siodmak. The film was produced by Ivan Tors, which led to Strock directing nineteen episodes of *Science Fiction Theatre* starting in 1955. These were also shot at Ziv by Tors's production company.

The absurdly short shooting schedule did not allow time for Strock to introduce any sort of art into either of the two films that he was slated to direct. He therefore needed some solid actors to carry them off. Bissell was brought back as Professor Frankenstein, while the role of his fiancée Margaret–essentially a cross between Hazel Court's Elizabeth and Valerie Gaunt's Justine in *The Curse of Frankenstein*–was given to Phyllis Coates, who was best known as Lois Lane in the 1951 feature film *Superman and the Mole Men*, and in the first series of the *Adventures of Superman* TV show, which had George Reeves in the title role.

As a television actress, Coates was used to working at a fast pace. So was Robert Burton, a veteran of series such as *The Lone Ranger* and *Broken Arrow*, who was cast as Dr Karlton, Frankenstein's ill-fated assistant. The youngest, most inexperienced member of the cast was Gary Conway, who was to portray the titular monster (albeit that the title actually referred to its creator!). Conway had worked as a male model for 'physique' photographers, so he had the necessary physical qualifications for the role, if nothing else.

It was a fairly open secret during Herman Cohen's lifetime that he was gay, though he could not be openly out of 'the closet' in the 1950s. His niece, Gail Cohen, gave an interview to a Dr Abner Mality some years ago for an e-magazine called *Wormwood Chronicles* in which she noted, 'I am sure my uncle was gay.. When I mentioned this years ago to his niece Eleanor, she said I was crazy and that he had just never found the right girl. I don't buy a word of it.. His brother Kenny, too, is sure that Herman was gay.'

This adds an interesting dimension to Cohen's AIP horror films, almost all of which involve an older adult who 'corrupts' a younger one of the same sex. It can fairly be held that Cohen was the one responsible for this formula, as he had written *I Was a Teenage Werewolf*. In an article in *Senses of Cinema* entitled 'Fear and Self-Loathing: Horror and Homophobia in the Films of Herman Cohen', Wheeler Winston Dixon wrote, 'In *Teenage Frankenstein,* the monster.. becomes so obsessed with his newly constructed body that he spends most of his time simply gazing into a mirror at his newly acquired face, lost in a narcissistic dream world.' Indeed, Bissell seems to have more than a professorial interest in Conway's physique and the sense that one gains from the interaction of the two is that the older man is sexually drawn to the younger man's virile power.

Teenage Frankenstein, the shortened title of the film in the UK, was very nearly

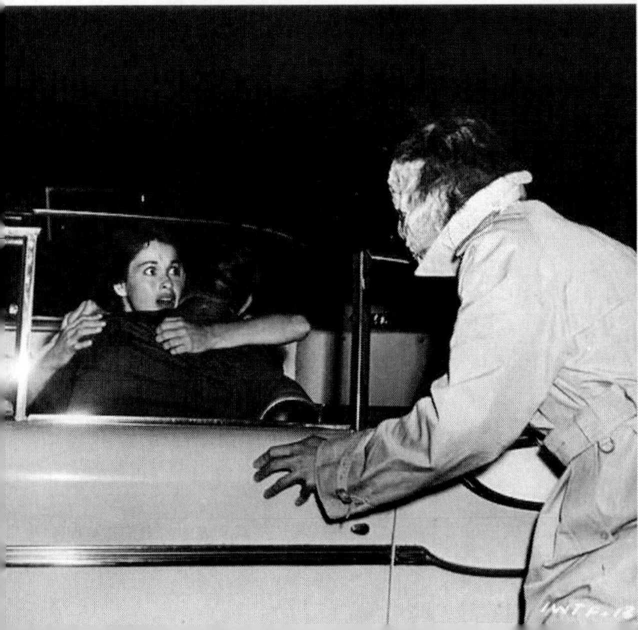

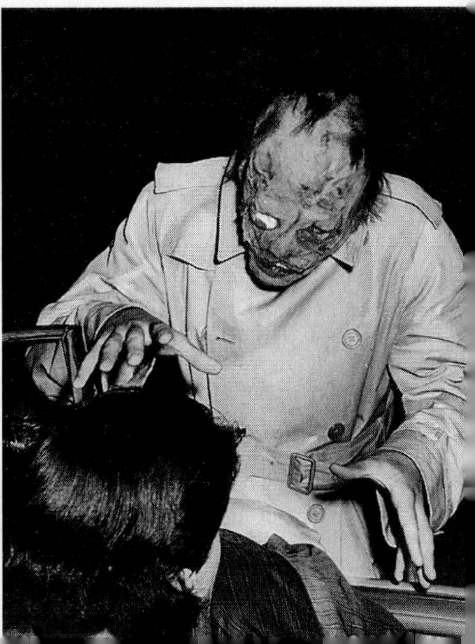

I Was a Teenage Frankenstein (Gary Conway, Angela Blake)

a remake in modern dress of *The Curse of Frankenstein*. Bissell's character is every bit as amoral as Peter Cushing's baron and as much of an egomaniac: at one point he says to his assistant, 'In this laboratory, there is no death until I declare it so.' As with the Hammer production, there is also some wry humour. In the vein of the famous 'Pass the marmalade' exchange in *Curse,* Bissell's Professor Frankenstein, frustrated with his creation's silence, admonishes him: 'Speak! I know you have a civil tongue in your head because I sewed it back myself!'

The Professor disposes of Margaret, his meddling fiancée, in exactly the same way as Hammer's Frankenstein did with Justine, by locking her in the lab with his creation. But instead of using an acid bath to dispose of the bodies, as in *Curse,* he casually tumbles them into his handy alligator pit–shades of Ed Wood's immortal *Bride of the Monster*–where they are promptly devoured.

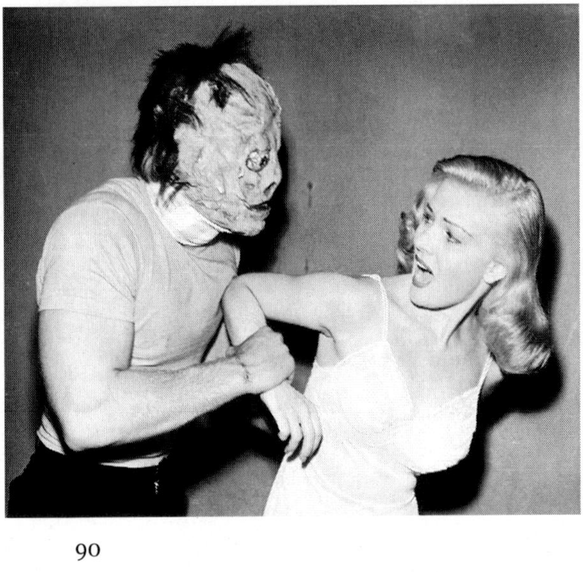

Philip Sheer, who had done such an original job on Landon's werewolf make-up, provided a much less effective one for Gary Conway, which was obviously based on Phil Leakey's work on Christopher Lee in *Curse* but with too much of a *papier mache*-and-putty look to be truly frightening. *I Was a Teenage Frankenstein*'s ultimate homage to *Curse* may have been in the tongue-in-cheek aside of stamping the address of Hammer's head office–113 Wardour Street–on its Professor's crates of lab equipment.

On its release in November 1957, *I Was a Teenage Frankenstein* received some reviews which were downright hostile, not because of the picture's quality but its supposed 'message'. In *The New York Times,* critic Richard W Nason was positively irate: 'If you discount any immediate connection between the mass media and the temper of the culture, then the film warrants little attention.. (The) automaton.. is a teenager assembled from the limbs of other teenagers. This is, in one sense, abhorrent. It forces one to acknowledge the impression that such films may aggravate the mass social sickness euphemistically termed "juvenile delinquency". Before one such act of surgical perversion, the mad doctor's assistant says, "I have no stomach for it". That would be a plausible reaction for any adult who had read the day's headlines about teen-age crime.'

The Curse of Frankenstein

Filmed mostly in black and white, *Teenage Frankenstein* nevertheless featured a full colour ending, as per *War of the Colossal Beast.* It is, quite literally, shocking, as it involves a death by electrocution as well as a gruesome scene of the alligator crunching on what is supposed to be human flesh. According to Cohen, interviewed by Tom Weaver in his book *Attack of the Monster*

Movie Makers, the alligator employed in the film had been acquired for that very purpose in life: Cohen claimed that it had been used to dispose of corpses by a serial killer operating out of Dallas, Texas. This is no doubt an apocryphal story, but it was an appropriate one!

Blood of Dracula (UK: *Blood is My Heritage)* might just as well have been called *I Was a Teenage Vampire,* but AIP would have known that Hammer's follow-up to *The Curse of Frankenstein* was to be a remake of *Dracula*, and it titled its new film accordingly.

The script, again by Kandel, is a virtual all-female remake of *Teenage Werewolf,* with a bit of *Reform School Girl* thrown into the mix. In a boarding school for girls, wayward teenager Nancy is taken under the wing of science teacher Miss Branding, who has evil designs upon her. She makes Nancy the subject of her experiments into the workings of the human mind and its ability to release awesome powers. Miss Branding employs an amulet, which she tells Nancy has come from the Carpathian Mountains, in order to hypnotise the girl and release those urges, which in Nancy's case involves metamorphosing into a monstrous bat-thing and committing vampiric murders during nights of the full moon.

For the starring role of Nancy, Strock and the producers cast Sandra Harrison, a young television actress who had also appeared in the *Adventures of Superman*, as well as *Father Knows Best*. Tying the film even more closely to *I Was a Teenage Werewolf* was the casting of Louise Lewis as Miss Branding; Lewis had previously played the kindly Principal Ferguson in *Teenage Werewolf*, and her genre credits included the same year's Paul Landres's *The Vampire*, with John Beal, Coleen Gray and Kenneth Tobey.

Others in the cast were Gail Ganley, who had appeared in Roger Corman's *Not of this Earth* (1957) for Allied Artists, Jerry Blaine, a songwriter who had written 'Eeny, Meeny, Miny, Mo' for *Teenage Werewolf* and who would write and perform 'Puppy Love' for *Blood of Dracula*, and veteran character actor Malcolm Atterbury,

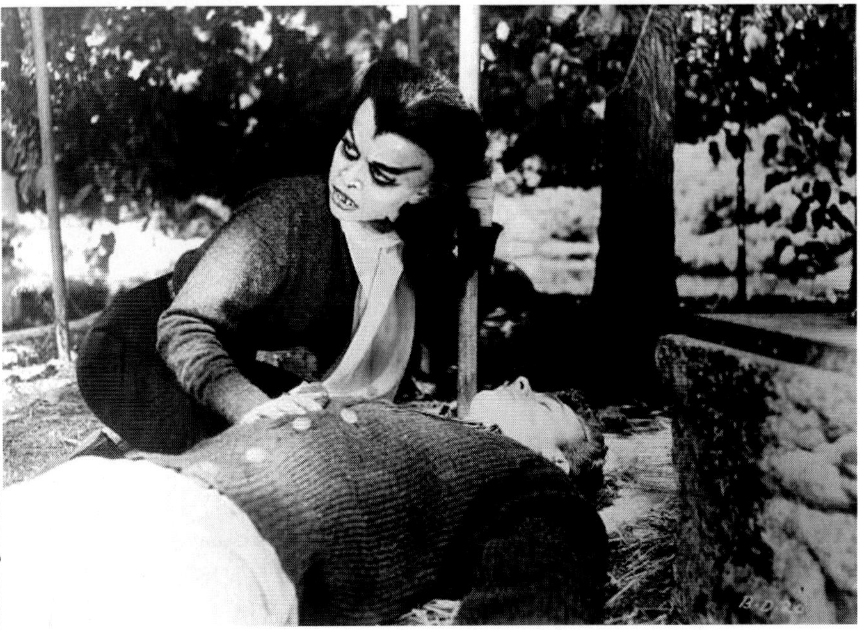

Blood of Dracula (Sandra Harrison, Jerry Blaine)

another cast member from *Teenage Werewolf,* who had appeared on television shows such as *Alfred Hitchcock Presents.* Far down the list was Richard Devon, who had played none other than Satan himself in Corman's *The Undead.*

As had been the case with *Teenage Frankenstein,* the shooting schedule for *Blood of Dracula* was extremely rushed, but Monroe Askins's cinematography was at least more atmospheric than Lothrop B Worth's on its companion-piece. Philip Scheer's make-up for Harrison-as-vampire is genuinely alarming; when the film was released to DVD, e-zine *DVD Verdict* noted, 'Her wild bat make-up is memorable, looking closer to *Nosferatu* with big hair than anything else.' While Valerie Gaunt in Hammer's *Dracula* is usually considered to be the first female vampire to sport fangs in a film, Harrison actually beat her to the punch by six months!

Again, the film features strong overtones of same-sex erotic attraction, as Dixon has pointed out: '...There is an unmistakable air of lesbianism in the film in the relationship between Nancy and Miss Branding, which is continually held up as being inherently manipulative and destructive, in contrast to the reassuring hetero-normality of Nancy's affections for the somewhat clueless Glenn (Michael Hall). As in the previous two films, Nancy is a young person who places her trust in an adult who seeks only her destruction, and views her as an expendable commodity in the name of science.'

The ending of *Blood of Dracula* is as weak as the dénouement of *Teenage Werewolf:* Nancy kills Miss Branding and is then killed herself by being impaled, as befits the vampire myth. There are elements of feminism in the film–Branding is driven to make a name for herself in a male-dominated field–but by the tale's finale, the suggestion that ambition could drive a woman to do awful deeds only underlines the time in which the movie was made: heterosexual relationships are the sole conduit of meaning in the world of the 1950s; anything else is an aberration to be stamped out. Whether this message was intentional or not is a matter of conjecture, but it is unmistakably there.

During that decade, the Catholic so-called 'Legion of Decency' attempted to hang on to its control over the faithful by 'condemning' movies which it felt should not be viewed by the devout. They had their work cut out for them as the fifties wore on, feeling the need to condemn such now-classic works as Henry Cornelius's *I Am a Camera* (1955), Roger Vadim's star-making *And God Created Woman* (1957) with Brigitte Bardot, and Elia Kazan's *Baby Doll* (1957) with Karl Malden, Carroll Baker and Eli Wallach. Although the Legion did not condemn *Blood of Dracula,* it strongly

Robert H Harris

cautioned Catholics to beware the film's 'stylised violence, hokey menace and sexual innuendo' and awarded the film an 'Adults Only' rating, long before there were any official rating systems in the US.

Cohen's next film for AIP was, in a sense, a follow-up to both *Teenage Werewolf* and *Teenage Frankenstein*. Again written by himself and Kandel, *How to Make a Monster* (1958) is perhaps the first authentically post-modern horror film inasmuch as it delivers shocks while at the same time spoofing the genre; complete with inside jokes, its scenario was loosely based on a real-life Hollywood story.

Make-up artist Jack Pierce had created all of the classic monsters for Universal Pictures, from Boris Karloff's Frankenstein monster and Mummy to Lon Chaney Jr's Wolf Man. Unfortunately for Pierce, a craftsman who became set in his ways, make-up artists in the 1940s had begun to use more modern techniques like foam latex, which were quicker and cheaper to apply. Pierce stuck to his old, familiar ways with cotton, collodion, mortician's wax and gum and ultimately, he paid the price: when a new regime took over Universal in 1946, Pierce was unceremoniously sacked after more than a decade of creating the studio's greatest monster make-ups. Bud Westmore would take over the make-up duties for comedy-horror film *Abbott & Costello Meet Frankenstein* (1948), but Pierce's departure, for all intents and purposes, brought an end to Universal's horror cycle.

The plot of *How to Make a Monster* parallels this event: Pete Drummond, head make-up artist for 25 years at 'American International Studios', is fired after the studio is taken over by another company. The new regime has no interest in making horror pictures and intends to produce only comedies and musicals 'with lots of

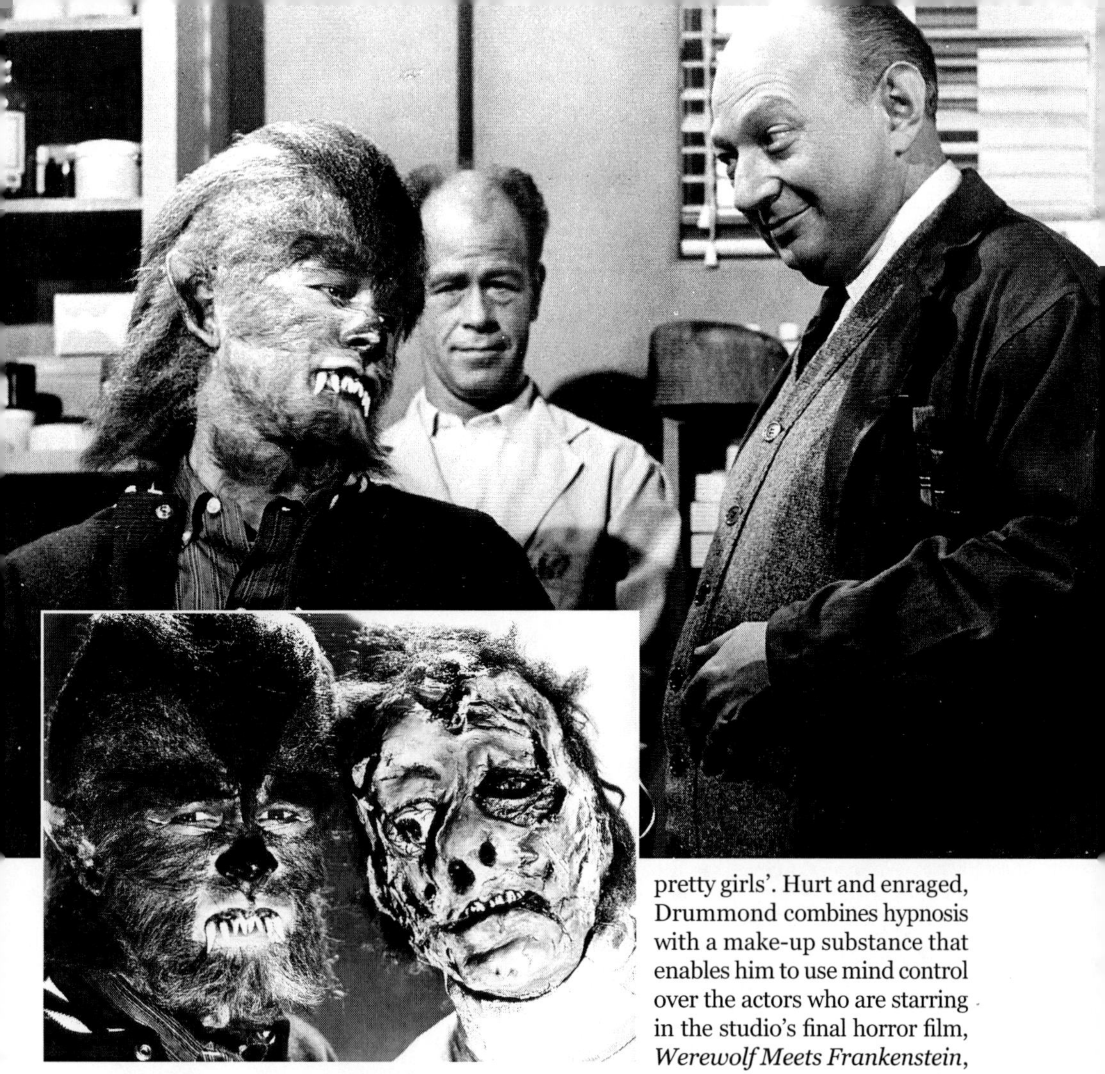

pretty girls'. Hurt and enraged, Drummond combines hypnosis with a make-up substance that enables him to use mind control over the actors who are starring in the studio's final horror film, *Werewolf Meets Frankenstein*, to turn them into real-life versions of his cinematic creations, through which he can then exact a proxy revenge.

Cohen cast John Ashley in the role of a singer–there always had to be at least one rock 'n' roll song in an AIP teenage monster picture–at the request of Nicholson, who had him under long-term contract. Nicholson's daughters admired Ashley, who had made a few mildly successful records in the fifties. He had also sung the tunes 'Hit and Run Lover' and 'Annie Laurie' in *Hot Rod Girl*, among others. (The song he sings in *How to Make a Monster*, 'You've Got to Have Ee-Ooo', is ghastlier than any of the murders in the film.)

Originally, Arkoff had wanted Bela Lugosi for the role of Drummond, having been unaware that Lugosi had died in 1956 until someone told him. Instead, veteran actor Robert H Harris was cast; Harris was a noted stage performer who had played in *Richard III* on Broadway, and he had just completed a feature role in *Peyton Place*, directed by Val Lewton protégé Mark Robson. In truth, Harris was too young for the part as written–other characters in the film refer to him as an 'old man', when in fact he was only in his forties at the time–but his characterisation overcomes the issue.

Gary Conway returned in the Teenage Frankenstein make-up, this time as an actor named Tony Mantell. Michael Landon did not reprise his Teenage Werewolf role as he was now finding success elsewhere; instead, the role of actor Larry Drake,

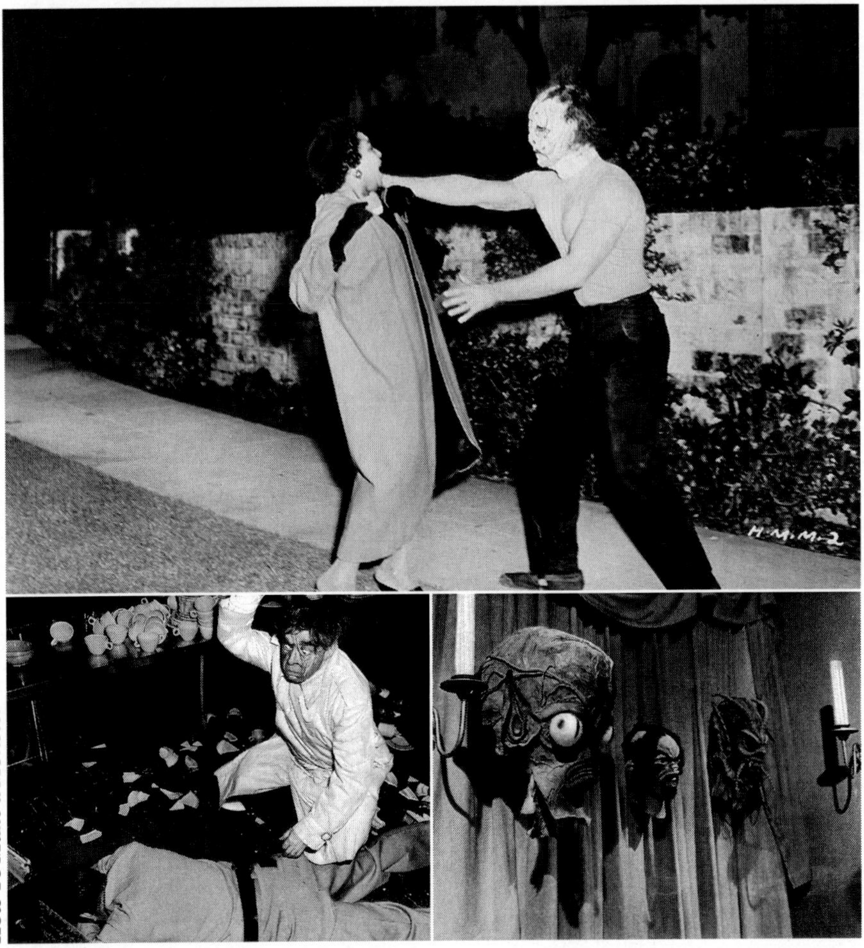

How To Make a Monster

who dons the werewolf make-up, was given to Gary Clarke, a young actor who had previously appeared on television in *Alfred Hitchcock Presents* and *Sky King*. The ubiquitous Morris Ankrum made an appearance in *How to Make a Monster*, while Robert Shayne, who had featured in such films as *Invaders From Mars* (1953) and *The Neanderthal Man* (1953), also showed up in a role. Producer Cohen appeared in the film uncredited, as a director in a projection room.

American International did not actually have a studio complex, so the scenes at the fictional studio were actually filmed at Ziv. In a neat promotion for Cohen's next production, tourists visiting the studio in the film are told by a tour guide that they are to be taken to the set of *Horrors of the Black Museum*–a plug for the movie that Cohen would make the following year.

Directed once again by Strock, *How to Make a Monster* is a worthy follow-up to its predecessors, highlighted this time by a good central performance; Harris is excellent in the role of Drummond, both sympathetic and cold-blooded by turns. Given the fact that the new studio heads are equally ruthless, viewer sympathy tends to lie with Drummond throughout the film, despite the fact that he sends innocent teenage boys to do his fiendish work.

Although the film was again shot in black and white, the entire final reel is given over to colour to highlight the flaming destruction of the fiery climax. In that climax, several of Drummond's creations–whom he refers to as his 'children'–are melted by the flames, and easily recognisable are Paul Blaisdell's masks and props from earlier AIP films *The She-Creature, It Conquered the World, Invasion of the Saucer Men, Voodoo Woman* and *Attack of the Puppet People.*

How to Make a Monster had cleverly spoofed the rock 'n' roll monster movie sub-genre which AIP had created. But it was considered innocuous enough by the British censor to be awarded only an 'A' certificate, so it now seemed as though that ship had somehow sailed. The question for the company became: where do we go from here? The answer quickly arrived–England.

Back in 1957, American International had truly gone 'international' when it co-produced *Cat Girl* in Britain with Nat Cohen and Stuart Levy's Anglo-Amalgamated. The film, a remake of sorts of Val Lewton's *Cat People* (1942) had been a first horror vehicle for Barbara Shelley, who would go on to star for Hammer in the likes of *The Gorgon* (1964), *Dracula Prince of Darkness* (1965) and *Quatermass and the Pit* (1967). AIP had put up $25,000 of the film's budget and provided a script by Lou Rusoff in exchange for distribution rights. Directed by Alfred Shaughnessy, *Cat Girl* was an atmospheric chiller with an excellent performance by Shelley in the title role. It was released in the US on the bottom of a double bill with *The Amazing Colossal Man* and sold on the tagline, 'To caress her is to tempt death!'

Anglo-Amalgamated, a British distribution company which occasionally made low-budget features at Merton Park Studios, achieved lasting success in 1958 when it produced *Carry On Sergeant,* the first in what would become a long-running film series. Anglo-Amalgamated was riding high as a result and open to suggestion from AIP, many of whose films they had already distributed in the UK.

Herman Cohen, interviewed by Tom Weaver for the book *Attack of the Monster*

***Cat Girl* (Ernest Milton, Lily Kann, Barbara Shelley)**

Movie Makers, said that he came up with the idea for *Horrors of the Black Museum*–the title mentioned in the course of *How to Make a Monster*–when he read a newspaper article about Scotland Yard's infamous Black Museum, the repository for a macabre collection of criminal memorabilia, including murderous implements which had belonged to such notorious killers as John Reginald Halliday Christie, John George Haigh and Neville Heath, along with death masks and other paraphernalia.

Cohen determined to visit the museum, which is not open to the general public. He supposedly knew a Scotland Yard inspector who enabled him to see some of the grisliest exhibits. The one that fascinated him most was a pair of binoculars used as a murder weapon; the slightest pressure on the binoculars' focussing ring released two metal spikes into the eyes of an unfortunate victim. According to Scotland Yard, the binoculars had been a 'gift' to an unsuspecting woman from a crazed stable boy whom she had jilted.

Inspired, Cohen wrote a treatment and had Kandel collaborate with him on the screenplay: Edmund Bancroft, a writer of thrillers, desires to include more unique and gruesome crimes in his books. To this end, he hypnotises his young assistant (in the by-now familiar plot twist) to commit them on his behalf in the guise of a monster; if it were not for the 'museum' element ringing the changes in the formula, the film would have been a logical follow-up to Cohen's previous 'teenage' monster jamborees, effectively 'I Was a Teenage Jekyll and Hyde'.

Half the money for the $164,000 budget was put up by Nat Cohen and Stuart Levy, with AIP contributing the other half. It was to be the first AIP horror in both CinemaScope and colour–not merely colour in the final reel.

The credited producer on the film was Jack Greenwood, but that was merely to ensure that the film qualified for the Eady Levy, a tax subsidy linked to box office receipts in the UK, which was intended to help support the British film industry. Cohen actually produced the film, with Greenwood acting as associate producer.

***Horrors of the Black Museum* (Michael Gough, Shirley Anne Field)**

Originally, Cohen wanted to hire Vincent Price for the role of Bancroft. At the time, Price was 'hot', having just appeared in *The Fly* for Fox and in William Castle's *House on Haunted Hill* for Allied Artists. There was also talk of hiring Orson Welles for the role, but Anglo-Amalgamated insisted on a British actor, as they worked for less money! That bottom line-thinking certainly appealed to AIP, which had decided to make the film in Britain in the first place because it would be cheaper.

The role went instead to Michael Gough, who had just played Arthur Holmwood in Terence Fisher's *Dracula* for Hammer. Gough had been in films since 1948, when he made his debut in *Blanche Fury* opposite Valerie Hobson and Stewart Granger. He had also played one of the murderers of Clarence in Laurence Olivier's *Richard III* (1955). Gough had been a conscientious objector during World War II, but he was now to embark on a career as one of the most unsympathetic villains in the history of the horror film.

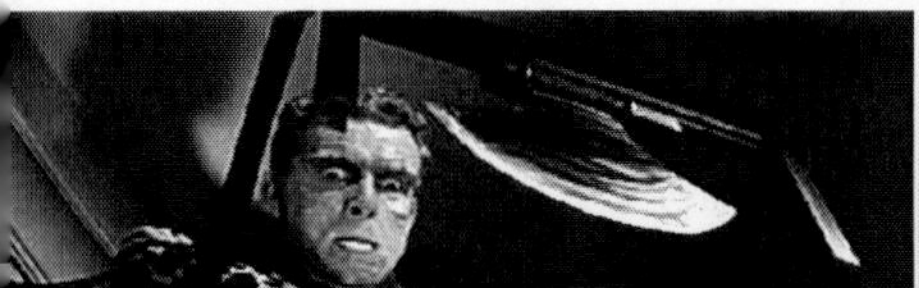

Second-billed in the film was London-born June Cunningham, a busty blonde who had studied at the Aida Foster School of Drama. In January 1957, her looks had got her on to the cover of *Picturegoer*. That same year, she had appeared in Basil Dearden's *The Smallest Show on Earth* with Virginia McKenna, Bill Travers and Peter Sellers, as well as in Wolf Rilla's *The Scamp*. In *Horrors of the Black Museum,* she was cast as Bancroft's restless young wife.

Graham Curnow, at 29, was cast as Rick, Bancroft's unsuspecting assistant and the film's reluctant 'teenage' Jekyll-and-Hyde. Curnow's previous credits included Ken Annakin's *Three Men in a Boat* (1956), but his playing was marked by a lack of experience that belied any prior history in films and gave *Horrors of the Black Museum* more of an affinity with its lower-budgeted American stable-mates than should have been merited by its upscale British production values.

Former model Shirley Anne Field was only 20 when she was asked to play the role of Angela, Rick's ill-fated girlfriend, but other performers were mostly veterans: Geoffrey Keen had been in such distinguished British films as Carol Reed's *Odd Man Out* (1947) with James Mason, as well as Reed's classic *The Third Man* (1949),

and busy character actors such as Sydney Bromley and Vanda Godsell filled in the supporting roles.

Cohen decided to hire Arthur Crabtree as his director. Crabtree had been in the business since 1936 and had recently directed the sci-fi/horror thriller *Fiend Without a Face* (1958) for Anglo, which had been released in the US by M-G-M. Cohen later told Tom Weaver, 'The price was right and the old guy needed a job, so I hired him. And he was exactly what I wanted and needed as a good craftsman.'

When filming was complete, a 15-minute prologue featuring real-life hypnotist Emile Franchele was shot in 'HypnoVista' for the American market by Jim Nicholson, who felt that the film needed an added gimmick. He was perhaps taking a page out of William Castle's book, who had employed gimmicks like 'Emergo' and 'Percepto' in *House on Haunted Hill* and *The Tingler* (1959). 'HypnoVista' really did not add up to much, being more or less a primer on how to hypnotise people, although Cohen claimed that when the film was later released to television, the prologue was removed 'because it does hypnotise some people'.

Horrors of the Black Museum was a blatant attempt by AIP to beat Hammer at its own game and on its home turf. Of course, AIP could not afford to make a Gothic period piece, so it made the most of scenes of sex and sadism and the film became notorious in the UK as the first of Anglo's 'Sadean' trilogy, the completing two being *Circus of Horrors* and *Peeping Tom* (both 1960). Gough's performance is ripe to the point of fermentation; he completely overshadows all of the other performers and makes their own contributions almost superfluous. His megalomaniacal playing and cold-eyed relish at the murderous goings-on caused a scene in which he disposes of a blackmailing shop-owner (Beatrice Varley) with a pair of oversized pincers to be cut by the British censor.

Gerard Schurmann's music is suitably overwrought and Desmond Dickinson's cinematography, while over-lit, highlights the lurid Eastmancolor effects that fans would come to love. Artistically, it was not a patch on the average Hammer horror of the time–and that year was a big one for Hammer, including such features as *The Mummy, The Hound of the Baskervilles* and *The Man Who Could Cheat Death*–but the emphasis on sex and violence (the eye-piercing binoculars being a memorable example) helped to propel *Horrors of the Black Museum* to financial success.

In his 1997 book *Monsters in the Closet: Homosexuality and the Horror Film,* Harry Benshoff wrote that the homosexual undertones in Cohen's films echoed the cliché that 'older homosexuals were out to recruit young people into their ranks'. Cohen denied this in his commentary for the *Horrors of the Black Museum* DVD release: 'I've had several friends of mine who've seen *Horrors of the Black Museum* recently who asked me, "Did you think this had sort of a gay, homosexual undertone as you wrote the picture?" And Aben and I never thought of that at the time. In those days, a lot of [American] critics would say that Herman Cohen made good, clean horror films. Of course, now, in the '90s, it certainly does look that way, especially in Bancroft's speech to his young assistant, Rick. Mind you, there's a lot of truth to what he's telling him...'

The speech in question reads, in part: 'As you know, I have no offspring, no kin. Someday, all of this will be yours–everything I possess: my home, my money, my books and our private Black Museum. Your future–my destiny–our very lives are menaced by Angela, who stands in our way. One must never trust a woman; it was no accident that Satan was able to tempt Eve before Adam.'

Dixon writes of this scene in *Senses of Cinema:* 'The underlying message here seems absolutely clear. Whether the result of willful denial or personal myopia, Cohen perversely chose to deny the driving force behind the narratives he created. Just as Cohen's films exploited youth by their very nature, being 'exploitation films', so the adults in his films mimicked Cohen's own attitude towards his teen audiences, relentlessly and ruthlessly exploiting the teens who trust them.'

During the production of *Horrors of the Black Museum,* Nicholson asked Cohen to produce a second film as a supporting feature. His instructions were to make the second feature quickly, cheaply and in black and white. In his interview for Weaver's

The Headless Ghost (Richard Lyon, Liliane Sottane, David Rose)

book, Cohen related: 'I told him I'd see what I could come up with. I started thinking, "What the hell can I do?" and I thought maybe I should do a comedy. So Aben Kandel and I wrote this picture…'

The film was *The Headless Ghost,* a not-so-rollicking comedy-horror about a group of teenagers who visit an old English castle and encounter a ghost or two, helping one to retrieve his missing head so that he can rest in peace, rather than in pieces. It was filmed at the same studio–Merton Park–as *Horrors of the Black Museum,* with some additional shooting, according to Cohen, 'at an actual castle', although he never specified which one.

The Headless Ghost went into production while *Horrors* was still being edited and Cohen needed a director who could bring it in quickly. He hired Peter Graham Scott, a former editor who had started directing in 1948 with a film called *Panic at Madame Tussaud's,* a cheapie mystery featuring none other than Harry Fine, who would go on to co-produce *The Vampire Lovers* for Hammer and AIP in 1970.

Richard Lyon was cast in the leading role of Bill. Lyon was one of radio and TV's 'Lyons' family, whose escapades had also featured in a pair of films for Hammer-Exclusive in the early fifties. 'I got great publicity for using Richard Lyon in one of the leads–Louella Parsons gave us a headline story–because he was Bebe Daniels and Ben Lyon's son,' Cohen said subsequently. I met him and he needed a job badly, so we hired him.'

The Headless Ghost was a forgettable trifle that felt overlong despite the fact that it ran only 62 minutes. When Shakespearian stage veteran Clive Revill is onscreen as the titular ghost, interest perks up, but Revill aside, the dreary goings on are dire in

the extreme. Revill's 'headless' persona is obviously a dwarf in a costume enlarged to normal size so as to make him appear so, and other 'effects' are of similar quality. As usual with AIP, the poster was beautifully wrought but it made promises that were not to be kept ('Head-hunting teenagers lost in the haunted castle!') and the film never once elevates itself above its second-feature status. One of the few scenes to keep viewers awake involves Josephine Blake as a 'Kooch Dancer Ghost', cavorting in gratuitous style to pad out the film's abbreviated length. Even its producer was less than fond of it, as Cohen told Weaver: 'We knocked out that picture very, very fast; that's why the running time is so short. But I honestly don't recall too much else about (it), it was so bad.' Cohen also said that he found the film unfunny–something of an understatement–and that he 'never liked it'.

The double feature was reviewed by Richard W Nason in *The New York Times* under the headline 'Hypno-Vision Bows'. '*Horrors of the Black Museum* has more significance as a promotional stunt than as a motion picture. Herman Cohen produced the film and also helped with the script, whose dialogue shows a convenient disregard for motivation and dramatic technique,' Nason noted. 'On the same bill is a pale and protracted bit of miscast whimsy entitled *The Headless Ghost,* about some college students in an English castle who assist the spirit of a baron in getting his head back. On the same programme there is a filler made by a telephone company. All in all, it's a pretty dismal show to see on an otherwise sunny day.'

Michael Gough was brought back for Cohen's next picture, *Konga* (1961), which was originally titled, naturally, *I Was a Teenage Gorilla.* The working title was no more than that as the teenage monster craze had well and truly run its course, and an allusion to the title ape's illustrious giant predecessor was soon deemed to be the

Konga (Claire Gordon, Michael Gough)

way to go in terms of the box office. Cohen had long been a fan of *King Kong* (1933) and he thought that a movie featuring a giant ape in colour would be a sure bet with a contemporary audience. Accordingly, he paid RKO, owner of the *Kong* copyright, $25,000 for the rights to use the name in his advertising.

Cohen would claim that the special effects for *Konga*–which had now to follow in the saurian footsteps of the King Brothers' spectacular dino-romp *Gorgo* (1960)–took eighteen months to complete. When one looks at the film now, that seems hard to believe; the effects in *Konga* are primitive, even by the standards of the time.

Shot again at Merton Park Studios, with some location filming around London, *Konga* is one of Cohen's–and Gough's–silliest, most over the top movies. The wild plot concerns Dr Decker (Gough), who has returned from Africa after spending a year there, having been presumed dead. During his time in the jungle, Decker has discovered a method of growing plants (and animals) to immense size. He has brought with him a chimpanzee on whom he intends to experiment and finding that he has 'enemies' in London, he uses the chimp–enlarged to the size of a gorilla–to eliminate them. After a series of murders, Konga is given an overdose of the serum and he grows to gigantic proportions and goes on the loose, causing panic in the streets of the capital.

Again written by Cohen and Kandel, *Konga* has Gough overacting to the point of making his *Horrors of the Black Museum* performance seem a model of restraint by comparison. Joining him in the fray were some distinguished names, including Jack Watson and George Pastell, as well as lesser-known players such as television actress Margo Johns, who is rather effective as Decker's long-suffering assistant. Token totty Claire Gordon, as Decker's student and the object of his lust, is quite dreadful, however, but no more so than Jess Conrad, a minor British pop star whose turn as Gordon's

Konga (Margo Johns, Michael Gough)

boyfriend was one of several that he would make over the next few years in an abortive attempt to break into acting. Konga himself, when grown to full size, was actually bit-part actor Paul Stockman in an ape-suit which had been rented from famed Hollywood 'gorilla-man' George Burrows; Stockman's previous credit had been as a living corpse in Sidney J Furie's *Dr Blood's Coffin* from a year earlier.

The climax of the movie, in which the now-giant ape escapes onto the streets of London, is highly exaggerated on the poster art, with Konga seemingly towering over the city. 'Not since *King Kong* has the screen exploded with such might, fury and spectacle!' screamed the copy. What amounted to only a few last-reel scenes, with dozens of extras running screaming through the city, were achieved only after Cohen was able to talk the relevant authorities into allowing the production to stage the 'panic' late at night on more-or-less empty streets. Canadian-born director John Lemont, a television veteran who had helmed a mere two features, *The Shakedown* and *And Women Shall Weep* (both 1960), had his work cut out trying to make the reality of the film match the promise of the poster with the limited resources that Cohen and AIP alotted him for the task.

HOLLY'S CAFE

Every night for a week, between 11pm and 6am, Lemont and his crew filmed scores of extras supposedly fleeing from the king-sized Konga, who was of course to be matted in later. The production team waited until the final night of location shooting in the London borough of Croydon to photograph Konga's death scene, which involved the use of anti-aircraft guns and bazookas. The mayhem that resulted was alarming to the residents, who awoke to the sound of heavy gunfire, and some of them thought that they were under attack. The phones rang off the hook at Scotland Yard. For the following few days, Cohen and his crew offered local citizens a *mea culpa*: flowers and boxes of chocolate.

The climax goes a long way to make *Konga* appear to have a bigger budget than it actually had. The combination of moderately-convincing miniatures, Stockman in the suit and decent travelling mattes give the final scenes a certain schlocky grandeur, even if Decker, clutched Fay Wray-like in Konga's huge hand, can too easily be seen to be a doll (except in the doctored publicity photographs).

Konga was released in January 1961, as always as part of a double feature, with *The Hellfire Club* in the UK and with *Master of the World,* starring Vincent Price, in the US. Needless to say, the reviews were not kind, a typical one by Eugene Archer in *The New York Times* stating, in part: 'The children attending yesterday's new neighbourhood theatre double bill greeted *Konga* with misplaced guffaws.. The British *Konga* is nothing more than an overblown King Kong, hammily played by Michael Gough and an improbable-looking ape.'

While *Konga* is indeed an overblown, under-budgeted film, it is never boring,

Konga (Claire Gordon)

thanks to sheer drive-in bravado and Gough chewing all the scenery that he can find. The film's nonsensical plot was a late-entry throwback to the 'mad scientist' cheapies of the 1950s, colour and scope being the only things that separate it from the likes of *The She Creature* or *I Was a Teenage Werewolf*. It is campy fun despite itself, but it represented the end of a particular era for AIP, and the end of a cycle of horror films aimed specifically at the teen market.

Konga was the last film that Herman Cohen made for American International. Nicholson and Arkoff wanted to shave the amount of his percentage in the picture so like Bert I Gordon before him, he left for pastures new. His next film, *Black Zoo* (1963), was made for Allied Artists but still starred Michael Gough. He then went on to produce British horrors such as *A Study in Terror* and *Berserk!* (the latter with Joan Crawford–and, of course, Gough!). His last British film was *Craze* (1973) with Jack Palance. Herman Cohen died of throat cancer on June 2, 2002.

Konga's American co-feature, *Master of the World*, was the second AIP film to star the company's latest acquisition, Hollywood B-lister Vincent Price, whose future role in the AIP story had not yet been assured by the returns from his debut outing, *House of Usher* (about which more in chapter 4). Price played Robur, Jules Verne's aeronautical version of his own Captain Nemo from *20,000 Leagues Under the Sea*, who had featured in two of the French author's 19th-century science fiction yarns: *Robur the Conqueror* and *Master of the World* (1886 and 1904). Verne had come to the fore in film adaptations in recent years, thanks to the release of major studio films like *Around the World in 80 Days* (1956), *From the Earth to the Moon* (1958) and the Cinemascope production of *Journey to the Centre of the Earth* (1959). AIP may not have had the financial resources of Hollywood's 'Big 5', but it had creativity to spare and it forged ahead on its own Verne adaptation on a $½ million budget, commencing in 1960 just prior to the opening of *House of Usher*. It was AIP's first attempt to mount

Master of the World (Vincent Price)

Master of the World (David Frankham, Charles Bronson)

a 'prestige' picture, boasting more location work and a larger cast than ever before, and it was the company's most expensive production to date.

Veteran William Witney was picked to direct. Witney had made *The Bonnie Parker Story* (1958) and *Paratroop Command* (1959) for the company, but he was mainly known for westerns and his tightly-choreographed fight sequences, patterned after the structure of the musical numbers in the thirties' films of Busby Berkeley. Author Richard Matheson, who had penned the script for *Usher*, was brought in to adapt the novel(s) and Price was given the plum role of Robur; Charles Bronson, who had played 'Machine Gun' Kelly for AIP and was now beginning to find fame in the likes of John Sturges's *The Magnificent Seven*, was cast as Robur's nemesis, John Strock. (Bronson had previously appeared with Price under his real name of Charles Buchinsky in 1953's *House of Wax*.) Henry Hull, who is possibly best-remembered for the title-role of Universal's *Werewolf of London* (1935), was persuaded out of retirement to play the role of the industrialist kidnapped by Robur in his flying machine, the Albatross. Hull's screen daughter was to be Mary Webster, and bringing up the rear was David Frankham. Frankham's role was to have gone to Mark Damon, who had co-starred with Price in *Usher*, but Damon had other plans.

David Frankham recalled, 'Vincent was at the studio getting wardrobe fittings for filming the following Monday when he was told that a crisis had arisen: Mark Damon had apparently decided at the last minute to quit the picture and move to Rome. Panic ensued–until Vincent recommended a young actor he had worked with just the year before–me. Consequently, later that day I was sent out to the studio to meet William Witney (the director) and was told the part was mine.'

The film on which Frankham had worked with Price was *Return of the Fly*, and his memories of filming *Master of the World* are still vivid. He recalled: '*Master of the World* was filmed at the old Republic Studios in the San Fernando Valley in the

summer of 1960. There was no air conditioning and the cast and crew rushed for the outdoor exits the moment William Witney hollered "Cut". We had the luxury of a three-week shoot although being AIP, it was still fast and low-budget. On the first day of filming, we spent the morning shooting the opening scene–the aftermath of the crash in the volcano, with Vincent standing over us with his cape fluttering in the wind–and then without a break, we moved up to Paradise Cove to shoot the final scenes. It was a very happy set, and Henry Hull and I hit it off especially. He had the energy of a man half his age. Months after the shoot I got a call from Shelley Hull, a casting director (and Henry's son), offering me a guest role on the *Wells Fargo* TV series. He said his dad insisted he find me one. And, as it turned out, it was to be directed by William Witney! Henry Hull often led sing-a-longs among the cast.'

Not singing along quite so merrily as the rest of the cast was Charles Bronson, as Frankham revealed. 'Charles hated doing interviews and repeatedly turned them down–"Get Dave to do it"–and I was more than happy to oblige. He seemed shy and stayed to himself. He didn't really socialise with us much, and preferred to go to a neighbouring set where his friend Steve McQueen was filming. Vincent, who liked a social set, once said to me, "I just don't get that guy." He wasn't criticising Charles, but Vincent was so gregarious that he was genuinely puzzled by Charles' introverted personality. Vincent always called me "Kid" - even as late as 1990. During filming he gave me a copy of his book on art, *I Like What I Know*, and signed it, "Master of the World–and don't you forget it!"'

Price was known for his sly sense of humour. 'While we were filming the closing scenes, in which Robur is injured, Vincent took great delight in stopping traffic as we crossed the street to the Tahitian restaurant for lunch with bloodstained bandages around his head,' Frankham recalled.

The special effects team for the film comprised of Wah Chang and Gene Warren, whose Projects Unlimited company would win an Academy Award for its work on George Pal's *The Time Machine* (1960). For *Master of the World*, they had to design and build a working model of the Albatross from Verne's description but despite the

David Frankham, Mary Webster, Vincent Price, composer Les Baxter / CENTRE: Frankham ..with James Nicholson and wife / TOP: ..with Henry Hull

film's high budget, stock footage had to be utilised to convey the machine's assault on the cities of the world, such as shots of Elizabethan London from Olivier's *Henry V*, standing in unconvincingly for that in the (Victorian) period of the novel. Other shots of the Albatross destroying warships in a naval battle were taken from London Films' *Lady Hamilton* (1941)–even less convincingly as the original was in black and white!

When the film was released in May 1961, AIP's publicity department sent several of the actors around the US to talk up the production, including Frankham: 'AIP had me going the rounds of Los Angeles radio stations and doing interviews. I carried along the model of the airship–as if anyone could see that on the radio! They also sent me to an American Bandstand-type live TV program with the airship, where all the teenagers stood around shaking their heads in disbelief and total disinterest at this square standing there with a weird model.'

In many respects, *Master of the World* is an impressive film, especially for AIP. At 102 minutes, it has an epic feel by the company's previous standards and it features one of Price's better performances. His Robur is megalomaniacal, to be sure, but his intention, like that of his forebear Captain Nemo, is to end war forever. His way of ensuring it is draconian, but his purpose is high-minded. When the morality of what he is doing is is remarked as 'mad', he responds: 'All well and sane to be the owner of factories, the products of which cause the violent deaths of millions in wartime and in peace. But to kill hundreds or even thousands with the aim of ending such deaths for all time? This is "madness"?'

Matheson is on record as feeling that Bronson was 'miscast'. He certainly looks uncomfortable in period costume and appears to have little rapport with the others in the cast. But 'house' composer Les Baxter contributed a spectacular score and Daniel Haller's production design is first rate, his Albatross interiors gleaming with just the right combination of Victorian 'modernity' and antiquated mechanical artefacts.

The cinematography by veteran Gilbert Warrenton was another plus, its vivid hues helping to give the film the 'big budget' look which it sometimes achieves. But AIP did not really have the wherewithal to mount such a high-concept fantasy, and the effects too often vary from the adequate to the poor (painted backdrops and sub-par matte work, though the Albatross itself is superb).

Master of the World is no masterpiece, but it is a highly entertaining fantasy adventure which, while not in the same rank as Verne adaptations like *20,000 Leagues Under the Sea* (1954), does still manage to capture its author's sense of *Boys Own* fantastic melodrama. But the film was only modestly successful and even played as a mere second feature (to *On the Fiddle*) in the UK. Despite talk of it at one time, it did not lead to a sequel–but as Matheson's script had already combined both Robur novels into one, such an eventuality could only have been wishful thinking.

By the time *Master of the World* opened, AIP had other things in mind for Vincent Price. He was about to become its biggest, most popular star, but not in anything as lighthearted as a Jules Verne fantasy. Price would soon be Hollywood's number one purveyor of all things moody and macabre–AIP's very own 'Merchant of Menace', and the screen's great interpreter of the Gothic world of one of America's most illustrious literary figures, Edgar Allan Poe.

4

AIP GOTHIC

CORMAN, POE AND PRICE

Amid all the activity with other producers and directors, Roger Corman was hardly being put out to pasture by AIP. On the contrary, he was as prolific as ever and his cinematic technique appeared to become more polished with every picture he made, despite the fact that Arkoff and Nicholson rarely gave him much of a budget with which to work. That was because they knew that their star director could still turn in a well-made production on next to nothing that would likely turn a profit.

One of Corman's most interesting black-and-white films was an oddity called *The Undead* (1957), starring Pamela Duncan as another innocent whisked back to a previous life, Allison Hayes as a sexy witch, and Billy Barty as her familiar. The script, again inspired by Bridey Murphy, was written by Charles B Griffith entirely in iambic pentameter (a favoured Shakespearian verse-form), which Corman loved at first but then asked to be changed. Elements of the original dialogue remain in a sequence set in the Middle Ages, which gives the film a quirky feel. Adding to the strangeness is the fact that the bat into which Barty (as an imp) transforms was actually a leftover 'alien' from *It Conquered the World.*

Filmed in a converted supermarket, *The Undead* (which was originally called *The Trance of Diana Love*) was completed in six days. It was Corman's first venture into the genre for which he would become best-known: Gothic horror. The medieval scenes, despite their low budget, reflect a real flair for the outré, especially an eerie diversion to a witches' sabbat.

Corman continued to branch out into other genres in the late fifties. In 1958, he directed *Machine Gun Kelly,* a highly-fictionalised biopic of the Prohibition gangster starring Charles Bronson. French critics praised the film, proclaiming Corman to be the next American 'auteur'. He was flattered by the French reviews, though not by those of the American critics who dismissed the film as 'sordid', but he continued to churn out exploitation product for AIP. Next up was a script by R Wright Campbell called *Prehistoric World,* with the leading role played by a future star of *The Magnificent Seven* and TV's *The Man From UNCLE,* Robert Vaughn.

Machine Gun Kelly (Charles Bronson)

Ultimately released in 1958 as *Teenage Caveman,* the movie featured the usual 'surprise' ending: the 'prehistoric' world is actually a post-apocalyptic one in which the ancestors of the survivors of a nuclear holocaust have reverted to living in caves! The cautionary tale ends with a voice-over asking soberly, 'Will humanity someday repeat its nuclear folly after civilisation has once again risen to its former heights?'

Corman invariably did his best to inject sub-text into his genre films, no matter

what assignment AIP gave him. One such project–and one of his most intriguing at the time–was 1959's *A Bucket of Blood,* written by Charles B Griffith. It came about because AIP had wanted Corman to produce another horror film but only gave him $50,000 and a five-day shooting schedule in which to do it. An additional caveat was that he had to use leftover sets from *Diary of a High School Bride,* another teenage throwaway directed by Burt Topper to co-feature with a comedy-horror called *Ghost of Dragstrip Hollow.* The leftover sets included a coffee house, an apartment and a police station interior. Corman asked Griffith to write something for those sets, but something out of the ordinary. Between them, they came up with the idea of shooting a satire about the then-current beatnik sub-culture. Interviewed for the book *Roger Corman: Blood Sucking Vampires, Flesh Eating Cockroaches and Driller Killers,* Griffith told author Beverly Gray that Corman had balked at the idea of making a comedy (despite the comedic elements in other of his films, such as *Viking Women*, which he had directed the previous year). 'You have to be good,' he said. 'We don't have the time or money to be good, so we stick to action.' Griffith eventually talked him into doing it because it was such a tiny amount of money on a short schedule that he could not fail to make a profit from it. 'Just shoot it straight,' Griffith said, when Corman asked how he should approach the material.

The genesis of the film was an evening that Corman and Griffith 'spent drifting around the beatnik coffee houses, observing the scene and tossing ideas and reactions back and forth until we had the basic story,' Corman revealed in a 2007 article for *LA Weekly*. They built the structure on Michael Curtiz's 1933 horror classic *Mystery of the Wax Museum,* which had already been remade as *House of Wax*. The movie was shot under the title *The Living Dead.*

The plot concerned Walter Paisley (Dick Miller), who works at clearing tables in a coffee house and envies the 'arty' regulars who frequent the place. He yearns to impress Carla (Barboura Morris), a bohemian whom he secretly desires. When

A Bucket of Blood (Dick Miller)

he accidentally kills his landlady's cat, Walter covers the body in plaster to hide the evidence and, after displaying the results as a 'sculpture', is acclaimed as a brilliant artist. His new-found 'friends', who previously had ignored him when not making fun of him, ask to see more of his work. Walter has no artistic talent, so he resorts to murder to furnish him with additional 'sculptures'.

The notion of setting *Mystery of the Wax Museum* in the world of the beatniks turned out to be inspired. Shot in May 1959, *A Bucket of Blood* was released by AIP in October of that year. *Variety* did not quite know what to make of it, opining, 'During the first half of the picture, there are many opportunities for gruesome humour, of which writer Charles B Griffith takes full advantage. In the latter half, the humour

Creature From the Haunted Sea (Antony Carbone, Betsy Jones-Morland)

becomes lost...' The reviewer clearly missed the point of the black comedy in the second half of the film, but he did single out Dick Miller as being able to 'sustain a sense of poignancy while acting conceited and committing atrocities.'

Years later, Miller said, '*A Bucket of Blood* is still my favourite picture. None of these are great pictures, understand. But I always thought if *A Bucket of Blood* had had another chunk of money in production it would have ranked with any of the top horror films. It's the best script Chuck ever wrote.'

Corman himself liked the movie so much that he made another one just like it, the more famous *The Little Shop of Horrors* (1960), which he released through his own company, FilmGroup, when AIP declined to distribute it on the grounds that some of the characters could be interpreted as anti-semitic. Mel Welles, who played Gravis Mushnick in the film, considered that there was no intent to defame any ethnic group. In any case, the film was released, became a cult classic (in part because it featured one of Jack Nicholson's earliest performances) and was subsequently remade as a stage and film musical.

Corman followed up *The Little Shop of Horrors* with a third comedy-horror in *Creature From the Haunted Sea* (1961), a parody of spy and gangster movies mixed in with an underwater monster. It, too, was released by FilmGroup.

Corman was not abandoning AIP; he was just trying to get them to think outside the box. The market for black-and-white genre films was diminishing. Colour films like *Horrors of the Black Museum* were taking more money than the impoverished second features which had been the company's bread and butter since its inception. The facts are disputed as to who initiated the upgrade in AIP production quality–Corman claimed that it was his idea, and Arkoff claimed it was his–but the long and short of it is that AIP gave Corman $350,000, along with colour and CinemaScope, to bring Edgar Allan Poe's short story 'The Fall of the House of Usher' to the screen.

The success of Hammer's Gothic horror films undoubtedly played a role in this change of tactic at AIP. Hammer's films had already spawned imitations–a sure sign

House of Usher (Vincent Price)

of success–such as Tempean's *Blood of the Vampire* (1958). Corman insisted that the idea to adapt Poe, *the* great American writer of horror tales, was inspired by a bound volume of his short stories that his father had given him when he was a child. Corman's version was that Arkoff initially rejected the idea of adapting 'The Fall of the House of Usher' because there was no monster in it. He told Arkoff that the house itself was the monster.

Arkoff's account differed with Corman's. He told Mark McGee, 'There's a story out about me that I didn't want to do the Poe picture. That's all bullshit. If people want to believe that old business that I didn't want to make *House of Usher* because it didn't have a monster.. It's so ridiculous.'

Whichever is correct, Nicholson contacted Richard Matheson, the author of the classic genre novels *I Am Legend* and *The Shrinking Man* (the latter of which had been made into a successful film by Universal-International in 1957) to write the screenplay. Matheson was made aware of both the budget and the fifteen-day shooting schedule but was not fazed by either. The story was essentially a three-hander, which all took place in a single, forbidding mansion, so there was not a great deal on which money needed to be spent.

House of Usher (Mark Damon, Myrna Fahey)

With a crew that included art director Daniel Haller and cinematographer Floyd Crosby, *House of Usher* went into production in January 1960. Much of the budget went on the salary of its leading man, Hollywood actor Vincent Price. In the 1950s, Price had become America's most prolific horror star, lending his arched eyebrows and velvet voice to *House of Wax* (1953), *The Fly*, *House on Haunted Hill* (both 1958), *The Tingler*, *Return of the Fly* (both 1959) and more. Cast as Roderick Usher, Price threw himself into the role, shaving off his trademark moustache and dyeing his hair white to suggest the character's sensitivity to sunlight.

The other cast members were Mark Damon and Myrna Fahey. Damon played Philip Winthrop, in effect the narrator of the story in print. Born in Chicago, Damon had worked mostly in American television before entering into films with *Inside Detroit* (1956) starring Dennis O'Keefe. Prior to *House of Usher*, he had appeared as a thug in a teenage gang movie called *This Rebel Breed*. Fahey was cast as Madeline Usher, Roderick's ill-fated sister and the object of Philip's affections. Most of her previous experience was also in television. The only other major role was that of Bristol, the Usher family retainer. He was played by veteran actor Harry Ellerbe, who had been appearing in Hollywood films since the 1930s.

With the film in the can, AIP launched a more 'prestigious' advertising campaign than its theatrical partners were used to. The sales department sent a letter to sub-distributors that read, in part:

'I.. enclose a proof of the newspaper campaign that has been prepared for the Edgar Allan Poe classic House of Usher in CinemaScope and colour starring Vincent Price. As you will note from these proofs, we have included a little bit of everything to reach the largest possible audience.

'At this time I would also like to advise you that the radio campaign for House of Usher was prepared by Gordon McLendon, who has a reputation for turning out some of the most powerful radio campaigns ever heard. The radio spots on House of Usher are among the most impressive he has ever done.

'We are sure that.. House of Usher will be one of the top grossers of the year.'

The radio spots, unlike those for earlier films, were subdued and elegant: 'Only once did I risk the most distant glimpses of the grim and foreboding House of Usher. The mere sight of that awesome structure, huge and menacing, struck me chill with fear. It lay like a malignant sore that festered in the middle of the wasteland. Overhead, the clouds hung low and a ghastly vapour rose from the ground. It seemed that the roots of the house touched the very coals of Hell.' This voice-over was followed by Price quoting from the film, after which the announcer returned to intone, 'Edgar Allan Poe's demonic tale of the ungodly, the evil *House of Usher*!'

This was a very different kind of campaign for AIP, and it worked like a charm. Audiences flocked to see the new colour Gothic despite the fact that in many venues, it was teamed with a more typical AIP potboiler, *Attack of the Giant Leeches*. It was *Usher* that brought people into the theatres, however, and it was *Usher* that brought in the biggest percentage of the profits. In some cinemas, it was paired with *Psycho,* and queues stretched around the block.

Eugene Archer's review in *The New York Times* was less than kind. 'American International, with good intentions of presenting a faithful adaptation of Edgar Allan Poe's classic tale of the macabre.. blithely ignored the author's style. The producers have made a horror film that provides a fair degree of literacy at the cost of a patron's patience.' Other reviews were more favourable, however. *Variety* noted, 'It is a film that should attract mature tastes as well as those who come to the cinema for sheer thrills. All things considered.. the fall of the *House of Usher* seems to herald the rise of AIP.' In the *Los Angeles Times,* Betty Martin gave it full marks for its 'fair amount of suspense throughout,' and thought that Haller's settings were 'lavish' and Crosby's cinematography 'flamboyant'. In addition to screening in cinemas where AIP films did not usually play, *House of Usher* received the best reviews overall of any movie that had been made by the company.

Corman was still making films for his own company, but AIP would not let him free of its clutches. After the runaway success of *House of Usher,* another Poe picture was a no-brainer. Arkoff and Nicholson asked Corman to follow up with *Pit and the Pendulum,* again from a screenplay by Matheson. As Poe's original was slighter even

House of Usher (Vincent Price, Mark Damon, Harry Ellerbe)

Pit and the Pendulum (Luana Anders, John Kerr)

than 'The Fall of the House of Usher', Matheson used it only as the climax to the film and came up with a new back story to lead up to it.

Again, the film utilised a single setting–a castle by the sea in 16th-century Spain. Price was naturally invited back to play the role of Nicholas Medina, the owner of the castle and a man tormented by guilt over the death of his wife. The protagonist this time was John Kerr, a stage actor who had achieved considerable acclaim for his sensitive portrayal of Tom Robinson Lee in the 1953 Broadway production of *Tea and Sympathy,* which he recreated for the 1956 film version directed by Vincente Minnelli. Most recently, he had played the lead in Joshua Logan's film version of the musical *South Pacific* (1958). As Medina's 'late' wife, Corman cast British actress Barbara Steele, who had just become an overnight horror sensation in Italian director Mario Bava's *Black Sunday,* which AIP had released a few months earlier. (Steele's English accent was later dubbed, and her career with AIP was short-lived as a result!)

Others in the small cast were Luana Anders and Antony Carbone. Anders had appeared in the supernatural anthology series *One Step Beyond* before making her film debut in Curtis Harrington's fantasy *Night Tide* (1961), and Corman regular Carbone was fresh from *Creature From the Haunted Sea*; Italian-born, he was raised in New York and had been a prolific performer on television.

The crew was virtually identical to that convened for *Usher,* as was the fifteen-day shooting schedule. Whereas *Usher* had stayed close to Poe's original, Matheson had to invent most of *Pit and the Pendulum.* His version aped the conceit of *Usher* and had an Englishman named Francis Barnard (Kerr) arrive at the castle in search of the truth about his sister's recent demise. Investigation reveals that she may have been buried alive, having submitted to a cataleptic trance brought on by extreme terror. The third act of the film takes an unexpected turn and culminates in Barnard being strapped to a plinth in Medina's dungeon as a huge pendulum blade swings down towards him...

The pendulum of the title was designed by Daniel Haller. It had a rubber blade, which unfortunately stuck to Kerr's stomach when they tried it out. Haller switched to a metallic blade, which had to be set up in such a way that it could slash the actor's shirt without harming him. A steel band was wrapped around Kerr's waist and four technicians had to work the pendulum manually in order to control it properly.

Kerr was understandably nervous so in order to demonstrate that it was safe, Corman himself stood in for Kerr while things were being prepared. As Mark McGee observed, 'The actor was a good sport about it all but Dan (Haller) noticed that he perspired a lot'. To increase the suspense in the scene, editor Anthony Carras removed every other frame, which made the blade appear to swing twice as fast.

When *Pit and the Pendulum* was released in August 1961, it garnered good reviews. *Variety* opined, 'A physically stylish, imaginatively photographed horror film which, though needlessly corny in many spots, adds up to good exploitation... (Matheson) has rendered it in some fruity dialogue. If audiences don't titter, it's only because veteran star Vincent Price can chew scenery while keeping his tongue in his cheek'. In *Limelight,* Len Simpson wrote: 'Edgar Allan Poe would have been proud of the treatment American International has given his short story'. *The New York Times* raved about its 'rich colours, plushy decor and eerie music,' and *Time* magazine thought it 'a literary hair-raiser'. *Pit and the Pendulum* was even more successful at the box office than *House of Usher* had been, proving to Arkoff and Nicholson that their first Poe film was no fluke. From now on, the company's new cash-cows would be Corman, Price and the collected works of Poe, but even they had no idea that the beast would thrive for the rest of the decade.

Meanwhile, Corman felt that he was entitled to a bigger piece of the pie. And his thoughts on the matter happened to coincide with those of the good people at Pathe Labs, who processed most of AIP's films. They were interested in starting their own

distribution company and thought that a Corman 'Poe' might be an excellent way to begin. They offered the director a deal on a new feature.

Corman decided to adapt Poe's 'The Premature Burial' as his first production for Pathe. It would look exactly like the AIP Poe pictures, with art design by Haller, cinematography by Crosby and costumes by Marjorie Corso, but music by Corman regular Ronald Stein. It would be set in the same 'country of the mind' as the other two Poes, with swirling mist, gloomy graveyards and a gaunt mansion, all filmed on interior sets. There was an exception, however: Vincent Price was under contract to AIP and Corman could not cast him in his 'runaway' Poe; according to a piece in New York's *Herald Tribune,* Price was receiving $125,000 per film under his AIP contract, plus a percentage of the profits, and the company was not about to loan him out. Instead, Corman hired one-time Oscar-winner (for *The Lost Weekend,* 1945) Ray Milland to play the lead.

Welsh-born Milland had had a career in the British Army before playing his first major role in *The Flying Scotsman* (1929). This had led to a contract with M-G-M, for whom he appeared in supporting roles, but it was at Paramount where he achieved success opposite Dorothy Lamour in *The Jungle Princess* (1936). By the mid-fifties, with his star on the wane, he had started directing in the new medium of television. When Corman came calling, Milland was freelancing and he liked the Chuck Beaumont/ Ray Russell script. Although he was as interested in directing as acting by this time, he and Corman got along well and he agreed to star in the film.

Milland's leading lady in *The Premature Burial* was a familiar face to fans of Hammer Horror. Hazel Court had starred in both *The Curse of Frankenstein* (1957) and *The Man Who Could Cheat Death* (1959) but had since moved to Hollywood, where she had appeared in episodes of *Alfred Hitchcock Presents, Thriller* (hosted by Boris Karloff) and *The Twilight Zone.* Corman cast her as Emily, the duplicitous wife of Milland's Guy Carrell.

The supporting roles were filled by Alan Napier, a veteran of genre films such as *The Invisible Man Returns* (1940), *Cat People* (1942) and *Isle of the Dead* (1945) (Napier would become better-known as Bruce Wayne's butler Alfred in the TV series *Batman*) and Richard Ney, who had recently appeared in the Doris Day thriller *Midnight Lace* (1960). The film would also feature a final screen outing for Heather Angel, who had starred in John Brahm's atmospheric werewolf thriller *The Undying Monster* (1942). But the pair who would steal the show were John Dierkes and Dick Miller as two sardonic grave-robbers. Dierkes's 6'6" frame made a memorable contrast with that of the diminutive Miller in their scenes together.

A mere two days into production, Arkoff and Nicholson arrived on the Pathe sound stage to inform Corman that he was once again working for AIP! It transpired that Arkoff had pointed out to Pathe that AIP was one of its biggest customers and if it was going to compete in the distribution business, then AIP would find another lab to process its films. As a result, Pathe had sold the production to AIP before principal photography on *The Premature Burial* had even begun. Corman received $500,000 plus an immediate $50,000 profit on his 50% interest in the film, and AIP was able to continue with its new sub-genre without further interruption.

Beaumont and Russell's screenplay had again to create a narrative where none exists in the Poe original. Guy Carrell has an obsessional fear of burial alive. To that end, he constructs a crypt designed to prevent premature interment by enabling him to free himself should his worst fear be realised and he falls prey to cataleptic seizure. His nightmare becomes a reality and despite his precautions, he is lowered into his grave while still alive. But... enter the two grave-robbers, and the treachery of someone close to him is revealed. The film's indebtedness to Poe was acknowledged in passing by a speech from Milland: 'Can you possibly conceive it? The unendurable oppression of the lungs, the stifling fumes of the earth, the rigid embrace of the coffin, the blackness of absolute night and the silence, like an overwhelming sea.'

In her autobiography *Hazel Court: Horror Queen,* Court wrote of the film, 'I was very excited about working with Ray Milland. Being Welsh, he wrote outstanding poetry, and being half Welsh myself, I loved talking to him. At the end of the picture, I had to be buried alive. Roger asked me if I would do it or if I would rather have someone double for me. I said, "Heavens, no! I will do it." Well, I lay in the ground, with a straw in my mouth so that I would have air, as they shoveled the earth over me. The straw was removed and when the director said, "Action!" I was to hold my breath for as long as possible. I made it for over one minute–long enough to get the shot. As I got to the end of the minute, the pressure on my body began, as the claustrophobia was setting in. It was one hell of an experience.'

The Premature Burial is considered by some to be 'second-rate Poe' because of the absence of Price, but Milland carries the film and is highly effective in conveying the pathos and the intensity of the long-suffering Guy. Stein's score

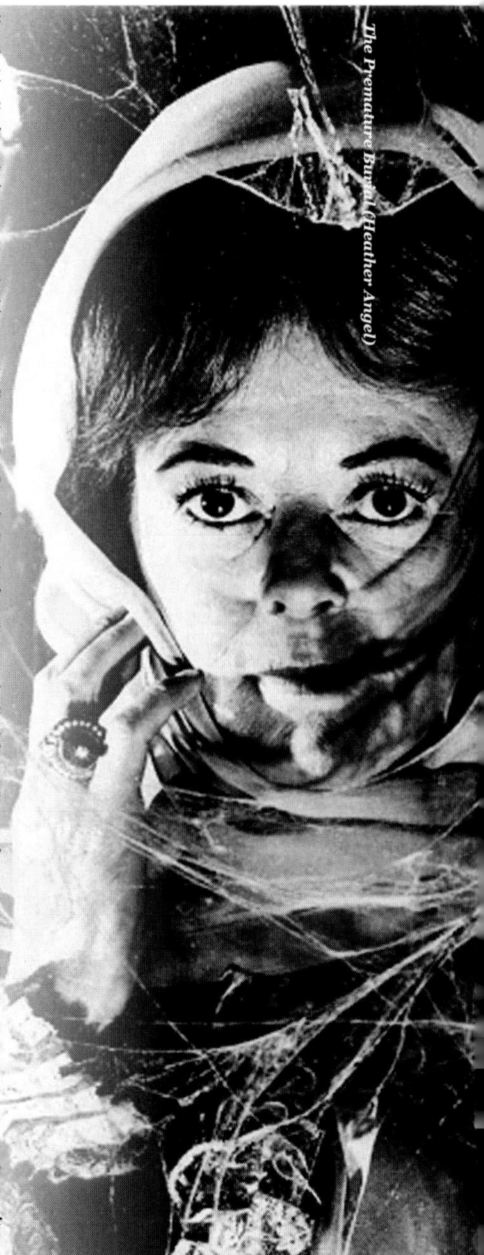
The Premature Burial (Heather Angel)

is outstanding, with much use of the folk-tune 'Molly Malone' as a motif for the impending events. Haller's art direction included hanging clumps of Spanish moss over dead trees like macabre Christmas decorations, which gave the studio Poe-scapes a genuine air of death and decay.

Now that AIP owned the film, it unleashed its usual publicity ballyhoo. The press-kit included the following suggestion for theatre owners: 'Key exploitation stunt for *The Premature Burial*... is an actual burial alive demonstration by a man or pretty girl. Should you have difficulty in contacting a stunt-man or woman in your area for this purpose, get in touch with the publicity department, American International Pictures, 7165 Sunset Blvd, Hollywood, Calif.'

On its US release in March 1962, *The Premature Burial* received more mixed reviews, and they were a sign of things to come. *Variety* noted, 'By this time, many film fans... are as familiar with Corman's downstairs dungeon as they are with their own basement hobby shops.' *The New York Times* was kinder, remarking that the film was 'no less attractively designed or tastefully coloured' than the two previous Poe pictures. Court's own thoughts were objective: '*The Premature Burial* was not as successful as the other horror films. Some critics felt it was because Vincent Price was not in it. I felt it might have been because a lot of people have fears of being buried alive–or of developing the condition of catalepsy in which one would be alive but accidentally presumed dead. The film was kind to me... a very good part.'

Milland's casting in Corman's film brought a career renaissance of sorts. It led to him directing and starring in a dystopian survival story called *Panic in Year Zero!* (1962). Originally titled *Survival*, the project was first announced in *The Hollywood Reporter* on January 4, 1962: '*Survival* will star Ray Milland, who also directs, with Frankie Avalon and Jean Hagen, rolling Feb 21.'

Written by Jay Simms and John Morton, *Panic in Year Zero!* reflects the very height of Cold War paranoia and, for Arkoff and Nicholson, it was in some respects (such as its lensing in black and white) a return to the post-atomic scenarios of bleak, exploitational fare like *Day the World Ended*. A family of four (Milland, Hagen,

The Premature Burial (Hazel Court, Ray Milland)

Panic in Year Zero (Frankie Avalon, Jean Hagen, Ray Milland)

Avalon and Mary Mitchel) head out of Los Angeles for a camping trip just before a nuclear bomb (of unspecified origin) obliterates the city. It takes only a short time for authority and the law to break down and Milland's character has to fight to keep himself and his family alive. Looters and murderers prowl the streets of rural towns and the family is forced to flee into the mountains, but trouble follows them. Milland is reduced to robbing a store to obtain weapons and the four end up hiding out in a cave.

Elegantly shot in widescreen by Gil Warrenton (*Master of the World*), *Panic in Year Zero!* is a tough, brutal movie even by today's standards. Harry, Milland's character, is complex and conflicted, becoming a lawless thug even as he derides the lawless thugs surrounding him. After his daughter is raped by two of them, he shoots the hoodlums to death, then agonises over his actions. Harry is often brusque and uncompromising, but Milland succeeds in showing the 'civilised' man beneath. The playing is competent, with Avalon surprisingly good in a dramatic role. He becomes a little too eager at one point to 'blow the head off' one of the hoodlums with his rifle and is moderated by his father, who tells him, 'Don't get trigger happy but don't be gun shy, either. If you have to use it, use it.'

One of AIP's most unusual–and topical–films, *Panic in Year Zero!* still packs a punch and remains controversial in its alarmingly fascistic point of view. It takes Milland no time at all to conclude that those who are most heavily armed are those who will survive. While there may be some credence to that in an extreme situation, it is disturbing to watch such an overtly ordinary family man come to such a nihilistic 'truth'. In the UK, *Panic in Year Zero!* was co-billed with the next Corman/Poe film, which would feature the return of Vincent Price–times three.

By the time Corman got around to *Tales of Terror*, he had already become restless with the Poe formula as it currently stood and had asked screenwriter Matheson to turn 'The Black Cat' (along with 'The Cask of Amontillado') into one of a trilogy of tales which

***Tales of Terror* (Vincent Price, Maggie Pierce)**

would include 'Morella' and 'The Facts in the Case of M Valdemar'. The resulting film would team Price and old friends Peter Lorre and Basil Rathbone, and it turned out to be a fruitful collaboration. 'With *Tales of Terror*, we tried to do something a little different,' Corman recalled. 'The screenplay was actually a series of very frightening dramatic sequences inspired by several of the Poe stories. To break things up, we tried introducing humour into one of them.'

'The Black Cat' was the second tale in the trilogy, the first being 'Morella'–a more typical Corman Poe-scape in which a young woman arrives at her estranged father's run-down mansion to try to reconcile their differences after he has spent a lifetime blaming her for his wife's death in labour. But Morella's spirit does not rest quietly and she 'possesses' her daughter, using her to enact a long-suppressed revenge against her husband. Vengeance from beyond the grave had become a too-familiar *motif* of the Poe series by this time and 'Morella' is the weakest of the three segments, although Price gives his usual professional performance.

The casting of Lorre in 'The Black Cat' was fortuitous. Matheson was as keen as Corman to parody the clichéd elements of the series and could not resist the chance to send them up, as he would again in *The Raven*; 'The Black Cat' became a comedy vignette, with Lorre ad-libbing his way through the role of the drunken Montressor, walling up his adulterous wife and her wine-connoisseur lover in his cellar. 'What are you doing?' Price's Fortunato asks him as he hangs, chained, in the wall-cavity. 'I'll give you three guesses,' Montresor replies. Unfortunately for the cuckold, he walls up his black cat as well, whose miaowing soon gives the game away to the inquisitive local police.

The most chilling tale was saved for last. 'The Facts in the Case of M Valdemar' had the best cast of the three: Price, Basil Rathbone, one of the all-time great Hollywood

Tales of Terror (Peter Lorre)

villains, Debra Paget and David Frankham from *Master of the World.* Frankham's appearance was owed, in part, to him having stepped into Mark Damon's shoes in the Verne fantasy: 'As the result of the casting crisis with *Master of the World,* my agent, Maurine Oliver, knew she had AIP over a barrel, and suggested, "Well, you know, David's helping you out so much, what about giving him a two-picture deal?" That's what they agreed to, with the second picture to be completed by the end of 1961. That's how I got *Tales of Terror*. They had to use me, or pay me anyway.'

The story of a mesmerist who attempts to keep a man in a hypnotic trance even beyond the point of his death is one of the most chilling in the Poe *repertoire*. 'What exactly is it that occurs within the moment of death, especially to a man within that moment who is not permitted to die, as in the case of Mr Valdemar?' Price narrates, and as Rathbone makes a bee-line for the widowed Paget in the belief that his charge is permanently indisposed, the hapless Valdemar rises catatonically from his death-bed and oozes liquid putresence all over his duplicitous tormentor.

Corman recalled how the decomposition of Price's character was achieved in 'The Facts in the Case of M Valdemar'*:* 'We settled for an old-fashioned mud pack. It dries and draws the skin up and then cracks open.' For the climactic scene of Valdemar melting away, a mixture of glue, glycerine, corn-starch and make-up was heated and poured over the actor's head. The resulting mess was so hot that Price could stand it for only a few seconds.

Each segment in *Tales of Terror* was shot in five days, totalling Corman's usual fifteen-day schedule. On release, the film was less well received by the critics than its forerunners had been. The *New York Herald Tribune* declared, 'Aficionados of the weird, the strange, or what Poe called the 'grotesque' and 'arabesque' can troop, I think with good heart, to *Tales of Terror*', but *The New York Times* was not so enamoured: '...A dull, absurd and trashy adaptation of three Edgar Allan Poe stories, broadly draped around the shoulders of such people as Vincent Price, Peter Lorre and Basil Rathbone (who at least bothers to act).'

Nevertheless, the film made $1.3 million in domestic gross rentals, a tidy sum if not on a par with those achieved by *House of Usher* and *Pit and the Pendulum*, but more than enough to ensure the continuation of the series. And there was no question by now: Corman and AIP had effectively created a franchise out of the works of Edgar Allan Poe, and a growing fan-base of 'monsterkids' now eagerly awaited each new instalment.

***Tales of Terror* (David Frankham, Debra Paget)**

Tales of Terror was the first in the series to be turned into a comic book by Dell, although *Pit and The Pendulum* and *The Premature Burial* had been produced as movie tie-ins by Monarch Books. These were early attempts by AIP to break into the kind of merchandising that no film nowadays can afford to do without.

The most successful segment of *Tales of Terror,* and the one most talked about by the critics, was determined to be 'The Black Cat', and it was decided that the next Poe film would be *all* comedy, reuniting Price and Lorre.

Arkoff and Nicholson settled on *The Raven,* Poe's most famous poem and the one with the greatest name-recognition. The fact that it was a poem and not a story

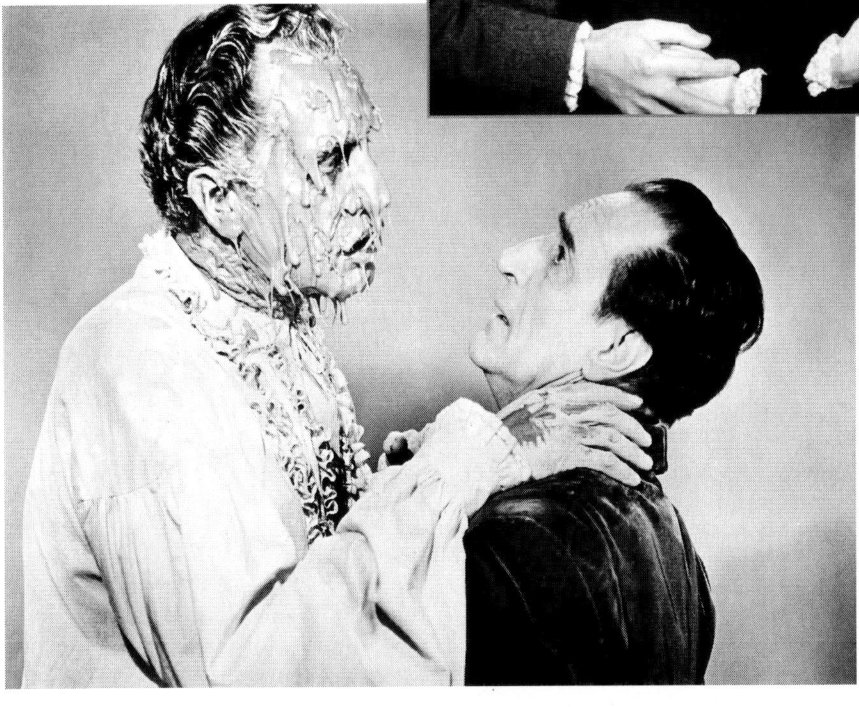

did not seem to bother them in the slightest. Interviewed for the book *The Making of the Raven,* Matheson told author Lawrence French, 'After I heard they wanted to make a movie out of a poem, I felt that was an utter joke, so comedy was really the only way to go with it.'

Starring alongside Price and Lorre was none other than Boris Karloff, who had spent the last few years on American television but still possessed name-value. The novelty pop song *Monster Mash,* by Bobby 'Boris' Pickett, had gone to number 1 in the US charts at Halloween, and the monsters of old were suddenly back in fashion. Karloff was in his seventies and not in the best of health, but he was willing to do all that was asked of him–which turned out to be quite a lot.

Karloff had recently turned down an offer to be in the Hammer/William Castle remake of *The Old Dark House* because 'the new version... was not to my liking,' he said, but he did like Matheson's screenplay for *The Raven* (he and Bela Lugosi had starred in *The Raven* for Universal in 1935), and he was pleased that Price and Lorre would be joining him. Hazel Court returned from *Premature Burial,* and Corman cast a young actor whom he had worked with before, Jack Nicholson.

Matheson's script was a medieval fantasy along the lines of Bert I Gordon's *The Magic Sword* (into which Basil Rathbone had side-stepped): a wizard named Bedlo (Lorre) has been turned into a raven by the evil Dr Scarabus (Karloff) and seeks the help of Erasmus Craven (Price) to return him to his former self; along the way, Craven discovers that his lost-believed-dead love Lenore is, in fact, alive and living with Scarabus, so he and Bedlo set off for the castle of the sorcerer...

The film begins with Price reciting Poe's poem, but when he asks rhetorically of the newly-arrived raven, 'Will I ever see my lost Lenore again?', and Lorre replies, 'How the hell should I know?', it quickly becomes clear that irreverance is to be the name of *The Raven*'s game. Much has been said about how Lorre improvised his lines. As Corman explained, 'Peter kept everyone on their toes, myself included. He

The Raven (Jack Nicholson, Olive Sturgess, Hazel Court, Vincent Price)

would just begin to improvise unexpectedly. Vincent was always willing to play along with it, but Boris, who was very methodical about his craft, was befuddled. Amused, but befuddled.'

'A gentle, very sweet man,' Hazel Court said of Karloff when I interviewed her. 'Peter Lorre wouldn't always know his lines. Boris would, but the others would come on and kind of make it up a little. But it was always alright. Peter was very funny.' She was less impressed with young co-star Nicholson, however. 'I always remember him saying, "I'm going home to write tonight." He was always talking about this great writing talent he thought he had. I never suspected he would become a great movie star. It was strange; he was this little person who popped around in a funny costume, with knee breeches and a funny hat. He looked rather like one of those little stone statues you can buy to put in your garden!'

'Strictly a picture for the kiddies and the bird-brained,' sniffed Bosley Crowther in *The New York Times*, though *Variety* was more positive: '...A skillful, imaginative narrative. Corman takes the premise and develops it expertly as a horror-comedy, climaxing with Price and Karloff engaging in a duel to the death.' *Time* magazine singled out Court in unforgettable style: 'She is a lusty redhead with a cleavage that could comfortably accommodate the collected works of Edgar Allan Poe and a bottle of his favourite booze besides.'

Somewhat surprisingly, *The Raven* turned out to be the most successful Poe film up to that time and Corman was so taken with Daniel Haller's castle set that when he had finished shooting, he paid actor Leo Gordon $1,600 to come up with a script that could be shot on the set in the few days that were left to the schedule. He also made a deal with Karloff for three days filming at a nominal salary, plus a deferred payment of an extra $15,000 if the resultant film took more than $150,000. The 'three-day' wonder that Corman produced and (partly) directed in the wake of *The Raven* became the infamous *The Terror*.

The Terror (Sandra Knight, Jack Nicholson)

In *The Making of The Raven,* Karloff explained, 'Corman had the sketchiest outline of a story. I read it and begged him not to do it. "That's alright, Boris, I know what I'm going to do. I want you for three days on this." I was in every shot, of course. Sometimes I was just walking through and then I would change my jacket and walk back. He nearly killed me on the last day. He had me in a tank of cold water for about two hours... (The sets) were so magnificent. As they were being pulled down around our ears, Roger was dashing around with me and the camera, two steps ahead of the wreckers. It was very funny.'

Audiences found *The Terror* funny as well, although it was not intended to be. And the film, contrary to legend, was by no means shot in three days. Karloff's scenes were completed in three days, but then Corman sent assistant Francis Ford Coppola to Big Sur for another three days to shoot more material. Coppola ended up staying for eleven days in total, trying to work something up that made sense in the context of the rest of the story. Future directors Monte Hellman *(Two-Lane Blacktop,* 1971), Jack Hill *(Spider Baby,* 1967), and even Nicholson himself also pitched in on some of the additional scenes.

The plot, some of it co-written on the fly by Corman and Hill, is a confused mix that mystifies viewers to this day. In 18th-century France, a young lieutenant follows a mysterious woman to the castle of Baron Von Leppe (Karloff), where he discovers that she looks exactly like the Baron's late wife, who has been dead for twenty years. The Baron eventually admits to having murdered his wife when he found her in the arms of another man, but has she now returned as a ghost? 'Some of the shots... have a Bergmanesque quality of imagination,' observed the critic of the *Western Daily Press*, but most reviewers were simply bemused.

In May 1966, Corman had to inform Karloff that he would not be receiving his deferred $15,000 as the film had failed to make the agreed figure. But he said that he would be paid the money if he worked on another, yet to be determined, production.

That film turned out to be the Peter Bogdanovich's *Targets* (1968), which was to garner Karloff some of the best reviews of his career. Bogdanovich had also worked, uncredited, on *The Terror*.

Tired of repeating himself with the Poe adaptations, Corman desired to wander farther afield and adapt a story by American fantasist HP Lovecraft. The Rhode Island author was a cult figure among afficionados, with his tales of cosmic horror set in the witch-haunted backwaters of New England; his most famous works fall into the broad category of 'Cthulhu Mythos', named after the devil-god around whom many of the stories revolve, and include 'The Dunwich Horror' and 'The Colour Out of Space'; Corman's interest was in adapting one of Lovecraft's later novellas, *The Case of Charles Dexter Ward*. Written in 1927, the story concerns the title character's obsession with a distant ancestor named Joseph Curwen, a notorious necromancer. Ward bears a strong resemblance to Curwen and attempts to bring his ancestor back to life by ritual magic. This arouses the suspicions of Ward's doctor, who investigates the affair and is horrified to find that Ward has summoned an ancient entity...

The tale's references to Lovecraft's pantheon of 'Mythos' demons, and his fabled grimoire the Necronomicon, were heady stuff for a populist horror film in 1963 and Arkoff and Nicholson were keener to extend their Poe franchise than embark on a new road with a much less well-known author. They asked Corman to downplay the Lovecraft connection and call the film *The Haunted Village* instead; ultimately, it became *The Haunted Palace*, derived, like *The Raven*–but more indirectly, from only a poem by Poe.

Most of the personnel from the Poe pictures returned to work on *The Haunted Palace*, including cinematographer Floyd Crosby, but Corman instructed him to use a darker colour palette to separate it from his other Poes. Price was entrusted with the dual roles of Ward and Curwen, and Debra Paget was brought back from *Tales of Terror* to play his wife. Also on board was Lon Chaney Jr, in his only appearance

The Haunted Palace (Vincent Price, Milton Parsons, Lon Chaney Jr)

for AIP. In Charles Beaumont's adaptation, the story begins with Curwen cursing the villagers who are intent on putting him to the stake; years later, Charles Dexter Ward returns to the village of Arkham to claim his ancestral home and, possessed by the warlock's spirit, he takes up where Curwen left off so as to enact his vengeance on the descendents of those whom Curwen had cursed. Beaumont may have reduced Lovecraft's complex narrative to convention, but he gives Ward some wicked lines in the process: 'I'll not have my fill of revenge until this village is a graveyard. Until they have felt, as I did, the kiss of fire on their soft bare flesh. All of them. Have patience, my friends. Surely, after all these years, I am entitled to a few small amusements?'

The justification for the film's title is a thin one; the poem itself was originally incorporated into Poe's 'The Fall of the House of Usher' and some lines from it are recited during the prologue by Price. A second stanza serves as a screen caption at the close, as had now become customary in AIP's Poe series: '...While, like a ghastly rapid river, through the pale door, a hideous throng rush out forever and laugh–but smile no more.'

Reviews were only so-so, with even the most fantasy-illiterate of critics catching on to the fact that unlike its more faithful predecessors, *The Haunted Palace* was a far cry from Poe. In *The New York Times*, Eugene Archer opined, 'Roger Corman is an old hand at turning out lurid horror melodramas in low-budget colour such as *The Haunted Palace*... Nothing about it calls for comment, except perhaps the proficient colour photography by another old professional, Floyd Crosby.' On its UK outing, it was relegated to second-feature status.

Corman also escaped the clutches of Boston's most famous son for his next AIP production, *X: The Man With the X-Ray Eyes*, an extraordinary sci-fi feature with elements of religious parable, scripted by Robert Dillon and Ray Russell. The director picked Ray Milland to star, along with Diana Van der Vlis and Harold J Stone, and the story told of a scientist experimenting on the limits of human eyesight; he fabricates

X: The Man With the X-Ray Eyes (Diana Van Der Vlis, Ray Milland)

a drug which enables him to see beyond the normal limits of vision and eventually into the very heart of the nucleus, which ultimately drives him mad.

The Man With the X-Ray Eyes is one of Corman's best films. Milland is excellent, and he dominates the film. 'What do you see?' his girlfriend asks him as they drive around to test out his new, improved vision. 'The city as if it were unborn,' he replies. 'Rising into the sky with fingers of metal, limbs without flesh, girders without stone. Signs hanging without support. Wires dipping and swaying without poles... Flesh dissolved in an acid of light. A city of the dead.'

But the best scene is reserved for the climax when, alone in the desert, Milland's Dr Xavier happens upon a revivalist meeting presided over by fire-and-brimstone preacher John Dierkes. Xavier stands before him like a penitent: 'I've come to tell you what I see,' he says. 'There are great darknesses. Farther than time itself. And beyond the darkness, a light that glows, changes. And in the centre of the universe... the eye that sees us all.' 'You see sin and the devil!' the preacher decries. 'If thine eye offends thee, pluck it out!' Xavier bows out of frame, and then rises again–having plucked out both of his eyes!

Sci-fi in the sixties did not come much better or more thoughtful than *The Man With the X-Ray Eyes*, and the fact that Corman shot it in his usual fifteen days for less than $300,000 is an even more impressive achievement. Its mix of science and metaphysics made it a precursor to Kubrick's *2001: A Space Odyssey* (1968), and its psychedelic effects prefigured the coming drug-culture. The film won the 1963 'Silver Spaceship' Award at the First International Festival of Science Fiction Film in Trieste, and it performed well at the box office. But Corman was not finished with Poe just yet. Arkoff and Nicholson made sure of that.

AIP announced in 1963 that its next Poe picture was to be *The Masque of the Red Death*, which Corman had wanted to film for some time but could never find a script

***X: The Man With the X-Ray Eyes* (Lorrie Summers, Ray Milland)**

that he felt was right. An early draft had been written by Robert Towne, who would go on to pen blockbusters like *Shampoo* (1976) and Roman Polanski's *Chinatown* (1974), but Corman was unhappy with Towne's version and the project was turned over to Charles Beaumont. Credit eventually went to Beaumont and R Wright Campbell, who completed the script when Beaumont fell ill (he died of a brain tumour in 1967, at the age of 38) and incorporated Poe's 'Hop-Frog' into the overall plot.

Concurrent with AIP's plan for *The Masque of the Red Death*, producer Alex Gordon was attempting to mount a rival version. Pressure was put on Gordon to withdraw, and the next Poe proved to be the most lavish of them all.

AIP's co-production deal with Anglo-Amalgamated gave Arkoff and Nicholson the idea to have Corman shoot *The Masque of the Red Death* in England. Ultimately, it was a financial decision; the film could qualify for Eady subsidy and the budget could be enlarged accordingly. This also created a more leisurely production: the film was shot on a five-week schedule, rather than Corman's usual three.

Price was cast as the sadistic Prince Prospero, a fuedal lord with a propensity for devil-worship, and Hazel Court was his mistress Juliana. British ingénue Jane Asher, currently the girlfriend of Beatles' band-member Paul McCartney, was the innocent Christian in whom Prospero takes a more than passing interest, and Nigel Green and Patrick Magee lent practised support. Daniel Haller designed the film, but he went unsung to allow it to qualify as a British production; Robert Jones is credited with the art direction.

The Poe story is little more than a moral fable, but the script stayed close to the spirit of the tale while adding enough satanic thrills to keep the traditional audience satisfied: Prospero invites his noble friends to stay in his castle while the Red Death ravages the countryside beyond its walls. As events move towards the titular masked

***The Masque of the Red Death* (Jane Asher, Vincent Price)**

ball, culminating in the fiery revenge of a dwarf against one of the guests, the plague edges ever closer. Comes the night of the ball and a mysterious figure in red appears among the revellers, even as Prospero has banned the wearing of red...

When *The Masque of the Red Death* was released in June 1964, it got some of the best reviews that Corman and AIP had ever had. In the *New York Herald Tribune,* Eugene Archer raved: 'On its level, it is astonishingly good... The film is beautifully costumed, the sets are lavish, the props exquisite.' (The 'lavish sets' were actually left over from Peter Glenville's *Becket,* which had finished shooting at Elstree Studios only weeks before.) 'Vincent Price is the very essence of evil...' *Variety* affirmed.

An unwelcome epilogue to the film's release arrived in the form of a lawsuit from Alex Gordon, who claimed that the script had been based upon one previously drafted by himself, his wife and two others. That version had at one time been submitted to AIP, he alleged. The judge, Macklin Fleming, dismissed the suit, claiming that the similarities between the two were 'coincidental'–which was hardly surprising, given that they were based on the same public domain source material.

Roger Corman on the set of The Masque of the Red Death

The Masque of the Red Death was not as financially successful as some of the previous Poe films, which the accountant in Arkoff blamed on it being 'too arty farty'. In his introduction to a later novelisation of the story, Corman reflected, 'I think that is a legitimate statement... The fault may have been mine. I was becoming more interested in the Poe films as expressions of the unconscious mind, rather than as pure horror films.' Corman still considered the movie to be one of his best, however, despite the fact that he was not entirely

The Masque of the Red Death (Hazel Court)

satisfied with the final 'masque' sequence, which he called its 'greatest flaw'. He shot it in a day, which he remarked would have been enough time in Hollywood, but that the British crew worked more slowly.

The Masque of the Red Death also suffered from censorship problems in the UK, primarily a hallucinatory sequence in which Court is assailed by demonic apparitions as she lies on a slab. In a 1977 interview with Steve Biodrowski for *Cinefantastique*, Corman recalled: 'From the standpoint of nudity, there was nothing. I think she was nude under a diaphanous gown. She played the consummation with the Devil, but it was essentially on her face; it was a pure acting exercise. Hazel fully clothed, all by herself, purely by acting, incurred the wrath of the censor. It was a different age...' It was not the hints of nudity that bothered the censor, but the blatant display of black magic; four years later, he was still making cuts to a scene of a woman lying prone on a slab during a satanic ritual, despite that also being a dream sequence. The film concerned was *Rosemary's Baby*.

For once, the critics were more taken by a Corman Poe film than the public and *The Masque of the Red Death* played at New York's prestigious Museum of Modern Art only a year after its release. 'Arty farty' it may have been, but it is also the finest of Corman's Poes, and its imagery–lensed by cinematographer Nicolas Roeg, who would become a noted film director in his own right–remains unsurpassed in the genre for its rich colour palette. If Corman had stopped at this point, he would have gone out on an unforgettable high, but he was persuaded to give the series one last shot.

Corman's final Poe film was *The Tomb of Ligeia*, also filmed in the UK, but in a very different style. The restless director wanted to get away from his usual technique of shooting entirely on sound stages; with *Ligeia,* he opted instead to film on location, to take full advantage of the beautiful Norfolk countryside. And with another 25-day schedule, there was plenty of time for artistic indulgence.

Poe's 'Ligeia' was published in 1838. An unnamed narrator suffers the death of his beautiful wife, Ligeia, but soon remarries; new bride Rowena also falls ill and

The Tomb of Ligeia (Vincent Price, Elizabeth Shepherd)

dies, and as the bereaved husband pays vigil over the corpse, he watches as Rowena slowly returns from the dead–but as the Lady *Ligeia*.

Corman hired Robert Towne to write the screenplay, which in pre-production was known as *The House at the End of the World*, the same title that had originally been proposed for *Monster of Terror*. *The Tomb of Ligeia* was another co-production with Anglo and in his quest to make this latest Poe 'different', Corman initially did not want Vincent Price for the lead role. He felt that Price was too old for the part, which in the script was a man of only 25 or 30. Richard Chamberlain was Corman's first choice; Chamberlain was the star of TV's popular *Dr Kildare* medical series and a national heartthrob. But AIP insisted on casting the contracted Price. Towne, for his part, had specifically requested that Price not be cast. When Corman informed Towne that Price would indeed be playing the role, he told him, 'Don't worry, Bob, I've got Marlene Dietrich's make-up man!'

***The Tomb of Ligeia* (Vincent Price, Elizabeth Shepherd)**

'What we ended up doing was giving Vincent a wig and using a bit more make-up on him than usual. We were trying to make him look younger,' Corman recalled in an interview for *Video Watchdog*. 'When we decided to use Vincent again, that did change the orientation of the film quite a bit.' Price's leading lady on this occasion was Elizabeth Shepherd–no spring chicken herself but a Shakesperean actress whose career encompassed the stage, film and television. (Shepherd had been the original choice to play Emma Peel in *The Avengers* but, after two episodes, she left the series and was replaced by Diana Rigg.)

The Tomb of Ligeia went into production in June 1964 at the 11th-century Castle Acre Priory in Swaffham, Norfolk. Price 'had always wanted to do a picture in a ruin', according to Mark Thomas McGee, but the unit was not allowed to install furniture in the priory because the building and its grounds were a conservation area and belonged to the National Trust. Only the exteriors were shot there, with the interiors filmed at Shepperton Studios. This proved fortutitous, as things turned out: 'The climax of the film called for the whole place to go up in flames,' McGee explained. 'Everyone was warned not to smoke. Vince and his co-star, Elizabeth Shepherd, were positioned under some debris, getting ready for the next shot, when somebody lit a match. All at once the place was an inferno. Vince dragged Liz to safety as fast as he could. Naturally, the shot and the set were ruined.'

Released in the UK in December 1964 and in the US in January 1965, *The Tomb of Ligeia* received some mixed notices. In *The New York Times,* Howard Thompson wrote, 'The least effective of the Poe films, it often drags and Price seems miscast...' But *Time* magazine was more forgiving: '*Ligeia,* like its predecessors, offers meticulous decor, shrewd shock techniques, and an atmosphere of mounting terror that fails to deliver on its promise. Again, the cream-centred menace is Vincent Price, an actor who appears to be swooping around in a cape even when he stands perfectly still.'

In *Video Watchdog,* Corman noted: 'Actually, all of the Poe films made money,

but *Tomb of Ligeia* made the least amount. I think it was because the series was just running out of steam and also because it was overly complicated.' Corman's final Poe was certainly the most blatantly romantic of them and its debt to Hitchcock's *Vertigo*, in which the protagonist tries to recreate a lost love by remodelling a new one, cannot be overstated. (Corman and Towne were both avid *cinéastes*.) But if *The Tomb of Ligeia* can be considered the end of the 'first wave' of AIP Poe adaptations, the series closed with more of a whimper than a bang. 'A tedious and talky additon to American International's series of chillpix based on the tales of the 19th century author,' *Variety* appraised. 'Roger Corman produced and directed a script that resists analysis and lacks credibility... colour lensing of no help. Endless repetitions of brief, ineffective horror bits involving black cat, saucer of milk, and dead fox.'

Early in 1964, AIP had also released *The Comedy of Terrors* which, while not a Poe film, still managed to look like one. Under the direction of Val Lewton alumnus Jacques Tourneur *(Cat People*, 1942; *Night of the Demon*, 1957), it reunited Price, Lorre and Karloff from *The Raven*, with Basil Rathbone from *Tales of Terror*, in a horror comedy about two bumbling undertakers (Price and Lorre) who try to boost their business by murdering people.

The Comedy of Terrors (screenwriter Richard Matheson's take on Shakespeare's *Comedy of Errors*) was one of the great comedy-horror films, its level of slapstick far outdoing anything in either *Tales of Terror* or *The Raven*. As a parody of all things Poe-esque, it was little short of sublime but its timing was unwise as it also damaged the veracity of the authentic franchise, making it increasingly difficult for AIP to return to the Gothic formula established by Corman without eliciting knowing chuckles from the intended audience. Consequently, *The Tomb of Ligeia* was the last of the 'true' Poes for more reasons than simply the departure of Roger Corman from the scene. Unfortunately for AIP, the film did not find favour with the public and was a commercial failure. 'I think they (AIP) were probably sorry they didn't use a Poe title, because Poe had a certain marketability,' Matheson said of it.

While Corman was filming *The Masque of the Red Death*, he had hired Charles B Griffith to adapt Poe's *The Gold Bug* into a comedy also. The script was written for Price, Lorre, Karloff and Rathbone, but Lorre's death from a stroke in March 1964 put an end to the project, and to any further comedy-horrors featuring Price and the trio of old-timers.

Roger Corman had one last hand to play in AIP Gothic, however, though it was not as a director. In 1969, he took another stab at HP Lovecraft, but he handed the reins of the film over to his former art director Daniel Haller, who had since switched to directing himself, helming AIP's first genuine Lovecraft adaptation *Monster of Terror* (see chapter 7) and a couple of late sixties' 'biker' movies: *Devil's Angels* and *The Wild Racers*.

As with *The Gold Bug* and other 'lost' AIP films, such as the on-off production of *The Sleeper Awakes* with Vincent Price (which was adapted from the novel by HG Wells and was originally to have followed *Master of the World*), *The Dunwich Horror* had been through numerous drafts before AIP had found one that gave it confidence enough to green-light the project–even then, it was the product of no less than three writers: Curtis (Lee) Hanson, Henry Rosenbaum and Ronald Silkosky, with uncredited contributions from Ray Russell and Charles Beaumont.

Of all Lovecraft's short stories, *The Dunwich Horror* is one of the most unfilmable, but that's Hollywood for you! The 1929 tale concerns a pair of twins, one of whom is a throwback and the other a half-human entity who is kept locked up in an attic; their back story is the union between their mother and one of Lovecraft's mighty 'Old

The Comedy of Terrors (Basil Rathbone)

Ones', the demonic 'Yog-Sothoth', and the climax involves an attempt to 'open the gates' to another dimension so that the 'Old Ones' can return from exile in time and space and repossess the Earth. No adaptative problems there, then.

By 1969, the difficulties in translating Lovecraft's 'Mythos' universe to the screen were thought to have been sufficiently ironed out for production on *The Dunwich Horror* to begin, and the story's Wilbur Whateley was transmogrified into the hippie form of former child-star Dean Stockwell, complete with Afro hair-do, Ché Guevara moustache and a cool line in Necronomic chat-up. Lovecraft's Miskatonic University in Arkham became any flower-power-promoting campus that one cared to name, and Wilbur's obsession with heathen gods was just another manifestation of the current youth culture's fascination with alternative religions. It should not have worked, and yet somehow, in a sign of the psychedelic times, it *did*.

The role of Wilbur had been offered to Peter Fonda, who opted instead to make *Easy Rider*, and Sandra Dee (who was known mainly as the star of the *Gidget* 'beach girl' movies) replaced Diane Varsi. Sam Jaffe, who played Wilbur's grandfather, was also second choice to Ralph Bellamy, who had been offered the role after his sinister turn as a warlock in *Rosemary's Baby*; when the idea was first mooted in 1963, it was Boris Karloff in the frame. Only Hollywood veteran Ed Begley, as Wibur's nemesis Dr Armitage, came to the film untarnished by compromise.

The screenplay overlayed a conventional horror narrative on Lovecraft's tale, as Matheson had to do in his Poe adaptations, and the more relaxed censorship regime of the late 1960s allowed for a strong dose of sex in the process: Wilbur's method of summoning the Old Ones now involved impregnating a virgin on a sacrificial altar, and Dee's drug-induced hallucinations on the way to her demon-birth gave plenty of scope for some trippy New Age nudity, as well as a fondled body-double of her own.

Stockwell, who had 'dropped out' himself earlier in the decade, gives a twitchy, mannered performance that stays just on the right side of camp, and as his antiquarian adversary, Oscar-winner Begley (who died soon after completing the film) manages to

The Dunwich Horror (Dean Stockwell)

The Dunwich Horror (Sam Jaffe)

look suitably awed by the weird goings-on. Haller's nods to genre forebears include an emulation of the dream-rape in *Rosemary's Baby*, but his depiction of the monster is novel and effective, all flash-frames and posterising effects. 'It's really happening, isn't it?' Lloyd Bochner's local doctor declares as Wilbur's twin heads inexorably and invisibly for the Devil's Hopyard and its appointment with Armageddon, aided by a majestic Les Baxter score, and the eeriness of its storm-torn, night-time journey almost persuades one to take Bochner at his word.

With *The Dunwich Horror*, AIP achieved with Lovecraft what it had with Poe. Even the reviews were favourable: 'Gripping, impressive and chilling' the *Hollywood Reporter* noted; 'Engrossing film of the supernatural,' said the *Los Angeles Times*; 'Better than average horror cinema,' *Cinefantastique* agreed. But the film was released on the lower half of a double-bill with the below-par *The Oblong Box*, and AIP finally abandoned the Gothic for a more satirical approach to horror.

After *The Dunwich Horror*, filmmakers gave up trying to adapt the notoriously difficult works of HP Lovecraft for the screen until director Stuart Gordon brought to the fore the sexual undertone that certain academics had always felt was hidden in the tales. Copious nudity and lashings of gore made a 'sleeper' hit of *Re-Animator* in 1985, followed by *From Beyond* (1986), *Dagon* (2001) and more, and neither Gordon nor Lovecraft have looked back since.

UK theatrical posters for Invasion of the Hell Creatures (Invasion of the Saucer Men) and (I Was a) Teenage Frankenstein

Konga (Michael Gough, Margo Johns) / ABOVE: Horrors of the Black Museum (Dorinda Stevens)

UK theatrical poster for The Premature Burial / US theatrical poster for Die Monster Die! (UK: Monster of Terror)

Publicity shot for Beach Party (Annette Funicello, Frankie Avalon) / ABOVE: Black Sabbath (Rika Dialyna)

Publicity shot for Dr G and the Bikini Machine (Vincent Price) / The Wild Angels (Bruce Dern, Nancy Sinatra, Peter Fonda)

Poster art for The Dunwich Horror (1970)

The Abominable Dr Phibes (Virginia North, Vincent Price) / LEFT: Foxy Brown (Pam Grier) / BELOW: Wuthering Heights (Timothy Dalton, Anna Calder-Marshall)

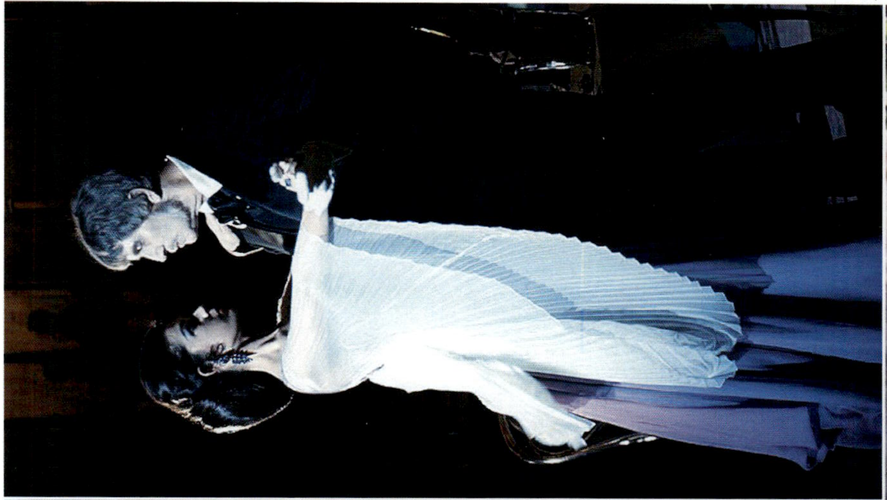

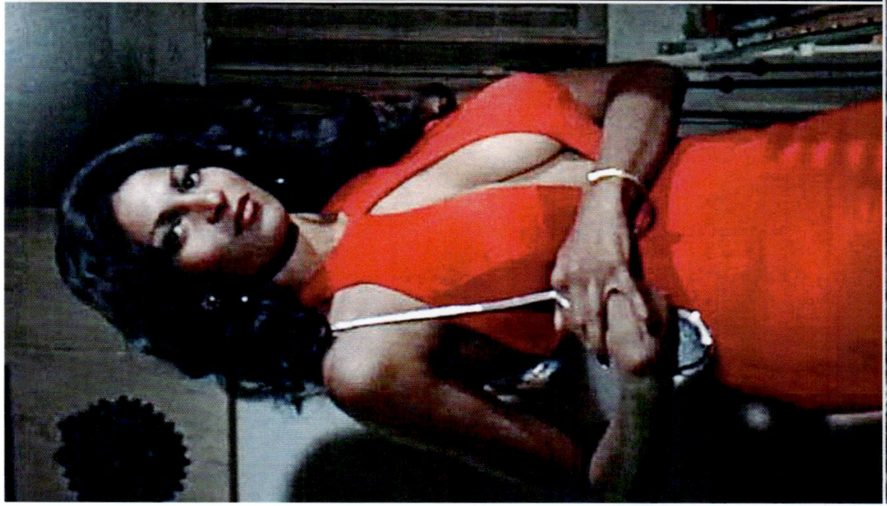

The Amityville Horror / ABOVE: *Love at First Bite* (George Hamilton, Susan Saint James)

5

AIP IN EUROPE

PEPLUMS, PLANETS AND SPACE VAMPIRES

In 1959, Joseph E Levine, who had been a Boston distributor for AIP, picked up the US distribution rights (for a very modest sum) of an Italian mythological adventure called *Le fatiche di Ercole* (US: *Hercules)*, which was loosely based on the Ancient Greek epic *Argonautica*, by Apollonius of Rhodes. Having acquired the film for peanuts, Levine, who had founded his own company Embassy Pictures in 1956 (and had cleaned up immediately by distributing the Japanese monster movie *Gojira*, which he retitled *Godzilla, King of the Monsters*), could afford to spend $1 million in promoting it. The movie made him a fortune.

At the time, AIP was itself moving into more expensive colour productions and abandoning its cheaper black and white titles. Arkoff and Nicholson were looking for new product to release while they waited for Corman to make *House of Usher*, and, like Levine, they wanted films that *looked* expensive but could be economically acquired. They found what they were seeking in Italy's burgeoning wave of 'peplums', as they soon came to be called.

The 'peplum' genre went back to the silent era in Italy. The term referred to the Greek or Roman togas worn by characters in films like the 1914 silent *Cabiria*, which also introduced the massively-muscled Maciste, played by Bartolomeo Pagano. The character of Maciste, usually played by Pagano, appeared in no less than two dozen silents from 1914 through to 1926.

In 1952, M-G-M producer Sam Zimbalist took advantage of the lower cost of film production in Italy and shot a remake of the silent epic *Quo Vadis* in Rome, which still became the most expensive film ever made up until then. This led to a home-grown clone called *Sins of Rome*, based on the story of Spartacus the slave, which was directed by Riccardo Freda with a wholly Italian cast and crew. It was dubbed into English and released by RKO in 1954.

Hercules (Steve Reeves)

The cross-fertilisation of 'runaway' Hollywood films and domestic Italian productions with imported American stars continued with the likes of *Ulysses* (1954), directed by Mario Camerini with Kirk Douglas as the titular hero, *Attila*, (also 1954) directed by Pietro Francisci and starring Anthony Quinn, and *Helen of Troy* (1955), directed by Robert Wise. So successful were these that the Italian industry decided to reclaim what it had created at the birth of the cinema and the 'peplum' was soon re-energised for a new generation.

The Italian/French co-production

of *Hercules*, was the real catalyst for the new cycle, however. A mere $120,000 had brought Levine a pay-day of more than $5 million–and that was just the beginning. A sequel, *Hercules Unchained* (*Ercole e la regina di Lidia*; 1959), was an even bigger success in the global marketplace.

With much of AIP's money currently tied up in *House of Usher*, Arkoff flew to Italy in the wake of Levine's windfall to check if there were other bargains to be had. He picked up two films: *Nel segno di Roma* and *Il terrore dei barbari*. On Arkoff's return to the States, Nicholson changed the title of *Nel segno di Roma* to the more commercial *Sign of the Gladiator* and promoted it on the star appeal of the voluptuous Anita Ekberg, who had just shot to fame in Federico Fellini's *La Dolce Vita*. With Ekberg in a variety of revealing costumes, the film's box-office appeal was assured.

Sign of the Gladiator (Anita Ekberg, George Marshal)

Sign of the Gladiator (Anita Ekberg)

Il terrore dei barbari was changed to *Goliath and the Barbarians,* and it starred ex-pat muscleman Steve Reeves, who had also played Hercules. The English dubbed version could have easily changed his character's name to cash in on *Hercules*, but Arkoff and Nicholson did not want to offend Levine (or be hit with a lawsuit), so they named the character 'Goliath'–an equally convenient catch-all for a mythic figure. They tried to have it both ways in radio advertising, however, by trumpeting, 'Steve Reeves, Mister Hercules himself, in his greatest role...'

Both films were typical *pepla*, with Ekberg portraying the lovelorn Queen of Palmyra in the first and Reeves portraying the beefy Goliath in the second (although in the film, the character is named Emiliano). The fact that there was no gladiator in *Sign of the Gladiator* did not disturb Nicholson or Arkoff one bit. A few changes in the dubbed dialogue created one, as Arkoff later told Mark McGee: 'We conceived that this man, this Roman consul, had been a slave tossed in the gladiators' ring. Anyway, the queen.. gives this Roman consul the old sex play to get him to betray himself. If he doesn't overcome the queen, who he's in love with, he could wind up back in the gladiator ring. Now there was a gladiator in the story. You didn't really have him in the picture but that made the thing work. And we had a modest success with that picture.'

The real test of how commercial the peplums would be for AIP was to come with the performance of *Goliath and the Barbarians*, with home-grown bodybuilder Reeves. The Montana-born health-and-fitness fanatic had won the 'Mr Universe' crown in 1950 but had since moved into acting and, in 1954, he had played opposite Jane Powell in the film *Athena*. Italian director Pietro Francisci had seen the film and contacted Reeves; the result was a trip to Rome to play the role of Hercules. American critics dismissed *Hercules* as 'muddled mythology' but audiences went crazy over Reeves's 'beefcake heroics'.

Goliath and the Barbarians was a historical rather than mythological adventure but it tapped into an escapist mood in cinemagoers with its simple revenge plot in which a barbarian horde invade Emiliano's village and murder his father. He then wages a one-man war against them, got up to look like some kind of forest demon, and under Carlo Campogalliani's direction, the emphasis was as much on sex (in the shapely form of Chelo Alonso) as it was on Dark Age barbarism.

Nicholson and Arkoff had more of an investment in *Goliath and the Barbarians* than they had had in *Sign of the Gladiator*. Production of the film had been shut down when finance ran out but after viewing the rushes, AIP agreed to not only buy the distribution rights but to advance the $20,000 needed to finish it. It turned out to be a wise investment: *Goliath and the Barbarians* was one of the biggest hits that AIP had ever had.

A typical response to the film from exhibitors arrived in December 1959 from Raymond Willie, the vice president and general manager of Interstate Circuiting. Addressed to 'Jim and Sam', the telegram read, '*Goliath and the Barbarians* opened in Dallas, Houston, San Antonio, Fort Worth and Galveston on Friday, December 18th, to the biggest grosses of any picture in the history of our company's pre-Christmas playing time. Thanks to American International for the availability of this attraction at this particular season.' The film earned $1.6 million in North America during its initial release.

At a press conference in New York early in 1960, James Nicholson announced that the success of their peplum features would lead AIP to switch from gimmicky exploitation pictures to 'blockbusters', which would be released every couple of months. This change in strategy necessitated an expansion of AIP's staff, especially in distribution and publicity. Regional sales managers were appointed from coast to coast and national advertising campaigns ranging from $500,000 to $1,000,000 were put in place for each major release for all media, including radio, television and the press. In some cases, ad campaigns would exceed the cost of the films themselves!

Goliath and the Barbarians (Steve Reeves, Chelo Alonso)

Goliath and the Dragon (Broderick Crawford)

AIP's follow-up to *Goliath and the Barbarians* was another Italian-French co-production, *La vendetta di Ercole* (literally *The Revenge of Hercules,* 1960), which the company retitled *Goliath and the Dragon* to tie in with the previous film. This one starred bodybuilder Mark Forest, with Hollywood veteran Broderick Crawford as the villain, and it featured 'special' make-up by Carlo Rambaldi, later a three-time Oscar winner for his work on *King Kong* (1976), *Alien* (1979) and *ET the Extra-Terrestrial* (1982).

The US version of *Goliath and the Dragon* was re-edited

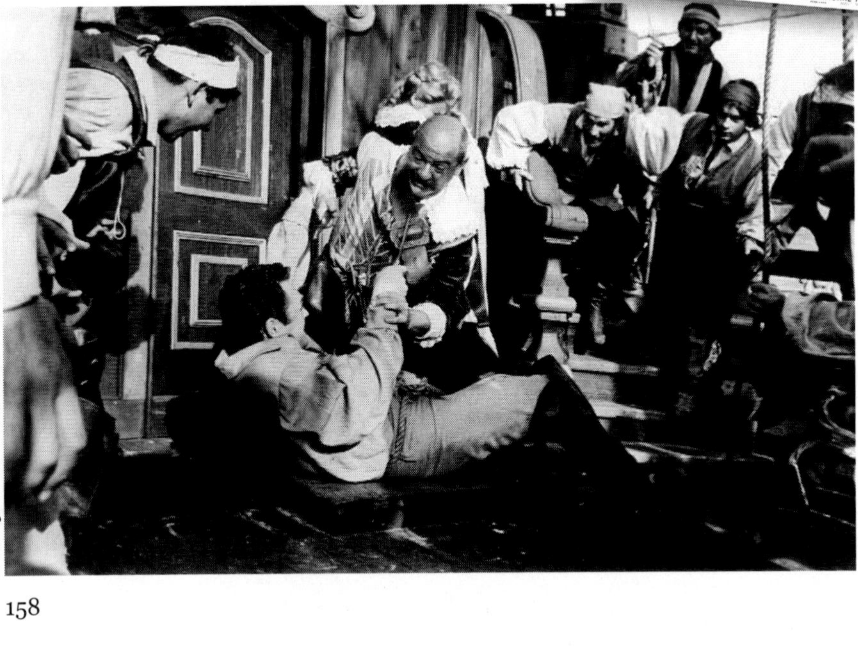
Guns of the Black Witch (Don Megowan)

to include a stop-motion sequence of a dragon, animated by Jim Danforth and Wah Chang, to 'complement' the original's cruder man-in-a-rubber-suit mechnical effects. The recut film also included a new score by AIP house composer Les Baxter. The plot was just as perfunctory: Goliath battles giant bats, the three-headed Cerberus and the titular dragon in order to save his wife (Gaby Andre) and countrymen from the evil schemes of King Eurystheus (Crawford).

Originally, AIP had announced plans for *Goliath and the Dragon* to be produced entirely by the company, from a screenplay by Lou Rusoff and starring Debra Paget. But this idea fell through and it ended up buying the Italian *Hercules* film, re-editing and re-dubbing it and adding the dragon sequence. The notion to use Paget had come from her fiery appearance in Fritz Lang's *Das indische Grabmal* (*The Indian Tomb,* 1959), in which she had performed an exotic dance. It was the second of two films to which AIP had obtained the rights in 1960, subsequently combining them into *Journey to the Lost City*.

***Goliath and the Dragon* (Mark Forrest)**

In 1961, AIP picked up a pirate adventure featuring French buccaneers called *Il terrore dei mari,* which it retitled *Guns of the Black Witch.* Starring Don Megowan and Silvana Pampanini, it was paired with a Filipino war film called *Lost Battalion*, directed by Eddie Romero. *Guns of the Black Witch* was not really a peplum but its appeal was to the same audience. The double feature did only average business, however, so the next Italian pick-up was a *real* peplum, *Marco Polo* (1962), which AIP sold as an *El Cid*-style spectacle. Directed by Piero Pierotti and Hugo Fragonese, it starred an unlikely Rory Calhoun in the title role, with Yoko Tani and Camillo Pilotto as the Grand Khan. *Marco Polo* supplied the lavish vistas that fans

of the 'epic' were curently paying to see, and Les Baxter provided a suitably majestic score for AIP's version.

To extract more mileage from the sets (not to mention Asian extras) of *Marco Polo*, the production company, Panda, asked writers Oreste Biancoli and Duccio Tessari to pen another epic in which Maciste (former screen Tarzan Gordon Scott) finds himself in China. Director Riccardo Freda, who had pioneered Italian horror films with *I vampiri* in 1957, was brought in to helm the project, which was originally titled *Maciste alla corte del Gran Khan*. Yoko Tani returned as the female lead, a Chinese princess whom Maciste rescues from a band of marauders. When AIP came on the scene, it changed the name of the title character and the film became *Samson*

***Samson and the 7 Miracles of the World* (Gordon Scott) / RIGHT: *Hercules and the Tyrants of Babylon* (Peter Lupus)**

and the Seven Miracles of the World; it was released in late 1962 with *Warriors Five,* an Italian-French-Yugoslavian war film starring Jack Palance.

AIP brought Samson back (this time played by Alan Steel) in *Samson and the Slave Queen* (*Zorro contro Maciste*; 1963) on a double bill with *Goliath and the Sins of Babylon* (*Maciste l'eroe più grande del mondo),* starring Mark Forest. As directed by Umberto Lenzi and Michele Lupo respectively, both films were undistinguished examples of the breed.

Finally daring to use the name Hercules, AIP released *Ercole contro i tiranni di Babilonia* as *Hercules and the Tyrants of Babylon* in 1964. But by then, the market for *pepla* had been exhausted by repetition. Directed by Domenico Paolella, *Hercules and the Tyrants of Babylon* starred Peter Lupus as Hercules–though he was billed as Rock Stevens, as per *Muscle Beach Party* (see chapter 6). In this latest epic, Hercules fights on behalf of the citizens of Babylon to save them from a wicked sorceress. The most memorable moments featured the alluring Helga Liné, who would grace many a Euro-Gothic, such as the Paul Naschy-starrer *Horror Rises From the Tomb* (1973).

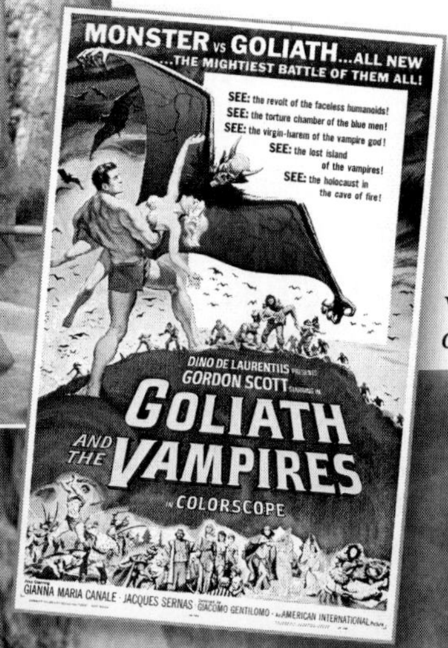

1964's *Maciste contro il vampiro,* which AIP was to retitle *Goliath and the Vampires,* was perhaps its best peplum of all. Released in the US on a double bill with Corman's *The Masque of the Red Death,* the film

Goliath and the Vampires (*Leonora Ruffo*)

Hercules in the Haunted World (Christopher Lee, Leonora Ruffo)

starred Gordon Scott as 'Goliath' and was directed by Sergio Corbucci and Giacomo Gentilomo. Moodily photographed by Alvaro Mancori, *Goliath and the Vampires* evinces the sure touch of Corbucci, who would go on to direct one of the most influential of Euro-westerns: *Django* (1966). Around the time of filming *Goliath*, he also contributed scripts for two Euro-Gothics–the Italian/Spanish *Horror* (US: *The Blancheville Monster*; 1963) and the Italian/French *Danza Macabra* (US: *Castle of Blood*; 1964), the latter of which he co-directed with Antonio Margheriti. Along with Mario Bava's *Ercole al centro della terra* (US: *Hercules in the Haunted World*; 1961), which had taken advantage of Christopher Lee's turn-of-the-decade tour of European studios in a bid not to become typecast in Hammer Horror, *Goliath and the Vampires* was the most effective of the occasional peplum/horror mashups.

AIP's final peplum was *War of the Zombies* (1965), a not uninteresting hybrid featuring John Drew Barrymore, the son of silent screen star John Barrymore. The fantastic plot involved a plan to conquer the world using an army of zombies, but there was not enough horror to satisfy fright-fans nor enough action to satisfy the *pepla* brigade. Peplums were now being replaced by Italian westerns made in Spain–the so-called 'spaghetti' westerns which had begun in earnest with Sergio Leone's *Per un pugno di dollari* (*A Fistful of Dollars*; 1964). AIP had long-since done with westerns, so it unwisely decided to pass on this new trend, lucrative as it turned out to be.

Arkoff and Nicholson were more than familiar with horror, however, given their fifties' teenage monster movies and the current success of their Poe series of films, and on one of their first shopping trips for *pepla*, they had picked up a Gothic called *La maschera del demonio*, from director Mario Bava. Bava (who had taken over the direction of *I Vampiri* in 1956 from Riccardo Freda) had decided to mount a Hammeresque adaptation of the Nicolai Gogol story 'Viy', about a young theology student who engages in a battle of wits with a witch. He and his co-writers, Ennio de Concini, Mario Serandrei and Marcello Coscia, had altered the story to give it a darker and more macabre tone, turning the witch into a vampire in line with the success in Italy of Hammer's 1958 *Dracula*.

Bava admired Gogol's tale and said that he used to read it to his children, whom it

Black Sunday (Barbara Steele)

frightened so much that they insisted on sleeping in bed with him. When he was given the opportunity to choose a subject to direct by the head of Galatea, Nello Santi, he immediately suggested 'Viy'. Santi, for whom Bava had just performed a 'salvage job' on Jacques Tourneur's *La battaglia di Maratona* (*The Giant of Marathon*; 1959), had given him a six-week schedule for *La maschera del demonio* in response, which had commenced on March 28, 1960. (Typical Italian productions of the period had three-to-four week schedules.)

When Arkoff and Nicholson were presented with *La maschera del demonio,* they could see that it was something special. Despite the fact that it was in black and white, the artistry and visual ingenuity of Bava's direction could not be denied, even by Arkoff, who did not care for what he termed 'arty-farty' pictures. But there were enough exploitable elements in the film to overcome any objections on that score.

The screenplay kept to the bare bones of Gogol's story and retained the Russian setting, but the rest was a far remove from its source: a vengeful witch is returned from the dead by a hapless entrant to her tomb and sets out to enact a gruesome revenge upon her near-identical descendant. A handsome young doctor battles with the vampire to save her soul.

La maschera del demonio provided a memorable introduction to an actress who would become a horror icon, Barbara Steele. Born in Birkenhead, Cheshire, Steele had been a Rank starlet and her feature film debut was in the comedy *Bachelor of*

Hearts (1958). After appearing in more domestic productions, including *Sapphire* (1959), *Upstairs and Downstairs* (1959) and *Your Money or Your Wife* (1960), her extraordinary looks and compelling screen presence led her to turn her back on the British industry and base herself in Italy, where she was cast in the dual role in Bava's film. Years later, her director recalled, 'A strange type was needed, and we chose Steele from pictures.'

Steele's leading man was another Briton, John Richardson, who had appeared opposite her in *Bachelor of Hearts*. Tall, handsome, with chiseled features, he would go on to appear in a number of home-grown 'peplums' for Hammer, including *She* (1965), *One Million Years BC* (1966) and *The Vengeance of She* (1968). Asa's vampire

Black Sunday (Arturo Dominici)

consort was played by Arturo Dominici, a veteran of innumerable *pepla* such as the original *Le fatiche di Ercole* (1958). He had also appeared in Freda's *Caltiki–il mostro immortale* (US: *Caltiki–the Immortal Monster*; 1959), another salvage job on which Bava received no screen credit. In *La maschera del demonio,* Dominici's real-life daughter Germana played a young girl sent out to milk a cow at night when her father's character claws his way out of a nearby grave!

Steele and Bava's on-set relationship was a difficult one, however. Steele did not see the script in advance and was only given the pages for scenes which would be shot that day. In a 2007 interview for *Video Watchdog* by Christopher Dietrich and Peter Beckman, she recalled, 'We had hardly any idea what was going down on that film. We had no idea of the end, or the beginning either, not at all.'

As a result, Steele sometimes refused to turn up on set because she did not like her wig, or the fact that Bava wanted her to show a little too much of her cleavage. At one point, she refused to appear because she was convinced that he wanted her to appear nude. In an interview with Tim Lucas in *Fangoria*, the director said that he found her to be 'somewhat irrational, afraid of Italians. One day she refused to come to the set because somebody told her I was using a special film stock that made people appear naked.'

In later years, Steele admitted that she had been 'difficult' on the film because of her inexperience and the fact that she barely understood the language: 'I didn't like my fangs; I had them changed three times. I loathed my wig; I changed that four times. I couldn't understand Italian. I certainly didn't want them to tear open my dress and expose my breasts, so they got a double that I didn't like at all. So I ended up doing it myself–drunk, barely over eighteen, embarrassed and not very easy to be around.' (In true Hammer fashion, both Steele and Dominici were fitted for vampire fangs but Bava decided not to use them in the end, although some publicity photos still show Dominici wearing them.) Steele would continue to work in Italy for many years, but she and Bava never worked together again.

When Arkoff and Nicholson picked up *La maschera del demonio,* they retitled it *Black Sunday* for the international market. Galatea had provided its own English-dubbed version of the film (titled *The Mask of Satan*), but Arkoff and Nicholson had found it 'technically unacceptable' and a new soundtrack was recorded in New York, in which Steele's voice was dubbed. Elements of the film were deemed too strong for the domestic audience, which in America had always included children, and some of the gore was trimmed–such as when Asa has a mask of spikes nailed to her face in the opening scene. Other cuts were made to tighten the pace, although references in the original to an incestuous relationship between Steele and Dominici were also removed from AIP's version. As a matter of course, Les Baxter's music unnecessarily replaced that of Roberto Nicolosi.

For its time, *Black Sunday*'s graphic visuals went further than anything previously

Black Sunday (Antonio Pierfederici, John Richardson)

seen. Bava's vampire-killing variant was a metal peg driven through the creature's *eye*, and flesh was seen to peel from a man's face as he burned to death in a fireplace. The air of decay and physical corrupton that hangs over Asa's tomb was very vividly realised and even after the cuts, AIP felt that the film should not be marketed to the under-12s and its ads emphasised the film's suitability for more mature audiences. In the UK, *Black Sunday* was banned outright by the British censor.

La maschera del demonio had been a modest success in Italy, premiering in Rome in August 1960. It was more successful in France and the United States. *Black Sunday* premiered in the US in Cleveland, Ohio, in February 1961 and reviews were

enthusiastic. Sam Burns of *Motion Picture Herald* wrote: 'A classic quality permeates this gruesome, shocking, horrifying story of a vengeful, blood-thirsty vampire. Effectively photographed in low key black and white against rich settings of macabre design.. (it) achieves frightful elements of surprise through clever makeup and performances.'

In the *Los Angeles Examiner,* Kay Proctor called the film 'a honey of a horror' for those 'who can take their macabre straight and strong'. *Variety* agreed: 'There is sufficient cinematographic ingenuity and production flair.. to keep an audience pleasantly unnerved'. *Time* called it '...A piece of fine Italian handiwork that atones for its ludicrous lapses with brilliant intuitions of the spectral'. *The New York Times* hated the movie, however, with Eugene Archer writing, 'Barbara Steele, a blank-eyed manikin with an earthbound figure and a voice from outer space, is appropriately cast as a vampire; not the Theda Bara kind, but the genuine blood-drinking variety. Mario Bava, ostensibly the director of this nonsense, allows this female Bela Lugosi to quench her thirst four times before she burns, screaming at the stake. As a setting for unadulterated horror, it will leave its audiences yearning for that quiet, sunny little motel in *Psycho*.'

After the success of *La mashera del demonio/Black Sunday,* Bava found himself in demand for more Italo-American co-productions. His next assignment was *Esther and the King* (*Esther e il re*; 1960), a co-production between Galatea, Titanus and 20th Century Fox, starring Joan Collins and Richard Egan. Bava directed the Italian version of the Biblical epic, while Hollywood veteran Raoul Walsh was credited with the English-language version. He followed this with a similar arrangement on *The Wonders of Aladdin* (1961), an Arabian Nights fantasy co-directed by Henry Levin and starring Donald O'Connor and Noelle Adam. It was released in the US by M-G-M and presented by Joseph E Levine.

AIP had not been able to pick up either of these for distribution, but it grabbed Bava's next, *Gli Invasori* (US: *Erik the Conqueror,* 1961), a Viking peplum starring

Erik the Conqueror (*Cameron Mitchell*)

Cameron Mitchell. The story borrowed heavily from Richard Fleischer's *The Vikings* (1957) and concerned two children, one of whom is raised by Britons and the other by Vikings; eventually they meet again as strife breaks out between the Vikings and the English.

B-lister Mitchell had relocated to Europe after a run-in with the Revenue Service and he would appear in numerous historical epics, spaghetti westerns and horror films; *Erik the Conqueror* was one of the first. In a 1991 *Fangoria* interview by Tom Weaver, he said of Bava: 'I loved Mario Bava; in some ways he may have been the best director. I've worked with Kazan, I've worked with Orson Welles.. I've worked with John Ford. Bava is right up there. And when I think of the limited money he had and the corners he had to cut, it's unbelievable!'

Erik the Conqueror is frequently dazzling. Photographed by Bava himself, in the rich colour effects which would become his trademark, scenes are bathed in gold, crimson, blue or green, and the opening battle is superbly choreographed. It gained added coverage by featuring the screen debut of *Life* magazine cover girls the Kessler Twins, German blonde bombshells who had performed at the Lido in Paris.

Bava's next film as director was *La ragazza che sapeva troppo* (*The Girl Who Knew Too Much*; 1963), a co-production between Galatea and Coronet s r l, another

The Girl Who Knew Too Much (*Letícia Román*)

Italian company. Bava was a fan of Alfred Hitchcock and he had wanted to make a Hitchcock thriller. The result was a seminal film in what would become known as the 'giallo' genre, a type of Italian slasher-*noir*. (The word 'giallo' means yellow and its employment as a label derives from its association with pulp mystery novels that were popular in post-war Italy, most of which featured yellow covers.) Starring John Saxon and Leticia Roman, the convoluted plot concerned an American woman in Rome who witnesses a murder. Neither Saxon nor the police believe her, as there is no corpse, but more murders follow which are linked to a decade-old series of killings where the victims were chosen in alphabetical order.

The Italian version had a sub-plot involving marijuana-smuggling but when AIP picked it up for the US market, it was not only retitled *The Evil Eye* but cut by several minutes, re-scored (Roberto Nicolosi's original once again replaced by another from Les Baxter), and all references to marijuana were removed. In either version, the film is still highly entertaining. The two leads play off well against each other, with Saxon a solid 'hero' and Roman a delectable damsel in distress. Bava also handled the camera and it became his last movie in black and white, its stylish look one of its most memorable aspects.

The Evil Eye was released in 1964, along with another Bava film which has since become a classic: *Black Sabbath* (1963).

Originally titled *I tre volti della paura (The Three Faces of Fear), Black Sabbath* came about as a result of AIP's deal with Galatea that they would contribute funds to nine co-productions over eight years. *Black Sabbath* (the title was intended to echo *Black Sunday*) followed the trend of films like the Sophia Loren-starrer *Yesterday, Today and Tomorrow* (1963) in that it was an 'anthology' composed of three short stories, mostly featuring European actors but with one international star courtesy of AIP: Boris Karloff. Mark Damon was also cast by AIP, while French co-production company Societé Cinématographique Lyre supplied Michèle Mercier and Jacqueline Pierreux; Mercier had previously worked with Bava on *The Wonders of Aladdin*.

***Black Sabbath* (Boris Karloff)**

Bava wrote the script with Alberto Bevilacqua and Marcello Fondato. It was based on three short stories: 'A Drop of Water' by Ivan Chekhov, 'The Telephone' by F G Snyder and 'The Family of the Wurdalak' by Aleksey Tolstoy. It was decided early on that Karloff would not only star in one of the tales but also host the film, as he had the horror anthology series, *Thriller*, on television from 1960 to 1962. When that ended, Karloff had signed a contract with AIP for several films, beginning with *The Raven*. *Black Sabbath* was his second.

Black Sabbath went onto the floor immediately after production wrapped on *The Girl Who Knew Too Much*, on an eight-week schedule through February and March 1963. AIP's involvement allowed Salvatore Billitteri of the Titra Sound company to ensure that the dialogue would be suitable for dubbing. Billitteri was also encouraged by AIP to suggest to Bava how to make the film more suitable for US audiences by moderating the sex and violence.

Both 'A Drop of Water' and 'The Wurdalak' were period pieces, but Bava wanted to include at least one contemporary story. That turned out to be 'The Telephone', his second attempt at a giallo. Unlike *The Girl Who Knew Too Much, Black Sabbath* was shot in colour (mostly by Ubaldo Terzano but with some participation by Bava himself). 'The Telephone' was an attempt to replicate the lurid style made famous by giallo paperbacks.

The final segment to be filmed was 'The Wurdalak', which commenced shooting at the end of February. Because of the inclement weather, Karloff came down with

Black Sabbath (Jacqueline Pierreux)

Black Sabbath (Michèle Mercier)

pneumonia during the shoot and had to rely on oxygen tanks in order to breathe by the time production ended.

Originally, Bava had planned to close the film on a bleak note, with Pierreux's character in 'A Drop of Water' found dead by the police, but Billitteri suggested that the film needed a less grim ending to counter the horror. Contemptuous of the need to pander to American sensibility, Bava shot a 'joke' ending which had Karloff's character on horseback warning the audience about vampires–but as the camera pulled back, he was revealed to be on a prop horse in a studio, with technicians holding tree branches for background effect.

That bizarre coda was removed by AIP, along with many other elements of the film. Alterations were made to all three of the stories. The most extensively changed was 'The Telephone', which starred Mercier as a call girl who is being harangued by phone calls from an apparent stalker. The Italian cut had implications of lesbianism and prostitution; AIP removed those with alterations in the dialogue and it changed the ending to infer a supernatural solution which Bava had never intended. AIP also changed the order of the stories. The original had begun with 'The Telephone' and had proceeded to 'The Wurdalak' followed by 'A Drop of Water'; Arkoff and Nicholson chose to open *Black Sabbath* with 'A Drop of Water', followed by 'The Telephone' and 'The Wurdalak'. The final story featured alternate, less gruesome cuts of some shots, but 'The Drop of Water' merely had 'spooky' sound effects added. The entire film was also re-scored, again by Baxter. AIP shot new introductions to each of the stories with Karloff, now recovered from his bout of pneumonia, in Los Angeles. Bava's version only had him introduce the film at the beginning.

'The Wurdalak' is epic in scope and could easily have been a feature on its own (it was effectively remade in 1972 as an Italian-Spanish production called *La notte dei diavoli*, aka *Night of the Devils*, by director Giorgio Ferroni). Karloff stars as Gorcha, the elderly patriarch of a Russian family. He returns home after destroying a wurdalak–a type of Russian vampire which drinks only the blood of its loved ones to survive–but it transpires that he himself has been infected and must now feed on members of his family to live. Gradually, they realise what he has become when his demeanour takes on a more ominous aspect. 'What's the matter, woman?' he asks his daughter. 'Can't I fondle my own grandson..?'

Black Sabbath (Boris Karloff)

'A Drop of Water' was also the stuff of nightmare. In Victorian London, a nurse (Pierreux) is summoned to prepare the corpse of an elderly woman for burial. As she dresses the body, she is distracted by two things: the face of the corpse is frozen in a hideous rictus (a mask sculpted by Bava's father, Eugenio) and an expensive ring resides on one of the woman's fingers. She steals the ring but, in doing so, knocks over a glass of water. Back in her own apartment, she is tormented by the slow drip, drip of tap-water until finally, the old woman's corpse appears to her, its face still contorted in that ghastly grin. Eventually, the apparition floats towards her and the nurse expires from a combination of guilt and heart failure. A second nurse is called, who also espies the ring and is tempted to procure it for herself...

Black Sabbath is considered by many to be a small masterpiece, from its evocative use of colour and lighting to Giorgio Giovanni's delirious production design. It was co-billed with *The Tomb of Ligeia* in the UK and the pairing provided audiences with a goodly quota of chills but the reviews, as usual, were mixed. Of AIP's version, the

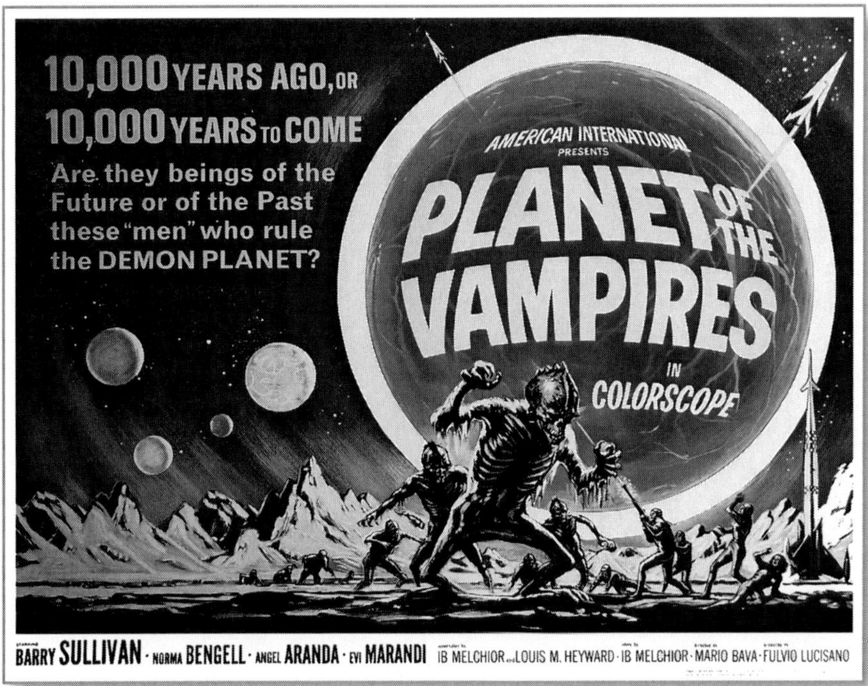

BFI's *Monthly Film Bulletin* opined, 'The eeriest thing about the picture is its decor'. It went on to state that Bava seemed 'determined to spell everything out with sudden zoom shots and shock cuts'. The film was better received by *The Globe and Mail,* which thought it 'a good deal more sophisticated than usual horror fare...'

Bava's next production for AIP was set in outer space. Titled *Terrore nello spazio* (*Planet of the Vampires*; 1965), it is one of his most visually inventive films. Based on Renato Pestriniero's short story 'One Night of 21 Hours', *Planet of the Vampires* was

Planet of the Vampires

co-produced by AIP and Italian International producer Fulvio Lucisano. AIP supplied screenwriter Ib Melchior, who had written (with Sidney Pink) and directed *The Angry Red Planet* (1959) and had co-written Pink's Danish-produced monster-fest *Reptilicus* (1962) for the company.

Barry Sullivan, who had been in Hollywood films since the 1940s and was prolific on stage and television, was imported to star. His screen debut had come in *Lady in the Dark* (1943), alongside Ginger Rogers and Ray Milland, but his best-known role was probably that of the film director in Vincente Minnelli's *The Bad and the Beautiful* in 1952. In *Planet of the Vampires,* Sullivan was cast as Captain Markary, the steely commander of deep-space starship, the Argos.

Brazilian-born actress Norma Bengell was cast as the female lead. Bengell had appeared in numerous international productions, such as *Mafioso* (1962) and *Eros* (1964), and she specialised in sexy roles. Her main claim to fame was that she had been the first actress to perform a full-frontal nude scene in a mainstream film, the Brazilian crime thriller *Os Cafejestes* (*The Hustlers*; 1962).

Supporting Sullivan was Spanish actor Ángel Aranda, as another of the Argos's crew. Aranda had appeared in the 1959 Steve Reeves peplum-starrer *The Last Days of Pompeii,* co-directed by Mario Bonnard and Sergio Leone. He had also enjoyed a sizeable role in Leone's *The Colossus of Rhodes* (1961), and he was in one of the first spaghetti westerns, Mario Caiano's *Bullets Don't Argue,* which had been produced by Jolly Film back-to-back with Leone's *A Fistful of Dollars*. The first of the crew to see her deceased companions rise from their graves as 'vampires' was Italian-Greek actress Evi Marandi. Marandi was also a veteran of peplums such as *Revenge of the Barbarians* (1960).

With such a truly international cast, *Planet of the Vampires* faced some unusual production problems. Each actor used his or her native language on the set and in many cases, each did not understand what the other was saying at any given point in the story; Sullivan spoke his lines in English, Bengell said hers in Portuguese, Marandi in Italian and Aranda in Spanish. Small wonder that even the dubbed version has a sense of the Tower of Babel about it!

As usual, Bava had little in the way of funds. There were a great deal of effects in the script, but he was unable to utilise any opticals due to the tiny budget. Forced to think outside the box, he employed miniatures and forced perspective to achieve the otherworldly ambience required, and fog and coloured gels to create the appropriate atmosphere. In an interview with Tim Lucas for *Fangoria*, Bava revealed just how little he had to work with: 'Do you know what that unknown planet was made of? A couple of plastic rocks–yes, two!–left over from a mythological movie made at Cinecittà! To assist the illusion, I filled the set with smoke.' In addition, he made do

***Planet of the Vampires* (Eva Marandi, Franco Andrei)**

with mirrors and double-exposure, so the scenes on the planet were quite literally a case of smoke and mirrors!

The story was a typically simple one: in search of another ship that has crashed on the planet Aura, the crew of the *Argos* begin to turn violently against each other, seemingly under some influence from the planet itself. They discover that the crew of the derelict had also died fighting each other and on further investigation, encounter the presence of invisible extraterrestrials who are trying to take them over so that they can leave their dying planet.

Two scenes in particular stand out: while exploring the derelict spacecraft, the crew find huge skeletons of the long-dead crew-members–a concept which inspired the similar scene in Ridley Scott's later *Alien* (1979)–and when the dead astronauts are possessed by the alien entities and return to life, they rise from their shallow graves wrapped in plastic shrouds, tearing themselves free of their body-bags in the process. Shot in slow motion with unsettling sound effects, it was Bava at his most poetic, recalling the scene in which Asa's henchman rises from his grave in *Black Sunday*.

AIP released *Planet of the Vampires* in the US on a double bill with *Die, Monster, Die!* in October 1965. Reviews for *Planet of the Vampires* were as varied as those for *Black Sabbath*. *Variety* noted that the 'plot is punctuated with gore, shock, eerie music and wild optic and special effects... smooth and first class.' But in *Films & Filming*, Richard Davis wrote, 'Bava is tied to a grossly synthetic studio set.. the piece on the whole is poor stuff.'

After the stylish *Planet of the Vampires*, it is depressing to contemplate Bava's next film for AIP, *Dr Goldfoot and the Girl Bombs* (1966).

***Dr Goldfoot and the Bikini Machine* (Vincent Price)**

Fulvio Lucisano, the head of Italian International, had wanted to make a sequel to his successful release *Due mafiosi contro Goldginger* (1965), a spoof of the James Bond film *Goldfinger* (1964) which AIP had picked up and dubbed into English for sale direct to TV as *The Amazing Dr G.* The film had starred the Italian comedy duo of Franco Franchi and Ciccio Ingrassia who, billed as Franco and Ciccio, were at the time the most famous comedians in Italy.

AIP agreed to co-finance the follow-up, but on one condition: it had to be turned into a sequel to its own successful sci-fi comedy *Dr Goldfoot and the Bikini Machine* (1965), which had starred Vincent Price. Lucisano agreed to this, although he had a condition of his own: the Italian version would highlight Franco and Ciccio, while the American version would emphasise Price as Dr Goldfoot, reprising his role from the original film.

Lucisano had Mario Bava under contract and assigned him to direct what would become *Dr Goldfoot and the Girl Bombs.* Bava did not want to direct the film but he could not get out of his contract. The result was what Price subsequently called 'The most dreadful movie I've ever been in'.

Frankie Avalon was originally scheduled to appear in the sequel, but he pulled out at the last minute due to the birth of his third child. He was replaced by Fabian, and filming commenced in April 1966 at Cinecittá and on location in Rome's Parco di Principe. According to AIP executive Louis Heyward, the script was rewritten nine times before production started as there was difficulty pleasing the Italian financiers as well as AIP.

The most noteworthy aspect of *Dr Goldfoot and the Girl Bombs* was its introduction of Laura Antonelli to American audiences. Antonelli went on to appear in a number of Italian sex farces such as *Malizia* (1973) and given the sexy image that she later cultivated, it was ironic that she refused to do a scene in the film in which she undressed. Arkoff later said that the box office failure of *Girl Bombs* was due to Antonelli's refusal to go *au natural* and that she had originally agreed to strip until Arkoff's nephew, Ted Rusoff, developed a crush on her and advised her not to go through

Dr Goldfoot and the Girl Bombs

with it. Truth be told, the lack of nudity in the film is the least of its problems. The plot, such as it is, involves Price's Dr Goldfoot once again coming up with a nefarious plan to conquer the world using female robots with bombs inside of them, who are sent out to blow up high-ranking NATO generals. Bumbling secret agent Bill Dexter (Fabian) is the only one who can stop him and the movie ends with a mad chase through the streets of Rome.

The Italian version runs some seven minutes longer than the AIP version and includes more screen time for Franco and Ciccio. It was called *Le spie vengono dal semifreddo (The Spies Who Came in From the Semi-Cold)*, a parody of John Le Carré's *The Spy Who Came in From the Cold.* The film was released in the UK as *Dr G and the Girl Bombs* because of the threat of legal action against AIP by a real Dr Goldfoot living in London.

The AIP cut is almost unwatchable. Franco and Cicchio mug throughout and their routines are unfunny in the extreme. The dubbing is atrocious and Price camps it up in three different roles, including one in drag. He was correct in stating that *Dr Goldfoot and the Girl Bombs* was the worst film of his career; it was also Bava's worst and it ended his six-year relationship with American International. But it was his biggest hit in Italy, which goes to prove that bad taste is an international phenomenon.

In addition to *Planet of the Vampires,* AIP released several other Italian-produced sci-fi films during the sixties, beginning with Antonio Margheriti's *Assignment Outer Space* (1960), a game attempt at a serious space adventure which was totally devoid of monsters and ray guns. Unfortunately, it made for a dull experience, which starred Rik Van Nutter (who would play agent Felix Leiter in the James Bond film *Thunderball* in 1965) and Gabriella Farinon. Margheriti, who often used the pseudonym Anthony Dawson, was a genre fan and he had co-written the script with Ennio De Concini. It was produced at the same time that Bava was filming *La maschera del demonio* on a Titanus sound stage next door.

Far from being one of Margheriti's best films, *Assignment Outer Space*–as with most Italian 'space operas' of the period–lacked the required budget to be effective. Nevertheless, the scenes set outside a space station are impressively handled and, in retrospect, appear like a warm-up for the more 'authentic' space scenes in Stanley Kubrick's later *2001: A Space Odyssey* (1968).

Corman was instrumental in importing three Russian science fiction films into

Assignment Outer Space

Voyage to the Prehistoric Planet

the US, re-dubbing and re-editing them and completely changing their plots. The first was *Nebo Zovyot,* a 1959 Soviet film about the race to be the first nation to land on the planet Mars. The original featured some splendid outer space effects, which were pretty much all that Corman kept when he 'westernised' it. He employed film-school student Francis Ford Coppola to do just that and had him prepare a dubbing script that eliminated the anti-American theme of the film. Coppola supervised the dubbing and shot an additional scene of two weird-looking alien creatures fighting each other, which he cut into the Russian print.

When the film was released in the US in 1962 as *Battle Beyond the Sun,* it failed to make much of an impact, although some critics were taken by the excellent effects. Undaunted, Corman adapted a second Soviet film–*Planeta Bur* (*Planet of Storms,* 1962)–into *Voyage to the Prehistoric Planet* (1965), this time assigning Curtis Harrington (*Night Tide,* 1961) to direct new footage with Basil Rathbone and 1950s' sci-fi doyenne Faith Domergue. Harrington was so displeased with the result that he ended up using the pseudonym 'John Sebastian' on the film's credits, but Corman,

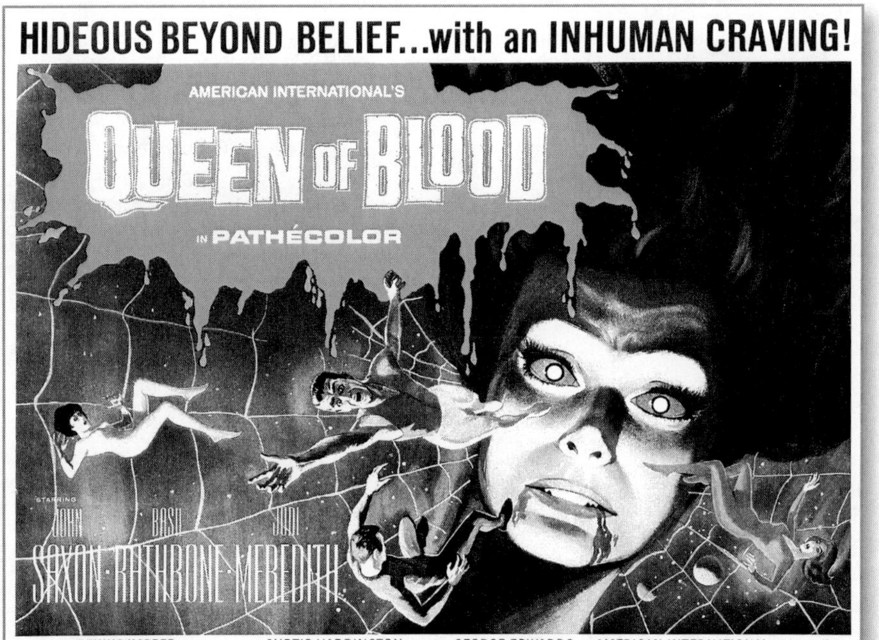

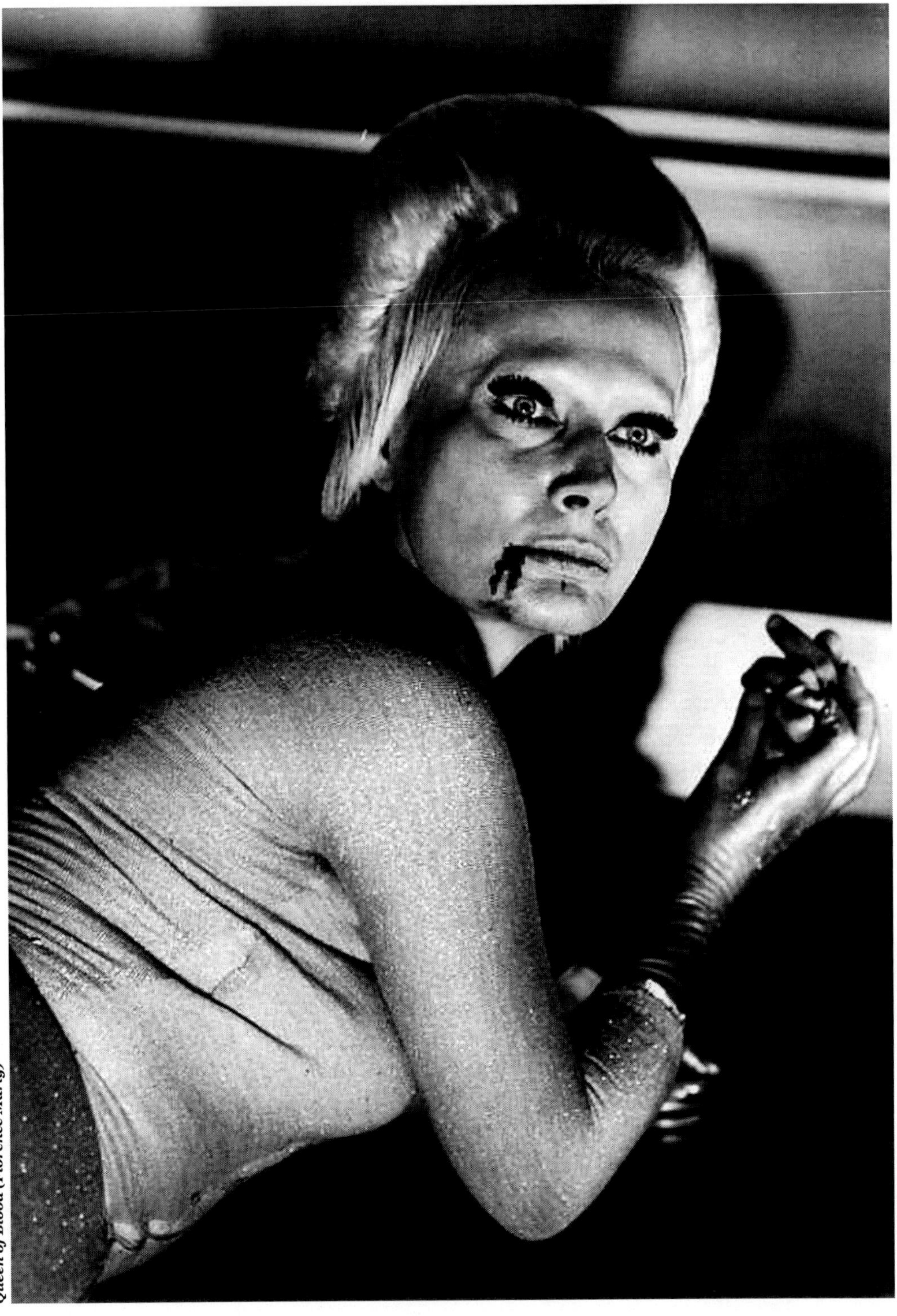

Queen of Blood (Florence Marly)

Queen of Blood (Florence Marly, Dennis Hopper)

with his usual economy, asked him to adapt both *Nebo Zovyot* and another Russian film, *Mechte Navstrechu (A Dream Come True,* 1963), into a sci-fi horror called *Queen of Blood* (1966). Harrington was pleased enough on this second occasion to retain his credit for the subsequent mashup.

Queen of Blood is seen by some as yet another of the inspirations for Scott's *Alien.* The plot has similarities: in 1990, an alien species makes contact with Earth, asking for help as they have crash-landed on Mars. Rathbone sends a team of astronauts (including John Saxon and Dennis Hopper) to the Red Planet to rescue them. On Mars, they discover only one survivor, a green-skinned female (Florence Marly). She is brought aboard the ship but is soon discovered to be a kind of space vampire, who drains the astronauts of their blood, one by one.

By far the best of Corman's 'Soviet trilogy', *Queen of Blood* is the only one of the three to have left any sort of cultural legacy. Harrington claimed that over 90% of the final film was his work and in a 2005 interview entitled *Retrospective in Terror: An Interview with Curtis Harrington*, he said, 'Ridley's film (*Alien*) is like a greatly enhanced, expensive and elaborate version of *Queen of Blood.*'

Both *Voyage to the Prehistoric Planet* and *Queen of Blood* were budgeted at a mere $33,052, but as many of the scenes were simply reused from the Russian films, it was enough to pay Rathbone (who appeared in both) $1,500 for a day and a half's work, although he ended up doing overtime and missing his meals. Saxon recalled that he shot his own scenes in seven or eight days and that throughout the shooting, Hopper, who had worked with Harrington on *Night Tide,* 'was trying very hard to keep a straight face'.

Although the meagre budget is obvious in the added scenes, Harrington's shots are crafted so that they blend well with the Soviet footage, giving the film a unique look. But the most memorable aspect of *Queen of Blood* is Florence Marly, a Czech actress of great presence, especially in the green make-up and bizarre hair-do that

she is required to wear here. While no classic as such, *Queen of Blood* is nevertheless another low-budget gem.

Eastern bloc movies were cheap to acquire and AIP snapped up the rights to a Czech sci-fi adventure called *Ikarie XB-1* (1963), which it recut and dubbed into a film called *Voyage to the End of the Universe* (1964). Given only a limited theatrical release, *Voyage to the End of the Universe* was ten minutes shorter than the Czech version and the names of the cast and crew in the opening credits were Anglicised. In the original, the spaceship's destination was the mysterious 'White Planet', but in the American version, that was changed to the 'Green Planet'!

AIP's cut of the closing scenes completely altered the ending of the original. In the Czech version, the *Ikarie* spacecraft approaches the White Planet to see, as the clouds part, a heavily-populated alien world. The AIP version eliminated the last few seconds and substituted stock shots of the Statue of Liberty and Manhattan Island, indicating, as per the 'twist' ending of *Planet of the Vampires,* that the Icarus and its crew are actually alien beings and that the 'Green Planet' is in fact Earth.

British trade magazine *Kine Weekly* was ambivalent about the film in its Czech guise–'Gadgetry and special effects are well contrived, but the picture has rather a job surviving its slow start, restricted setting and repetitive style'–but it won awards at the 1963 Trieste Science Fiction Film Festival and is now considered to be one of the greatest Eastern bloc science fiction movies of the period. If *Queen of Blood* is thought to have partly inspired *Alien,* then *Ikarie XB-1* must have had some small influence on Stanley Kubrick's *2001.* It has been reported that it was one of many 'outer space' offerings that Kubrick viewed before making his landmark epic.

The fact that foreign-language films released by AIP in the US and UK contained ideas which would inspire later bigger-budgeted productions was, in retrospect, an omen of what was to come. By the late 1970s, major studio offerings with 'B-movie' plots would be all the rage and it ultimately became impossible for independents

Voyage to the End of the Universe

like AIP to compete. But the sixties were still a time of expansion and excitement for Arkoff and Nicholson, and the popular bills in which they specialised were still some way away from running their course.

For most of the 'swinging' decade, American International Pictures had put as much effort into production in Britain as it did in Hollywood–and the 'runaway' features that resulted were some of the most memorable genre films in the company's entire history.

6

SEX, DRUGS AND ROCK 'N' ROLL

BEACH PARTIES AND BIKERS

As censorship throughout the world became more liberated in the 1960s, the cinema performed a slow striptease. Some British films included nudity in 'continental' versions, such as the topless shot of Pamela Green in Michael Powell's controversial *Peeping Tom* (1960), and June Ritchie bared her breasts in *Live Now, Pay Later* (US: *Flight From Treason*, 1962). But those were just the beginning. In 1966, Michelangelo Antonioni's *Blowup* became the first English-language film to feature female pubic hair, and not just in a 'continental' version.

By 1967, two ground-breaking Swedish films, *I Am Curious (Yellow)* and *Inga* broke new ground by featuring not only full frontal nudity but explicit sex-scenes as well. Meanwhile, British films continued to 'take it off,' with *Here We Go Round the Mulberry Bush* (1967), which featured an uninhibited nude swim by Judy Geeson, followed by *Three Into Two Won't Go* (1968), which exposed even more of the young actress. Ken Russell's *Women in Love* (1969) rounding out the decade with frontal *male* nudity in a wrestling scene between Alan Bates and Oliver Reed.

In the US, the puritanical Production Code was virtually obsolete by 1966. *The Pawnbroker,* released in 1964, had finally shattered it by fully exposing the breasts of actress Thelma Oliver. After that, the floodgates burst and the Code was replaced by a new rating system in 1968. Between the two extremes of the coy sex of the early

Beach Party (Bob Cummings, Annette Funicello)

1960s and the more graphic sexuality and onscreen drug use of the latter part of the decade came AIP's 'beach party' series, a sub-genre of its own that thrived for a brief period from 1963 to 1966. Though other studios eventually got in on the action, the lower-budget AIP efforts remained the most profitable at the box office.

In 1959, Columbia's *Gidget*–along with its sequel, *Gidget Goes Hawaiian* (1961)–had established the precedent, but AIP had actually been there first, with 1958's *Hot Rod Gang* and its 1959 sequel *Ghost of Dragstrip Hollow,* both written by Lou Rusoff. They were teenage comedies in which romance and music loomed large. The tone of adolescent sexuality actually loomed larger in M-G-M's *Where the Boys Are* (1960) and Paramount's *Love in a Goldfish Bowl* (1961), however, and it was these which would find echo in AIP's *Beach Party* (1963), the prototype for the series.

In his autobiography *Flying Through Hollywood By the Seat of My Pants,* Sam Arkoff related that he got the idea for *Beach Party* by viewing, with Nicholson, an unnamed Italian film that the two moguls screened in Rome in the summer of 1962. Arkoff felt that the film, which was set entirely on a beach, did not have much in it with which American teenagers could identify. But as he wrote of the event, 'The beach is a wonderful setting for a teenage movie. And it doesn't hurt to show girls in skimpy bathing suits.'

After this epiphany, Rusoff was assigned to research the southern Californian 'beach scene' and he was soon hard at work on the script for *Beach Party.* What he did was to take the *Gidget* template but follow AIP's oft-used formula of catering to the teenage audience with original songs performed by rock 'n' roll bands. The *Beach Party* films subsequently became the only American musical films not based on Broadway shows which were produced in the sixties, with the exception of Elvis Presley's movies for M-G-M.

As parental involvement was to be totally absent, the teens onscreen had to live in their own insular world, free to express their sense of fun and 'innocent' sexuality without having to answer for the consequences. Rusoff's first draft was a little 'raw' for AIP's nominated director, however. When it was shown to William Asher, he agreed to make the film if it was more of an upbeat musical about teenagers having a good time rather than just another movie about kids getting into trouble. Arkoff and Nicholson agreed to his request, and Asher rewrote the script with Robert Dillon.

Years later, Asher told author Mark Thomas McGee: 'They had a screenplay.. (that was) an exploitation thing, kids in trouble, parent-kid relationships, those kinds of things. And I didn't want to do that. I asked them if they'd do a film based on kids having a good time and not getting in trouble. Where they don't have to make up their minds right away about what they're going to do with their lives. The kids in the beach pictures were right out of high school, a time to be free before they made a commitment. I wanted to use that time and just let them enjoy themselves.'

Asher and Dillon were asked by Arkoff to let Rusoff have sole writing credit, as he had been diagnosed with a tumour on the brain. Lou Rusoff passed away in June 1963, a month before *Beach Party* had its premiere.

AIP's first and only choice for the female lead was Annette Funicello, a former 'Mousketeer' on Walt Disney's *The Mickey Mouse Club* television series. Funicello had grown into an attractive and effervescent young woman and her acting and singing abilities were not to be underestimated; the problem was that she was under contract to Disney which was very protective of its star and did not want her to be associated with anything remotely salacious.

Asher (who had directed many episodes of TV's *I Love Lucy,* among other shows), was initially concerned that Disney might not approve of Funicello appearing in an

Beach Party (Annette Funicello, Frankie Avalon)

AIP film. He told the Mouse House that there was nothing in *Beach Party* to offend anyone and Disney finally relented and said yes.

Arkoff and Nicholson's choice for the male lead was pop singer Fabian (Forte), but he was also under contract to 20th Century Fox, which would not let him appear. Instead, Frankie Avalon was cast. Avalon had first appeared on US television when he was only eleven years old. As a youthful trumpet player, he had performed on *The Jackie Gleason Show*. In 1959, after switching to singing, he had become a teen idol when his song 'Venus' went to number one for five weeks in the US. He followed that with several other hits, including 'Why?', 'Just Ask Your Heart' and 'I'll Wait For You', but his highest-profile screen role to date had been as the sole male survivor of the mission massacre in John Wayne's epic western *The Alamo* (1960), and AIP scored something of a coup by persuading him to star in *Beach Party*.

John Ashley returned to AIP to play the role of Avalon's best friend. Ashley told author Gary A Smith in *American International Pictures: The Golden Years*: 'We all had to wear body make-up because nobody had a tan. One day Frankie and I had some dialogue to do on our way to the water with our surfboards. It was colder than Hell that day and the water was freezing. We had our backs to the camera and Frankie said, "Man, can you believe us? Two 30-year old guys in body make-up playing teenagers!"'

However, the biggest stars in the original *Beach Party* were Hollywood veterans Robert Cummings and Dorothy Malone. Cummings was a film and television actor known for comedic roles in *The Devil and Miss Jones* (1941) and *Princess O'Rourke* (1943), but he had also been highly praised for two films in which he had starred for Alfred Hitchcock: *Saboteur* (1942) and *Dial M for Murder* (1954). More recently, he had been a favourite on American television in *The Bob Cummings Show*.

Morey Amsterdam (Cappy) was another face well known to US TV viewers. To millions, he was Buddy Sorrell in *The Dick Van Dyke Show* and his role in *Beach Party* was that of the beatnik who more or less runs 'Big Daddy's', a hipster coffee house. Harvey Lembeck was another TV regular, and Jody McCrea was the son of actors Joel McCrea and Frances Dee. But the most surprising cast-member was Vincent Price, as Big Daddy himself. Price (or a stand-in!) spends most of the film seated on a chair in the coffee house with his hat over his face and does not reveal his identity until just before the end-credits; at that point, he looks into the camera and in true hipster fashion, states that he has his 'pit' and now he needs a 'swinging pendulum'. AIP gave a 'special thanks' to Price for appearing and inserted a title card which read, 'Soon to be seen in *The Haunted Palace*', a cheeky example of cross-promotion.

Beach Party (Eva Six)

The plot of the film was calculated for maximum appeal to its core demographic: anthropology professor Robert Orwell Sutwell (Cummings) and his secretary Marianne (Malone) are studying the sexual habits of teenagers who frequent the nearby beach. The surfing teens are led by Frankie (Avalon) and Dolores (Funicello), and they *talk* a lot about sex but never seem to indulge. They also sing a lot, battle with a motorcycle gang and frolic to the music of 'Dick Dale and the Del Tones'. Shot at Malibu near the Pacific Coast Highway on a budget of $350,000, *Beach Party* quickly became AIP's biggest box office hit to date. It was heavily marketed to its teenage audience and its promotion extended into the film itself. In one scene, Malone says to Cummings in reference to their anthropology project: 'I hope you keep the picture rights. Sell it to American International and make a fortune.'

Although Asher, Arkoff and Nicholson always insisted that their *Beach Party* films were just good, clean, wholesome fun, close inspection of them indicates that a spin was put on the truth. The films themselves do not feature nudity, and nor is there the depiction of any sexual act, but the *Beach Party* cycle positively teems with sexual innuendo. Frankie and Dolores constantly dance around the sexual act as though they were a teenage Rock Hudson and Doris Day: a typical exchange occurs when Frankie says, 'The only thing I've studied this semester is you,' to which she replies, 'Well, I hope you don't flunk.' Frankie retorts, 'There's always summer school...'

Funicello, true to her Disney contract, is the most modestly attired of the beach bunnies, although she sports more cleavage than she ever did on *The Mickey Mouse Club*. The real sex in the movie is left to Eva Six, a blonde bombshell who gets fed up with Frankie when he refuses to canoodle with her. The other boys are so enamoured of her that one makes a sand-sculpture of her ample breasts. AIP's advertising also put the accent on sex: 'When 10,000 kids meet on 5,000 beach blankets.. something's bound to happen!' The company's marketing campaign paid off so handsomely that it found it had a new sub-genre on its hands and decided to make the most of it.

One of the strangest films inspired by the success of *Beach Party* was a shocker called *The Horror of Party Beach* (1964), produced independently in Connecticut by Alan V Iselin and its director, Del Tenney. Filmed on a shoestring in black and white, specifically for the drive-in market, with no names but a rock band called The Del-Aires, it featured atomic 'mutants' who menaced scantily-clad beachgoers and was a movie that could easily have been made by Arkoff and Nicholson themselves. Released on a double bill with *Curse of the Living Corpse* (Roy Scheider's feature debut), made by the same team, it wound up being distributed by 20th Century Fox which took several pages out of AIP's book with its lurid promotional campaign. If imitation is indeed the sincerest form of flattery, then the joint heads of American International must have felt very flattered indeed.

The Horror of Party Beach

Muscle Beach Party (*Frankie Avalon, 'Little' Stevie Wonder, Annette Funicello*)

After finishing *Beach Party,* Asher directed *Johnny Cool* for United Artists, which was a crime thriller starring Henry Silva and Asher's wife, Elizabeth Montgomery. As he explained to Mark Thomas McGee: '*Johnny Cool* went on to make its money back and maybe a little more. *Beach Party* took off. But I was not aware it was doing well until I got a letter from AIP that had a cheque in it.. Sam finally called and asked if I would meet with him on his boat in Miami to talk about another picture. I said sure.' The result was *Muscle Beach Party* (1964)–the mixture much as before, but with a few new faces. Dick Dale and the Del Tones were back, but the film also featured the screen debut of 'Little' Stevie Wonder, Motown's newest discovery. Other newbies included Don Rickles, who was fresh from Roger Corman's *X: the Man With X-Ray Eyes,* Italian actress Luciana Paluzzi (soon to appear in *Thunderball*) and comedian Buddy Hackett, one of the all-star cast of Stanley Kramer's comedy extravaganza *It's a Mad, Mad, Mad, Mad World* (1963).

Avalon and Funicello reprised their characters from *Beach Party,* though from now on, Funicello's character would be referred to as Dee Dee rather than Dolores. And John Ashley was back, but as a character called Johnny. This time the 'surprise' cameo was provided by none other than Peter Lorre, appearing as a character called Mr Strangdour. Peter Lupus, soon to become one of the leading characters on TV's *Mission: Impossible,* is billed as 'Rock Stevens' in *Muscle Beach Party,* in which he plays a bodybuilder called Flex Martian. He is the only one of the 'musclemen' in the film to have any memorable lines, not to mention acting talent.

Next in the series was *Bikini Beach* (1964) in which, true to its title, a little more flesh was on show. By this time, the *Beach Party* movies had also become more self-assured and Asher felt free to experiment. The plot is essentially the same: perennial teenagers Frankie and Dee Dee are on summer vacation (again) when millionaire newspaper owner Harvey Huntington Honeywagon III (Disney regular Keenan

Bikini Beach (Mary Hughes)

Wynn) becomes convinced that the beach partygoers are so obsessed with sex that their mentality is below that of the great apes (Honeywagon attempts to prove this with his pet chimp Clyde, who can surf, drive and even dance better than most of the beach-bums). Honeywagon's goal is to turn Bikini Beach into a senior citizens' retirement home. A sub-plot involves British 'pop star' Peter Royce Bentley, known as 'Potato Bug'–an oblique reference to The Beatles, who had 'invaded' America in 1964. The filmmakers' uneasiness with this new phenomenon is clear: as played by Avalon (in a dual role), Potato Bug is the most stereotypically-foppish British character ever committed to celluloid, with one of the worst-ever attempts at an English accent.

In an interview, Asher claimed that *Bikini Beach* was originally written for the The Beatles, which might explain its manic energy in the vein of Richard Lester's ground-breaking band romp, *A Hard Day's Night* (1964). According to Asher, the group had agreed to appear in the film but were forced to withdraw when their growing fame priced them out of AIP's range. However, doubt is cast on Asher's story by the fact that United Artists had signed The Beatles to a three-picture deal in late 1963.

With or without The Beatles, *Bikini Beach* is zanier and more anarchic than the first two films in the series. Supporting roles this time went to Rickles, Lembeck and Ashley, alongside newcomer Martha Hyer as Wynn's unlikely love interest. The weirdest moment in the film comes courtesy of nineteen-year-old Val Warren, billed as 'Teenage Werewolf' in the closing credits, who was the first prizewinner in Forrest J Ackerman's *Famous Monsters of Filmland's* National Horror Make-Up Contest.

The prize was a trip to Hollywood and an appearance in *Bikini Beach*. Warren had won out over a teenage Rick Baker, who would go on to a carreer in Hollywood and three Oscars for his make-up work.

When Ackerman died in 2008, at the age of 92, Warren was tracked down and interviewed by the *Los Angeles Times*, for which he recalled some of his *Bikini Beach* memories: 'When director William Asher requested that I growl during my brief sequence, my ever-protective agent, 'Uncle' Forry, quickly reminded them that said role had now become a 'speaking part' and, as such, I was entitled to a cast credit as well as the Screen Actors Guild pay standard of an additional 250 bucks. When Asher consented, Forry, like the big kid he was, expressed his delight by turning to face me with a beaming smile and an exaggerated wink.' (The scene in question took place in a pool hall and had the werewolf sitting incongrously in the background.)

Bikini Beach arrived at a pivotal moment in sixties cinema, when all the stops were being pulled out and onscreen anarchy was the order of the day. This time, the cameo in the film was provided by Boris Karloff as an art dealer, who finds much to admire in a chimp's paintings and says to camera, 'I must tell Vincent Price about this place!' (Price was a well-known collector of art.)

The apex of the *Beach Party* movies came in 1964. *Pajama Party* was the third entry that year, arriving late on (in November) and minus Avalon in the lead role; he was replaced by Tommy Kirk, a former Disney child star of films such as *Old Yeller* (1957) and *The Shaggy Dog* (1959). Funicello was back on board, but as a different character on this occasion. *Pajama Party* is not always considered to be part of the series proper, but AIP marketed it as such at the time of its release: 'The *Bikini Beach* Gang is warming up! For the 'Party' that takes off–where others poop out!'

Many of the other regulars appeared as different characters to those in previous films. Avalon showed up in cameo as a Martian, as did Don Rickles and Jody McCrea. Newcomers to the cast included Elsa Lanchester (Universal's *Bride of Frankenstein*) as Aunt Wendy, Susan Hart, in the first of several appearances that she would make

***Pajama Party* (Annette Funicello, Buster Keaton, Tommy Kirk)**

in the ongoing series, journalist Dorothy Kilgallen as herself, and the great silent screen comic Buster Keaton, who played Chief Rotten Eagle. In smaller roles were future star Teri Garr (*Young Frankenstein,* 1974) and singer-songwriter Toni Basil. Harvey Lembeck also returned as Eric Von Zipper.

The screenplay was even crazier than that for *Bikini Beach*. It had its genesis in a play written by famed animator Joseph Barbera (one of the duo who created *Tom and Jerry* and whose menagerie of cartoon characters were a television staple in the 1960s), which had debuted in Los Angeles in 1952. Capitalising on the sci-fi craze, the play was called *The Maid and the Martian* and concerned one Captain Derro, an invader from Mars, who goes to Earth on a scouting expedition but ends

up falling in love with an Earth girl. The production was directed by Gordon Hunt and starred Pat Priest, who would later achieve a degree of fame by playing Marilyn in TV's *The Munsters* (1964-1966). The play ran for only seven weeks but, in 1961, AIP announced that it would make a film version of *The Maid and the Martian* from a screenplay by Al Burton and Gordon Hunt, with Stanley Frazen producing. None of those names appear on the credits of *Pajama Party*, however, despite its almost identical plot. Funicello even recorded a song called 'The Maid and the Martian' for her album *Pajama Party*.

The main difference between *Pajama Party* and the first three films in the series is that it was directed by Don Weis, rather than William Asher. Weis was a television veteran who had helmed episodes of *The Twilight Zone* and *Alfred Hitchcock Presents*, among many other series; he had won two Directors Guild of America awards, one in 1956 and another in 1958. Asher was otherwise engaged, producing *Bewitched* as a vehicle for his wife, Elizabeth Montgomery.

Pajama Party was the first movie for AIP on which Louis M Heyward worked. 'Deke' Heyward would loom large in the company's middle years, writing several more teen comedies and eventually becoming the head of AIP's London office. He had previously been a comedy writer for television, honing his craft on series such as *The Ernie Kovacs Show*. He wrote the script for *Pajama Party* in two weeks, aiming it firmly at the 18-30 demographic.

It was Heyward who was instrumental in obtaining the services of the legendary Keaton. It was his idea, he claimed, as they had worked together previously on *The Faye Emerson Show*. Keaton was best known for his work in silents like *The General* (1926) but he had recently made something of a comeback in television, where he had had his own show in the 1950s and had later appeared in a memorable *Twilight Zone* episode called 'Once Upon a Time'.

Production on *Pajama Party* commenced on August 10, 1964, using the Warner

Beach Blanket Bingo (Buster Keaton)

Bros studio backlot for a car-chase sequence. The beach used for a volleyball game and a Donna Loren musical number was Surfrider Beach in Malibu. The film was one of the first to employ what is now called 'product placement'; Loren and others are shown drinking Dr Pepper, as she was known at the time as the 'Dr Pepper Girl' from a series of TV commercials.

With barely a pause for breath, *Beach Blanket Bingo* arrived like clockwork in April 1965, just in time for the American drive-in season. Asher was back at the helm and Avalon was back as Frankie, with Funicello once again playing Dee Dee. Support this time came from Deborah Walley, Marta Kristen, future *Dynasty* star Linda Evans and Donna Michelle, who was *Playboy*'s Playmate of the Year for 1964. Keaton was again on hand as a character aptly named Buster, and Rickles was back along with television comedy star Paul Lynde.

After the kooky sci-fi of *Pajama Party,* the script for *Beach Blanket Bingo* was a little more down to earth. A singer called Sugar Kane (Evans) is kidnapped by Von Zipper and his gang after he has fallen madly in love with her. Meanwhile, Frankie and Dee Dee have taken up skydiving and yet another sub-plot involves a mermaid (Kristen). Towards the climax, the film enters the realm of silent serial *The Perils of Pauline* when the villainous South Dakota Slim (Timothy Carey) ties Sugar Kane to a buzz-saw.

Each 'Beach Party' movie during these years was a huge success, due in part to AIP's clever marketing, which appealed not only to teenagers but to older audiences as well. Their casting of greats such as Price, Lorre, Karloff, Keaton, Lanchester and Dorothy Lamour (in *Pajama Party*) ensured that kids were not the only ones to go and see the films. The major studios were now joining in on the action, but Asher told Mark McGee that they largely missed the point: 'Every major studio made a beach picture, trying to capitalise on AIP's success, and none of them were successful.

How to Stuff a Wild Bikini

Columbia eventually wanted me to do one.. but I didn't want to.. Paramount made one, M-G-M, they all made a beach picture and none of them succeeded. They were doing all the things that were formula concepts that nobody wanted to see. They didn't go for the feeling of it, they went for the mechanics of it. They put in parents. The *reality* of parents. What would *really* happen if kids spent summer at the beach? Parents would be concerned about the whereabouts of their kids, their behaviour, what they were involved in and so on. Our pictures were fantasies.'

Asher and AIP's next 'fantasy' was *How to Stuff a Wild Bikini* (1965), the sixth 'official' entry in the series, featuring Avalon in a very reduced role as he was filming *Sergeant Deadhead* at the same time. The Hollywood veterans this time out included Mickey Rooney as Peachy Keane and Brian Donlevy as Big Deal McPherson. TV's 'Dobie Gillis', Dwayne Hickman, was cast as Ricky, with Buster Keaton as Bwana and Elizabeth Montgomery as Bwana's daughter. The two-week schedule commenced in April 1965 but Funicello was pregnant during production and had to be filmed wearing loose-fitting tunics or with a prop in front of her; in one scene, it is a bucket of Kentucky Fried Chicken. The film's opening credits were shot in ' claymation' by Art Clokey, the creator of *Gumby*.

In the new story by Asher and Leo Townsend, Frankie is on naval reserve duty in Tahiti. Away from Dee Dee, he fears that she will be unfaithful to him and so he hires a witch doctor named Bwana to conjure up a floating bikini. The bikini is then 'stuffed' with the voluptuous Cassandra (Beverly Adams), who is dispatched to distract advertising executive Ricky from chasing after Dee Dee.

How to Stuff a Wild Bikini was the final 'Beach Party' picture with Avalon and Funicello. Avalon had been phasing himself out of the series for some time and Annette Funicello was now a mother. In the next (and final) offering, *Ghost in the Invisible Bikini* (1966), they were replaced by Tommy Kirk and Deborah Walley as Chuck and Lili. This time round, the 'vets' included Francis X Bushman as Malcolm, Basil Rathbone as Reginald Ripper and Boris Karloff as Hiram Stokely. Patsy Kelly,

How to Stuff a Wild Bikini (Brian Donlevy, Mickey Rooney)

an old hand from the likes of *The Gorilla* (1939), played the role of Myrtle Forbush. Keaton was originally cast as Chicken Feather, but he passed away before production began and was replaced by veteran comic Benny Rubin. The youngsters also had a new recruit in the shapely form of Ol' Blue Eyes's daughter Nancy Sinatra. Susan Hart and Harvey Lembeck were becoming old hands in the 'Beach Party' stakes themselves.

The film was announced in January 1965 as *Pajama Party in a Haunted House*. It was also known in development as *The Girl in the Glass Bikini* and had been intended for Avalon and Funicello. William Asher was to have directed it, but he was now too busy with the highly successful *Bewitched* and was again replaced by Don Weis. During production, it was also known as *Bikini Party in a Haunted House*. Heyward wrote the screenplay along with *Three Stooges* veteran Elwood Ullman.

The crazy plot this time involved the recently-deceased Stokely (Karloff), who has twenty-four hours to mastermind a good deed without leaving his crypt so that he can go to his reward and have his youth restored. He enlists the aid of his long-dead girlfriend Cecily (Hart) to prevent his attorney (Rathbone) from claiming the estate for himself. Chuck and Lili, the true heirs, bring their friends to the mansion for a pool party, but the attorney and others are intent on terrifying the teens.

The original cut of the film featured neither Karloff nor Hart. After Nicholson

There's Something BLOOD CURDLING for Everyone!
...when a pretty GHOUL trades in her bed sheet for a BIKINI!
AMERICAN INTERNATIONAL'S
GHOST IN THE INVISIBLE BIKINI
IN PATHÉCOLOR AND PANAVISION®
STARRING TOMMY KIRK · DEBORAH WALLEY · ARON KINCAID · HARVEY LEMBECK · JESSE WHITE · CLAUDIA MARTIN
NANCY SINATRA · SPECIAL GUEST STAR BASIL RATHBONE · and PATSY KELLY
FEATURING PICCOLA PUPA · EXECUTIVE PRODUCERS James H. NICHOLSON and Samuel Z. ARKOFF · DIRECTOR Don WEIS
SCREENPLAY BY Louis M. HEYWARD and Elwood ULLMAN · STORY BY Louis M. HEYWARD · An AMERICAN INTERNATIONAL PICTURE
ALSO FEATURING
SUSAN HART as THE GHOST
BORIS KARLOFF as HIRAM STOKELY

and Arkoff viewed it, they ordered extensive reshoots which included the plot-point of Karloff's character having to perform a good deed and Hart's character helping him to achieve it; by then, Hart was married to Nicholson. As the ghost, her scenes were filmed with her in a blonde wig and black swimsuit against a black backdrop; they were directed by the editor, Ronnie Sinclair. Hart worked alone in this fashion for two weeks with Sinclair and then for another week with Karloff, whose scenes were shot on a separate soundstage. Neither of them worked with any others of the cast and their scenes were inserted into the film–not entirely seamlessly.

When released in April 1966, *Ghost in the Invisible Bikini*, despite its suggestive title, was a commercial disaster. In *The New York Times,* critic Vincent Canby called it 'a flop', while the *Los Angeles Times* predicted, '...(It) will be the last in AIP's long proliferating series...' In *Science Fiction Stars and Horror Heroes* by Tom Weaver and Michael and John Brunas, Heyward expressed his own disappointment with the

Publicity shot for Ghost in the Invisible Bikini)

Ghost in the Invisible Bikini

film, noting, '...There was no reason for it to be made, other than Jim (Nicholson) trying to prove that he could make Susan Hart into a star.'

The *Beach Party* movies were ultimately a victim of their own success; the formula did not allow for any real innovation and the tame sexuality of the films was beginning to look decidedly quaint against the sexual frankness of contemporaneous releases like *Who's Afraid of Virginia Woolf?* and *Blowup*. Not to mention a current AIP offering by Roger Corman called *The Wild Angels*...

The Wild Angels was inspired by a feature spread in a 1965 issue of *The Saturday Evening Post* concerning the infamous California motorcycle gang known as the Hell's Angels. After two AIP employees, Milt Moritz and Al Kallis, showed the feature to Arkoff, Roger Corman was contacted and within a matter of days, *All the Fallen Angels* was announced to the press. Corman hired 'Chuck' Griffith to write the screenplay. The first draft did not please his director; it had almost no dialogue and contrasted the lives of the bikers with that of motorcycle policemen. Griffith rewrote it, but Corman was still unhappy with the result and he gave it to his current protégé Peter Bogdanovich to rewrite. Corman paid Bogdanovich a mere $300 to work on the script and Bogdanovich claimed that he rewrote 80% of it.

George Chakiris was signed for the lead, mainly on the strength of his work in Robert Wise's *West Side Story,* in which he had played the leader of a street gang. Unfortunately, Chakiris did not know how to ride a motorcycle. He went for a quick spin and decided that motorcycles were not for him: he was willing to do the movie only if Corman hired a double.

At the same time, Peter Fonda, son of Hollywood veteran Henry Fonda, was in town trying to raise money to make a film of his own when he was offered the part of Loser, a character who spends most of the film in a coffin. *The Saturday Evening Post* cover had been of a biker funeral, and that was going to be one of the highlights of the film. Fonda was offered $10,000 to play a 'stiff', so he accepted.

Once Chakiris had revealed his lack of love for motorcycles, however, Corman decided to cast Fonda in the lead instead. Chakiris was out and Fonda was promoted to the role of Heavenly Blues, the leader of the gang. The character's original name was Jack Black, but Fonda came up with the new moniker after telling Corman that 'Heavenly Blue' was a drug made from Morning Glory seeds.

Much of the dialogue and many of the situations arose out of conversations with real Hell's Angels in a bar at Venice Beach called the Gunk Shop. The *machismo* of the bikers made Corman feel uncomfortable, but he still hired quite a few of them to appear in the film, which brought them all to the attention of the local police...

Another famous Hollywood offspring hired to appear was Nancy Sinatra. She had just had a number one chart hit with 'These Boots Are Made for Walkin'' and had already appeared for AIP in *Ghost in the Invisible Bikini*, as well as in the United Artists release *For Those Who Think Young* and M-G-M's *Get Yourself a College Girl* (both 1964). Sinatra was cast as the girlfriend of Heavenly Blues.

Bruce Dern was a young actor who had been knocking about Hollywood for some time but had recently received acclaim for small but significant roles in both Alfred Hitchcock's *Marnie* and Robert Aldrich's *Hush, Hush, Sweet Charlotte*. Corman cast Dern as Loser, the role originally intended for Fonda. Dern's wife Diane Ladd was cast as Loser's wife. Smaller roles were filled by up-and-comers Michael J Pollard and Gayle Hunnicutt, and behind the camera was Richard Moore, the cinematographer who had co-created Panavision in 1953. Peter Bogdanovich served as the second unit director and did other odd jobs on the production.

During shooting, cast and crew were on location in Mecca, a town not far from the Salton Sea in California, when the state police began to keep tabs on them. There were arrest warrants out for some of the Angels because of incidents in which they had been involved. Production manager Jack Bohrer pointed out that the Angels were earning an honest day's wage on the film, but the cops were unimpressed; they told him that the unit needed to finish the day's work as quickly as possible and get out of town.

The Wild Angels (Peter Fonda)

During the shooting of Loser's funeral outside a church in North Argyle, Dern was assaulted and beaten by two Angels. He tried to explain to them that he was in a movie, but the bikers (who were not a part of the cast) refused to believe him and simply knocked him out cold, leaving the actor lying on the sidewalk. Dern joked later, 'It was like, "Hey, I'm not even alive in the movie, I'm dead," and *still* they're beating on me.'

Corman completed the film in his usual fifteen days. Under its final title, *The Wild Angels* premiered at the Theatre Owners' Convention in New York City. It was an after-dinner showing and few of the audience were in the demographic for whom it was intended. Unsurprisingly, they were shocked by the violence and brutality. Arkoff and Nicholson, who were also in the audience, could see the writing on the wall and they walked out to the lobby to await the end of the screening. One of the owners remarked on his way out, 'It's too strong for my theatre', and then left. His wife was more forthright: she asked angrily, 'What kind of people are you to make a picture like this?'

Even the scenario was too much for some. The plot revolves around Heavenly Blues, Loser and their gang, who spend an inordinate amount of time getting high, beating people up and assaulting women. When Heavenly Blues tells Loser that he has located his stolen motorcycle in Mecca, they botch their attempt to retrieve it and Loser is shot in the back by a police officer and winds up in hospital. The Angels break him out, but he dies in the process. The action builds to the final third of the

film, in which Loser's funeral degenerates into orgiastic rite. There was no moral lesson to be had from *The Wild Angels,* which is one of the reasons that it received such a hostile reception in 1966. The film's freewheeling attitude towards traditional ideas of right and wrong can be summed up by a speech that Heavenly Blues makes in a church at the close: 'We wanna be free! We wanna be free to do what we wanna do. We wanna be free to ride. We wanna be free to ride our machines without being hassled by the Man! And we wanna get loaded. And we wanna have a good time. And that's what we're gonna do. We're gonna have a good time. We're gonna have a party!'

This was all too much for general audiences, who were finding the long hair and lax attitudes of advocates of counterculture to be an increasing threat to society. One of the theatre owners at the screening said testily to Arkoff and Nicholson, 'That was a dirty picture.' On the way to his car, Fonda was accosted by a woman who struck him with an umbrella, screamed at him and called him a Nazi. He made his 'escape' to Lincoln Center, where he was booed and hissed by exhibitors.

Nevertheless, AIP received an invitation to screen the film at the 27th annual Venice (Italy, not California) Film Festival. While it was not well received there, it did end up winning an award at the Cannes Film Festival. US critics were outraged. In *The New York Times,* Bosley Crowther called it 'a brutal little picture', although *Variety* at least recognised what Corman had been trying to do: 'The Angels, in vicious stride and without regard for law and order, operate in a Southern California beach community. Corman directs his clinical eye in dissecting their philosophical (?) rebellion.' *Newsweek* , like Crowther, simply dismissed it as 'an ugly piece of trash'.

Many exhibitors were at first afraid to book the film. In mainland Europe, where Corman was considered to be an *auteur* on the strength of his Poe adaptations, the critics were kinder and *The Wild Angels* did solid business, particularly in Italy and France. At that point, American bookings began to take off.

The fact that real Hell's Angels were employed in the film brought great publicity, especially when the Venice chapter sued Corman for defamation. Their complaint was that they were portrayed as 'an outlaw gang', which they insisted was untrue; they purported to be a 'social organisation' dedicated to spreading 'information about motorcycles'. They said that because of the way they were characterised in the film, they could no longer appear in public without being assaulted or jeered at. And they asked for $2 million in damages. They eventually settled for $2,000. Corman later claimed that they threatened his life.

The Wild Angels became the sixteenth biggest box office draw of 1966 in the US. It also grossed well in France, but it was refused a certificate in the UK and was not released in Britain until 1972, then only after cuts. The problem, so far as the British censor was concerned, had been aptly described by Bosley Crowther in his piece for *The New York Times*: 'A vicious account of the boozing, fighting, "pot"-smoking vandalising and raping done by a gang of "sickle riders" who are obviously drawn to represent the swastika-wearing Hell's Angels, one of several disreputable gangs on the West Coast. And despite an implausible ending and some rather amateurish acting by Peter Fonda and Nancy Sinatra in the leading roles, it gives a pretty good picture of what these miltant motorcycle-cult gangs are.' In other words, drugs, sex, violence, Nazi regalia and anti-social behaviour–the very things (apart from the Nazi regalia) which had caused Laszlo Benedek's *The Wild One* to be similarly banned more than a decade before. If Roger Corman had set out to wave a red rag in the face of the British Board of Film Censors, he could not have done a more convincing job. Of course, the result was predictable: *The Wild Angels* quickly garnered cult status for itself, regardless of any intrinsic merit.

The Wild One (Marlon Brando)

Once again, AIP found itself exploiting a new sub-genre: the 'outlaw biker film'. The prototype had been the aforementioned *The Wild One,* with Marlon Brando as the head of the Black Rebels Motorcycle Club. Also loosely based on actual events, the 1954 film had inspired a few imitators, such as AIP's *Motorcycle Gang* (1957), starring John Ashley, but none of them had anything like the impact of the controversial original until *The Wild Angels* came along.

Now that AIP's *Beach Party* franchise had drawn to a close, the company found that the culture was changing again; teen audiences were demanding harder action, more sex and more realism in general. The fantasy of the 'innocent' beachgoers was over; the gritty reality of bikers was here, and AIP would make many more such films to cater to that market. The company–and Corman–had taken the pulse of the cinemagoer and had discovered it quickening. AIP would cash in with film after biker film over the next few years, until even the most ardent cycle-nut would become sick to death of the smell of petrol fumes.

AIP followed up Corman's film with *Devil's Angels* (1967), directed by Daniel Haller. Written by 'Chuck' Griffith, *Devil's Angels* has the tone of a western, the first of many biker films to portray bikers as modern-day cowboys who ride motorcycles instead of horses.

Griffith's story was more conventional than the free-wheeling screenplay that

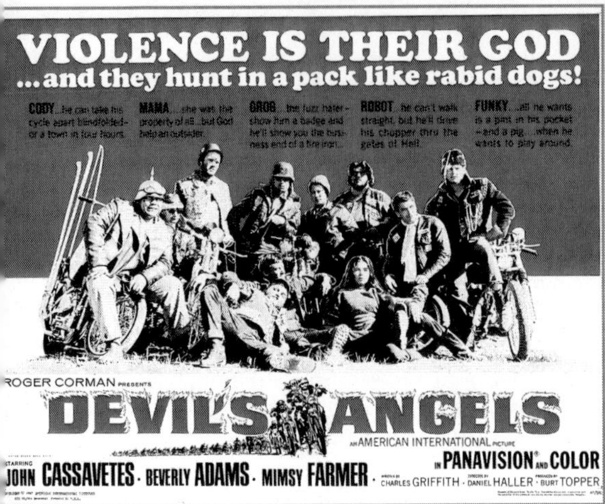

Bogdanovich had contributed to *The Wild Angels*. In the film, the 'Skulls', an exiled group of Hell's Angels, make a deal with the Sheriff of a small town, who agrees to let them stay to protect the citizens from another gang. However, the other gang also enters the town and a turf-war ensues. The western motif was further enhanced in

Devil's Angels (John Cassavetes, Beverly Adams)

the script by the Skulls familiarity with frontier outlaw Butch Cassidy and his gang, who took refuge from train-robbing in a place called Hole-in-the-Wall, where the only authority was their own. The Skulls, in consequence, are on a quest to find just such a hideway where they, too, can settle. The town in the story becomes the focus of that quest.

Devil's Angels went into production on January 10, 1967, with actor-director John Cassavetes in the lead role of Cody, head of the Skulls. Beverly Adams and Mimsy Farmer were local girls who catch Cody's eye, and AIP regular Leo Gordon essayed the role of Sheriff Henderson. Filming took place near Point Fermin in San Pedro, California, and in Patagonia, Arizona.

Cassavetes's presence sets the film apart from its peers; already the leading light in American cinema verité filmmaking, New York-born Cassavetes had taken the part in order to fund the post-production of his Oscar-nominated indie production *Faces*. A familiar face in supporting roles himself–most recently for Robert Aldritch in *The Dirty Dozen*–Cassavetes brings his Stanislavsky-trained earnestness to what, on the page, was a pale reprise of Brando's iconic pack-leader in *The Wild One*, and he would go from here into a starring-role in Roman Polanski's critically-acclaimed horror yarn *Rosemary's Baby* (1968). He would also go on to become one of the most celebrated directors in American cinema.

Featuring the tagline, 'Violence is their god.. and they hunt in a pack like rabid dogs!', *Devil's Angels* was a quick cash-in on *The Wild Angels* which did not make as much as its predecessor. But as it still brought in some $4 million for AIP, more biker films were clearly in the offing. AIP led the pack in this regard, but they were by no means the only producers of outlaw biker movies. A company called Fanfare produced *Hell's Angels on Wheels* (1967), starring none other than Jack Nicholson, while Four Star Excelsior distributed *The Rebel Rousers* (1970), with Nicholson, Diane Ladd, Bruce Dern and Harry Dean Stanton.

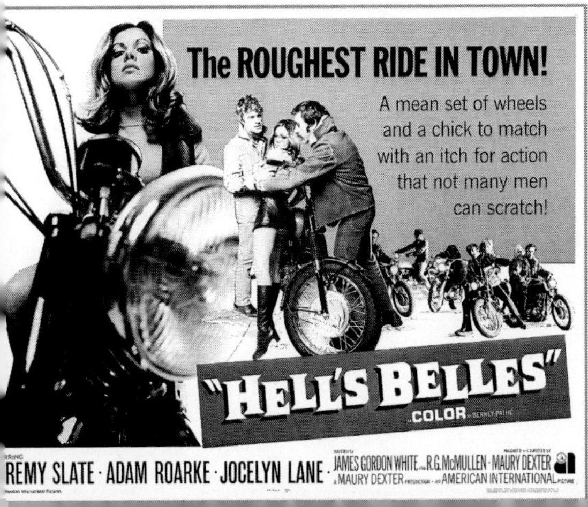

AIP's biker movies from the period include *The Glory Stompers* (1967), with Dennis Hopper, Jody McCrea and Jock Mahoney, directed by Anthony M Lanza, *The Mini-Skirt Mob* (1968), a novelty entry with Diane McBain, Sherry Jackson and Patty McCormack as members of an all-girl motorcycle gang, directed by Maury Dexter, *Angels From Hell* (1968), directed by Bruce Kessler and starring Tom Stern, Jack Starrett and Arlene Martel, and *The Savage Seven* (1968), directed by Richard Rush and starring Robert Walker Jr, Joanna Frank and Adam Roarke. Without Corman's influence–he was busy in the big league with *The St Valentine's Day Massacre* for Fox–all of AIP's subsequent biker films were both forgettable and undistinguished, but they remained popular drive-in fare.

One of the more influential films of this type was Tom Laughlin's *Born Losers* (1967), directed under the pseudonym of T C Frank. Since 1954, Laughlin had been trying to produce a script about a character called Billy Jack in a tale of discrimination towards Native Americans. When the biker films became popular in the late sixties, he decided to introduce the character in a script tailored to capitalise on that trend. The story was based on an actual incident in which members of the Hell's Angels had been arrested for raping five teenage girls in Monterey, California, in 1964.

In *Born Losers,* a brutal motorcycle gang harasses the residents of a small town in California, intimidating its citizens to prevent them from reporting to the authorities; among other crimes, the gang is responsible for the rape of four teenage girls. They pressure the victims into refusing to testify in court, but one of the girls is taken under the wing of Billy Jack (Laughlin), a half-breed Vietnam veteran. He takes on the gang, who are led by Danny (Jeremy Slate), which leads to a predictably violent showdown.

Born Losers (Elizabeth James)

The movie was shot on location in California at Seal Beach, Rancho Palos Verdes, Huntington Beach, Big Sur and Morro Bay. Filming took three weeks on a budget of $160,000. To keep costs down, a stunt scene of a biker flying head over heels into a pond was a stock-shot taken from AIP's *Ghost in the Invisible Bikini.*

Laughlin, who also produced the film, ran out of money during the post-production but showed the footage to AIP, who bought out the original financiers and gave him $300,000 to finish it. It proved a good investment for all concerned: *Born Losers* earned $2,225,000 in North American rentals and led to Laughlin raising the funds to produce his dream project, *Billy Jack,* which became a sleeper hit for Warner Bros in 1971. After the success of that film, AIP reissued *Born Losers* in 1974 with the tagline, 'The original Billy Jack is back!' Laughlin sued AIP at that juncture, and it was forced to include the disclaimer 'This is a re-release,' in all its advertising, to alert viewers that it was not a sequel to *Billy Jack.* Re-release or no, by 1976, *Born Losers* had earned a total of $11.5 million for AIP.

AIP went on to produce five more biker movies: *Hell's Belles* (1969), directed by Maury Dexter and starring Jeremy Slate, Adam Roarke and Jocelyn Lane, *Hell's Angels '69* (1969), a biker-heist movie involving a plan

The Trip / INSET: *Peter Fonda*

to rob Caesar's Palace in Las Vegas, again starring Slate, with Tom Stern and Conny Van Dyke and directed by Lee Madden, *Angel Unchained* (1970), directed by Madden and starring Don Stroud, Luke Askew, Tyne Daly and Aldo Ray, *The Hard Ride* (1971), with Robert Fuller and Tony Russell, and directed by Burt Topper, and *Chrome and Hot Leather* (1971), about Green Berets vs bikers, starring William Smith and Cheryl Ladd, directed by Lee Frost.

American International, like many film companies, had the knack of running its most popular themes into the ground. In an article in the *Atlanta Journal* in 1969, Jim Nicholson was quoted as saying: 'We make films until they quit paying, like the Poe horror shows. We made a number of them and they went great. Then one day, one didn't sell. We quit. The same with the beach party films. For three years they were great. Then one didn't sell. We quit.'

The company quit making biker movies in 1971. Again, as with the 'Beach Party' series, they were victims of their own success. In 1968, Peter Fonda, Dennis Hopper and Terry Southern had got together to write a new 'outlaw biker film', *Easy Rider,* which told of two 'hippie' bikers travelling through the American landscape. It came about in part because Jack Nicholson had written *The Trip* (1967) for Corman, which had co-starred Fonda and Hopper. Fonda had meantime become a counterculture icon as a result of *The Wild Angels,* and *The Trip* did for LSD what *The Wild Angels* had done for bikers.

In preparation for *The Trip,* an exploration of the drug-culture that was on

The Trip (*Peter Fonda, Dennis Hopper*)

the rise in certain sections of the teen community, Corman took an acid trip of his own, and found it to be somewhat life-altering (although, by all accounts, he never repeated the experiment). 'I was the most conservative of a very wild crowd,' he told Mark McGee. 'What started out was a couple of us going up to Big Sur and it ended up as a caravan when they found out I was going to take LSD. There must have been twenty people or more. We had to draw up the equivalent of a production schedule–who was going to be taking acid at what time.'

The Trip was produced in three weeks for $100,000. After post-production was complete, AIP got cold feet at the 'objective' treatment of LSD in the film and added a disclaimer about drug experimentation. Corman's original ending was also altered with an optical effect which looked like cracked glass over a shot of Fonda's face, suggesting that his drug use had resulted in a 'shattering' mental experience. Corman was unhappy with these changes and it led to a falling out between himself, Arkoff and Nicholson. He would direct only two more films for AIP (*Bloody Mama* and *Gas-s-s-s*, both in 1970), and within a couple of years, he had formed his own production and distribution company called New World Pictures.

To avoid that sort of interference, Fonda, Hopper and Southern determined to produce *Easy Rider* independently of Hollywood. Production began with an outline rather than a full script and much of the dialogue was ad-libbed. Fonda's idea, in true outlaw biker fashion, was to make the movie as a kind of modern western, in which two bikers travel the country but are eventually shot to death by rednecks.

At one point, *Easy Rider* was offered to AIP and Corman was to act as executive producer. Arkoff and Nicholson passed on the project and Fonda and Hopper took it to producers Bert Schneider and Bob Rafelson whose company, Raybert, had made the TV series *The Monkees* (1966-1968).

Had AIP gone ahead with *Easy Rider,* it would likely have been a very different film, yet Fonda and company owed most of their production savvy to their days with Arkoff and Nicholson. As things turned out, *Easy Rider* became both a box office sensation (to the tune of some $60 million) and a cultural touchstone, changing the way that films were produced in Hollywood for years to come. Arkoff subsequently went on record to say that he regretted turning down *Easy Rider.*

Fonda's breakthrough was an omen of things to come for American International Pictures. Within a few years, the major studios would be making the kinds of movies that AIP had always specialised in–horror, sci-fi and other forms of 'exploitation'–but with bigger budgets and better resources. Before that occurred, however, AIP still had a few more tricks up its corporate sleeve.

Roger Corman, Peter Fonda and Peter Bogdanovitch on the set of The Wild Angels

7

AIP IN BRITAIN

CO-PRODUCTIONS AND COSTUME HORRORS

In late 1956, Sam Arkoff and Jim Nicholson had paid a visit to Nat Cohen, who ran British distribution house Anglo-Amalgamated with his partner Stuart Levy. Anglo-Amalgamated had been the UK distributor for AIP's films and the pair now sought to return the favour by co-financing a British production with Cohen. AIP put up $25,000 towards the budget and provided the services of Lou Rusoff to write the screenplay–originally called *Wolf Girl*–in exchange for the US rights to the film. In the final script, the wolf became a cat and *Cat Girl* was born, along with the horror career of future Hammer Films star Barbara Shelley.

Not the most original of screenplays, *Cat Girl* was a thinly-disguised retread of Val Lewton's classic *Cat People* (1942). However, as directed by Alfred Shaughnessy, it was a moody, well-acted, psychosexual horror which AIP released as a second feature to *The Amazing Colossal Man* but which could, in truth, have been top of the bill. Shelley played Leonora, who is told by her uncle that she is the victim of a curse in which her soul becomes one with that of a leopard. Her husband soon falls prey to a 'big cat', and the same shadowy nemesis starts to threaten love-rival Kay Callard, but when Callard's husband Robert Ayres manages to run the leopard over with his car, Shelley dies also.

Born Barbara Kowin in London, Shelley was a former model whose film career began in Italy in the likes of *Luna nuova* (*New Moon,* 1955), in which she co-starred with a young Virna Lisi, and *Mio figlio Nerone (Nero's Mistress,* 1956), in which she was featured along with Vittorio De Sica, Gloria Swanson and Brigitte Bardot. She

***Cat Girl* (Barbara Shelley)**

returned to England for a comedy called *The Little Hut* (1957), appearing alongside Stewart Granger, David Niven and Ava Gardner, but *Cat Girl* set her on a course to be a heroine of the horrors.

Shaughnessy had worked at Ealing Studios in various capacities and had directed his first feature, a crime thriller called *Suspended Alibi,* in 1956. It starred Patrick Holt and Honor Blackman and was released by Rank in February 1957, just before he embarked on *Cat Girl.* In his autobiography, *Both Ends of the Candle,* Shaughnessy recalled of *Cat Girl*: '(It) was a sort of joke around Beaconsfield Studios... nobody wanted to direct it. So, keen as mustard to direct another film, I took a step forward. (It) was shot in three hysterical weeks with the gorgeous Barbara Shelley starring in her first British picture. By using her, I fear we condemned a very beautiful and talented actress to a long career in horror films.'

Cat Girl was something of a sexual breakthrough for British films. David Pirie, in his landmark book *A Heritage of Horror,* wrote: '...The ghostly cheetah, powered by all her repressed desire, begins to savage the lovers while she looks on in ecstasy... This first metamorphosis marks a crucially liberating moment in British cinema.' In *English Gothic,* Jonathan Rigby expressed more mixed emotions, referring to the film's 'clumsy handling' but waxing rhapsodic about Shelley. A sexually-suggestive scene in which she imagines herself possessed by her cat persona was 'embellished' by AIP to show her apparently transforming into a leopard, claws and all. AIP often seemed incapable of keeping its hands off a finished product, especially if it was shot in a foreign country.

Cat Girl was all-but dismissed by American critics. *Variety* opined that it 'lacks the ingredients to rise above a very minor entry for the exploitation market, where it is being packaged with *Amazing Colossal Man.* Barbara Shelley... tries hard to give some semblance of reality but doesn't stand a chance with what's handed her.'

After the smash success of the Herman Cohen-produced *Horrors of the Black Museum,* Arkoff and Nicholson were keen to co-finance more films in Britain. When Anglo offered them distribution rights to a film written by George Baxt and produced by the Rank team of Julian Wintle and Leslie Parkyn called *Circus of Horrors,* they snapped it up. Herman Cohen was nominated to keep an eye on things, but AIP's participation was otherwise that of eager onlooker, anticipating its next big horror hit.

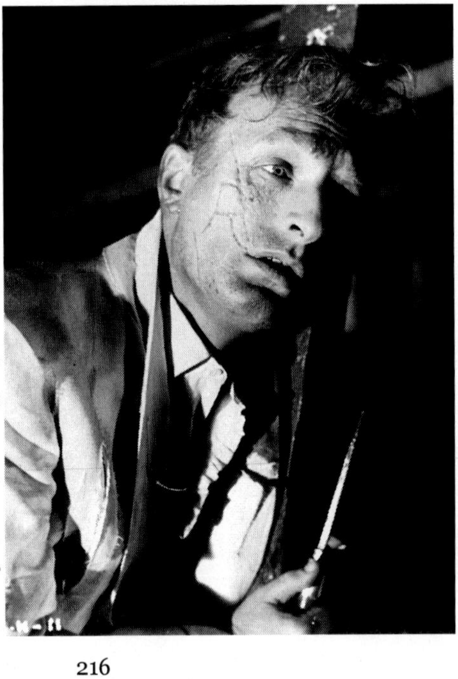

Circus of Horrors (Anton Diffring)

Baxt, a Brooklyn-born screenwriter, had just written a witchcraft film called *The City of the Dead* (1960), produced at Shepperton Studios by fellow Americans Milton Subotsky and Max Rosenberg, who would go on to form Amicus Productions. His plot for *Circus of Horrors* involved a plastic surgeon who flees England after a surgical mishap. In France, he uses a circus as cover for his activities, which involve restoring the faces of scarred beauties whom he then employs as circus acts. Returning to England, he starts to dispense with those who threaten to expose him, and Scotland Yard eventually comes calling.

Starring as the surgeon was German-born Anton Diffring, who had recently top-billed

Circus of Horrors (Anton Diffring, Yvonne Romain) / INSET: The Angry Red Planet

in Hammer's *The Man Who Could Cheat Death*. Diffring had appeared in numerous British war films, usually playing German officers, and his chiselled features, clipped delivery and aristocratic bearing easily lent themselves to villainy. He dominates every scene in which he appears in *Circus of Horrors*, and his cold, autocratic manner did much to assure the film of notoriety as one of the 'strongest' horrors to have been made in Britain up to this point in time.

Supporting Diffring was a bevy of voluptuous beauties, including French actress Yvonne Monlaur and soon-to-be Hammer starlet Yvonne Romain, and bringing up the rear were Jane Hylton, with whom director Sidney Hayers had worked on *Rebound,* character actors Kenneth Griffith and Donald Pleasence, and televisions's *William Tell*, Conrad Phillips. *Circus of Horrors* was shot at Beaconsfield Studios, with location shooting at Billy Smart's Circus on Clapham Common, in South West London. Billy Smart's provided the big top and many of the performers, and the cinematography was by the great Douglas Slocombe, who had distinguished himself on Ealing classics like *Kind Hearts and Coronets* (1949) and *The Lavender Hill Mob* (1955). Another outstanding aspect of Hayers's film was the score by Franz Reizenstein. The theme song, 'Look For a Star', became a Top Twenty hit for Gary Mills in the UK.

Released in America in August 1960, on a double bill with Ib Melchior's space opus *The Angry Red Planet, Circus of Horrors* cleaned up at the US box office, even though it was shorn of footage which had been seen by British audiences under an X certificate on its release in the UK in April. Typically, most of the American cuts involved sex, rather than the violence, for *Circus of Horrors* in its original form also showed as much female flesh as the British censor would allow. American reviews were mostly dismissive, but *Hollywood Citizen News* called it a 'better-than-average chiller-diller'. AIP's advertising was as lurid as ever: 'Spectacular towering terror! One man's lust... made men into beasts, stripped women of their souls!' screamed the poster.

The success of *Circus of Horrors* led to another AIP/Anglo-Amalgamated horror from a different British team, and one that was altogether more refined.

Fantasy and sci-fi author Fritz Leiber's novel *Conjure Wife* had previously been made into a film by Universal called *Weird Woman*, as part of its *Inner Sanctum* series in 1944. Leiber's novel, which dealt with a college professor who discovers that his wife is practicing witchcraft, was considerably watered down by screenwriters Scott Darling and Brenda Weisberg, with Lon Chaney Jr miscast as the professor and Anne Gwynne only moderately-witchy as his wife. Richard Matheson and Chuck Beaumont were fans of Leiber's novel and they were each paid $5,000 by AIP to adapt it for the screen, to be filmed in England as a co-production with Anglo. New producer Albert Fennell had George Baxt 'polish' their script.

With Sidney Hayers again at the helm, the leading role went to Peter Wyngarde, who had made an ominous mark as the spectral Peter Quint in Jack Clayton's film of Henry James's *The Turn of the Screw*, shot in 1961 as *The Innocents*. (The role had originally been offered to Peter Finch, who turned it down.) The role of Tansy, the professor's wife, was taken by American big band singer and actress Janet Blair, who was perhaps best-remembered for playing Rosalind Russell's sister in *My Sister Eileen* (1942). Blair was an unlikely choice to appear in a British horror film–indeed any horror film–but she rose to the occasion in what went before the cameras as *Night of the Eagle*, an unsubtle nod to Jaqcques Tourneur's 1957 witchcraft classic *Night of the Demon*.

Filming took six weeks, a leisurely schedule by AIP's standards, and *Night of the Eagle* was released in America as *Burn, Witch, Burn*–to which a prologue was added which had voice actor Paul Frees reciting a spell to protect the audience from witchcraft.

***Night of the Eagle* (Janet Blair, Peter Wyngarde)**

The Haunted and the Hunted (William Campbell)

Hokey opening notwithstanding, the US critics loved *Burn, Witch, Burn*. *The New York Times* praised it as 'the best outright goose-pimpler dealing specifically with witchcraft since *I Walked With a Zombie*', while Jonathan Rosenbaum in the *Chicago Reader* said that it was 'atmospheric and underplayed in the tradition of Val Lewton... eerily effective.'

Although filmed in Ireland rather than on the UK mainland, *The Haunted and the Hunted* (US: *Dementia 13*) is an important film of the period. Working as a sound man on Roger Corman's *The Young Racers* was 23-year-old Francis Ford Coppola, who previously had worked with the director on *Battle Beyond the Sun,* for which he was rewarded by being hired as dialogue director of *Tower of London* (1962). *The Young Racers* had been made in Ireland, and it was always Corman's policy to try to make two films while on location. Originally, he had planned to direct a 'quickie' himself but his schedule would not permit it (he was slated to make *The Raven* for AIP in Hollywood). Corman had $22,000 left from *The Young Racers*'s $165,000 budget, so he suggested instead that Coppola stay in Ireland with a small crew and turn out a low-budget psychological horror in the style of Hitchcock's *Psycho.* In J Philip DeFranco's book *The Movie World of Roger Corman,* Coppola recalled: 'Roger wanted to make (the film) cheaply. He wanted it to be homicidal, sort of a copy of *Psycho*. You know, gothic and psychological–with some kind of terrible knife-killing scene thrown in. So I wrote the script to order.'

After penning an outline in a night, Coppola described the film's most horrific sequence to Corman, in which a half-naked woman is murdered in a lakeside setting by an axe-wielding maniac. Corman was impressed enough to release the funds that Coppola needed to make the movie. Coppola's friend Al Locatelli became the film's

The Haunted and the Hunted (Luana Anders) / INSET: Mary Mitchel

art director and also helped him to finish the script in a mere three days. Considering its short gestation period, the plot of *The Haunted and the Hunted* is a convoluted one:

When her husband has a heart attack in a rowing boat on a lake and dies as a result, Louise Haloran throws his body overboard and informs his family that he has left on an important business trip. The reason for the deception: she can only inherit her part of the family fortune if her husband is alive. As she gets to know the Halorans better, she finds that they are still grieving over the death of their youngest daughter, who drowned in a pond when she was a child; the family holds a ceremony in her honour on the anniversary of her death. But this time, someone is murdering them with an axe. Who, and why..?

William Campbell, Luana Anders and Patrick Magee all agreed to stay on from *The Young Racers* to star in the film. Campbell had appeared in supporting roles in productions such as William Wellman's *The High and the Mighty* (1954), while Anders had co-starred with Vincent Price in *Pit and the Pendulum*. Magee had been a member of the Royal Shakespeare Company and was the most distinguished actor in the film, for which he (and everyone else) received very little money. The cast was rounded out with members of the Abbey Theatre, as well as friends of Coppola, and were paid minimum wages; they stayed together in a farmhouse in the countryside outside of Dublin.

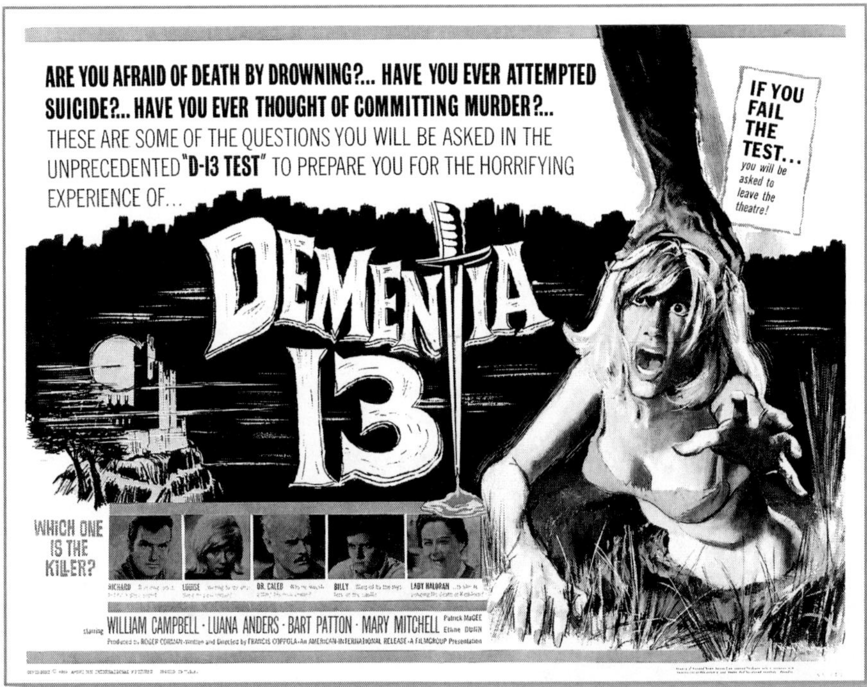

As shooting progressed, Coppola kept Corman informed by letter and telegram, promising that the film would be strong enough 'to make people sick'. Coppola was given his head and was left alone to direct. He had his work cut out for him but he rose to the occasion, impressing Campbell and the others with his professionalism and leadership abilities. However, when filming was complete, Corman demanded numerous changes which Coppola was unhappy about. In *Faster and Furiouser: the Revised and Fattened Fable of American International Pictures* by Mark Thomas McGee, Coppola recalled that Corman 'insisted on dubbing the picture the way he wanted it, adding voiceovers to simplify some of the scenes. Worse, he wanted some extra violence added, another axe murder at least...' Corman had Jack Hill shoot a scene involving a poacher who is decapitated by the axe-wielding killer.

Corman also considered that the film was too short, and he added a prologue in which a psychiatrist 'tested' the audience to ensure that they were 'mentally fit' to see what followed. This sequence was directed by Corman protégé, Monte Hellman. To add to the William Castle-style gimmicks, a quiz was handed out to patrons to determine if they were psychologically fit, which included such 'yes-or-no' statements as: 'The most effective way of settling a dispute is with one quick stroke of an axe to your adversary's head.'

On its release in the US as the supporting feature to *X–the Man With the X-Ray Eyes*, the retitled *Dementia 13* received poor reviews, if it was reviewed at all. *The New York Times* called Coppola's direction 'stolid' and went on to complain: 'Don't ask what that title means–or whatever happened to the first twelve dementias. One is enough. The picture stresses gore rather than atmosphere, and all but buries a fairly workable plot.'

Dementia 13 eventually fell into the public domain, along with several other films produced by Corman whose copyrights he failed to renew. As a result, it can often be found only in prints of varying quality. But when seen as it was intended, it reveals itself to be a work of genuine craftsmanship, despite its tiny budget. Coppola shows real talent and, with the help of cinematographer Charles Hannawalt, comes up with imaginative setups and inspired staging: the opening scene, for one, in which a radio belonging to Louise's husband is thrown overboard along with his corpse and floats to the bottom of the lake while still playing a rockabilly number called 'He's Caught', the music gradually muffled by the murky waters.

During this period, AIP also released a number of British films in the States that it did not co-produce, including Columbia's Hammer cast-off *The Two Faces of Dr Jekyll*, snipping several minutes from it, putting the accent on violence rather than sex, and releasing it as *House of Fright*. That kind of hatchet-job was fortunately not performed on John Krish's *Unearthly Stranger* (1963), a genuinely creepy exercise in thoughtful sci-fi starring John Neville, or on Basil Dearden's unusually adult Cold War psycho-drama *The Mind Benders* (1963).

City Under the Sea (Vincent Price)

After the side-step into juvenile fantasy that was *City Under the Sea*, an underwater adventure in the legendary Cornish 'Atlantis' of Lyonnesse, once more populated by Vincent Price and cynically cloaked in the threadbare robes of a Poe poem, AIP's next British production was *Monster of Terror* (US: *Die, Monster, Die!*). Roger Corman had turned to American *Weird Tales* author HP Lovecraft to try to breathe new life into his ailing Poe series and had adapted *The Haunted Palace* from a story by Lovecraft–*The Case of Charles Dexter Ward*–and only a poem by Poe. In another effort to advance Lovecraft as a replacement for Poe in the Gothic horror stakes, AIP decided to revisit the 'Gentleman from Providence' with an adaptation of his 1927 short story 'The Colour Out of Space'. With the provisional title *The House at the End of the World*, the film was shot at Shepperton Studios during February/March 1965, with 'house' art director Daniel Haller in the director's chair.

After featuring him in *The Raven*, AIP chose Boris Karloff to star as Nahum Witley, the patriarch of a strange family with a dark secret. Co-starring with Karloff was Nick Adams, who was best known for playing the title role in the US TV series *The Rebel*, and rounding out the cast were Suzan Farmer and Freda Jackson.

The script by sci-fi writer Jerry Sohl jettisons most of Lovecraft's cosmic horrors in favour of sci-fi cliches, but the plot of *Monster of Terror* still sticks fairly close to the story from which it was derived. Stephen Reinhart (Adams) visits his fiancee at the Arkham estate of her wheelchair-bound father (Karloff), a scientist who has discovered a radioactive meteorite that creates mutations in plants and animals. When the scientist's wife is mutated, he takes it upon himself to destroy the object. But he, too, becomes infected and turns into a psychotic madman...

Adams is like a fish out of water in Arkham (a New England town in Lovecraft's

Monster of Terror (Boris Karloff)

world but an olde English village in the film) but Farmer is a decorative screamer and Karloff and Jackson have plenty of scenery-chewing fun around Hammer's old stomping-ground of Oakley Court, which acted as the location for Witley's residence. Haller comes up with some nice Lovecraftian touches, such as the scene in which Adams and Farmer stumble upon the ghastly 'mutations' in Karloff's greenhouse, which the former aptly describes as being 'like a zoo in Hell'. Another nice visual touch comes when Karloff has himself been mutated and Adams follows his green, glowing hand-prints through the bowels of the mansion, in much the same way as Mark Damon followed the trail of blood in *House of Usher* (on which Haller served as art director).

Monster of Terror was released as *Die, Monster, Die!* on the top half of a double bill with *Planet of the Vampires* in the US, but with *The Haunted Palace* in the UK. Under either title, it did not set any new precedent for AIP and its horror films would continue to reference Edgar Allan Poe rather than Howard Phillips Lovecraft. The company did not look to Lovecraft for inspiration again until 1969.

In 1966, after a baptism of fire as the executive producer of *City Under the Sea*, Louis M 'Deke' Heyward was appointed AIP's Director of European Productions and was given a London office from which to oversee the company's foreign investments. Heyward's first film in the role was *Witchfinder General,* a watershed moment in British horror.

Not long before, film producer Tony Tenser had formed a company called Tigon Pictures. Tenser and former partner Michael Klinger had previously run Compton-Cameo, which had made both the lurid Gothic horror *The Black Torment* and the Sherlock Holmes/Jack the Ripper mystery *A Study in Terror*. One of the first films that Tenser produced for Tigon was *The Sorcerers* (1967), a contemporary horror thriller with Boris Karloff, Catherine Lacey and Ian Ogilvy, and directed by 21-year-old Michael Reeves.

To Tenser's delight, *The Sorcerers* ran for three weeks in London's West End, an unusual feat for a low-budget horror film. It did equally well in the provinces and in July 1968, it won the 'Grand Prix' at the Trieste Film Festival, with Lacey winning a Best Actress award. As a result, Reeves found himself playing the role of cinematic *wunderkind* and Tenser was keen to secure another vehicle for his young director's

Louis Heyward, Vincent Price, Sam Arkoff on the set of Witchfinder General

talents. Coincidentally, he had recently received galley proofs of a historical novel called *Witchfinder General* by Ronald Bassett, which was based on the life of Suffolk lawyer Matthew Hopkins, a self-appointed Puritan witch-hunter who had instituted a reign of terror during the dark days of the English Civil War.

Heyward knew little about Reeves but he liked the script for *Witchfinder General* and felt that it could be an opportunity for him to show his mettle to his bosses back home. Nicholson and Arkoff agreed to put up £32,000 of the total £82,000 budget in return for distribution rights in the US–and on the condition that the film would star Vincent Price.

Tenser, for his part, had no problem acceding to AIP's demands: Price–who was not so enthused of the script–would receive £12,000 for essaying the role of Matthew Hopkins. Contracts were signed and the project was given the green light.

The volatile Reeves made it clear from the outset that he did not want Price for the role, his preferred choice having been Donald Pleasence. Price's urbanity was at odds with Reeves's vision of the character, and he was concerned about the horror film 'baggage' that Price carried with him. But the agreement was final, and Reeves had no choice but to go along. The outcome was a fraught shoot, with Price and his 'young genius' director at loggerheads throughout–so much so that when star Ian Ogilvy's wife Diane spotted Price by the side of the road on her way to the unit's hotel and offered him a lift, he asked, 'Are you going to California?'

Principal photography was completed on November 13, on schedule but slightly over budget. When they saw Reeves's cut in the States, Arkoff and Nicholson were as impressed as Tenser and Heyward with their young charge. Nevertheless, they had the right to final cut and they chose to exercise it. Arkoff thought that the title was not commercial enough and felt that if the film could be tied to Poe, with Price as its star, it would be an unqualified hit. Drawing on a little-known Poe poem, *Witchfinder*

Curse of the Crimson Altar

General became instead *Edgar Allan Poe's The Conqueror Worm* in the US and Price was called back to read sections of the poem over both the opening scene and the freeze-frame that occurs at the end-credits, thereby linking the film–in a roundabout way–with AIP's 'Poe series'.

Witchfinder General was released in Britain and America in the autumn of 1968. It met with a considerable outcry in the British press because of its violence, but the controversy generated by the brutality only enhanced its box office success. 'Leave the children at home... and if you are squeamish, stay home with them!' blared AIP's advertising. The movie earned nearly $2 million on its US release, bringing about a second wave of 'Poe' films from the studio, again starring Price.

Heyward's first British production had knocked the ball out of the park, as the American saying goes. He segued immediately into another co-production with Tigon, *Curse of the Crimson Altar*, 'inspired' by (rather than based on) the short HP Lovecraft story 'Dreams in the Witch House'. The big names in horror that Tenser put together for this one were Christopher Lee, Boris Karloff and Barbara Steele, but the film was alotted to veteran director Vernon Sewell, who had just completed *The Blood Beast Terror* for Tigon, rather than the more inspirational Michael Reeves.

Curse of the Crimson Altar had little to do with Lovecraft beyond the basic plot of a man experiencing strange dreams about a legendary witch (indeed, the story's author is not even credited), and the screenplay by Mervyn Haisman, Henry Lincoln and Jerry Sohl is routine: in search of his sibling, antiques dealer Mark Eden travels to the country house where he was last seen. Occult expert Karloff regales him with tales of a local witchcraft cult and he uncovers strange goings-on in the old mansion, whose owner, Lee, is not all that he seems.

Having pushed the envelope of sex and violence with *Witchfinder General,* Tigon upped the ante in *Curse of the Crimson Altar* with flashes of nudity and a smattering of sado-masochism (all of which was deleted by the British censor, in the event). Despite this attempt at titillation, however, *Curse of the Crimson Altar* was a pedestrian affair in both scripting and direction. Even the presence of its eminent

The Oblong Box (Alister Williamson, Sally Geeson, Uta Levka)

stars failed to bring the affair to life and they are mostly wasted (especially Steele, who does not have a single line of dialogue). *Witchfinder General* cinematographer John Coquillon ensured that a certain polish was maintained, and setting the action in Grim's Dyke, the former home of WS Gilbert of Gilbert and Sullivan fame, made a welcome change from Oakley Court, but a cracker of an original idea was lost to insipid pacing and perfunctory staging. Due to the erotic nature of some of its scenes, AIP held the film back in the States until 1970, when it was shorn of its more contentious aspects, awarded a PG rating, and disposed of as *The Crimson Cult*.

(*Curse of the Crimson Altar* had a sad postscript. Karloff contracted pneumonia during a January shoot in inclement weather; he would recover sufficiently to star in four Mexican features in May the same year but he died on February 2, 1969, at the age of 81.)

For its next Poe, AIP wanted the wayward talents of Michael Reeves. Reeves was offered *The Oblong Box* by Heyward, was less than enthusiastic about the prospect, and promptly died of a drug overdose before production could begin. Another director was found in his stead: Gordon Hessler, who had worked in various capacities on the CBS/NBC-TV series, *Alfred Hitchcock Presents* and *The Alfred Hitchcock Hour*, from 1960 to 1965.

Price, Rupert Davies and Hilary Dwyer were all brought back from *Witchfinder General* to star. The screenwriter, Lawrence Huntington, also died as shooting began and the script was hastily rewritten by Hessler and Christopher Wicking. Following in the footsteps of Reeves by including more sex and gore to the mix as before, *The Oblong Box* proved a successful addition to the series; it made over $1 million in the US and Poe and AIP were together again, with Arkoff and Nicholson ready to make the most of the reunion.

Spirits of the Dead

Spirits of the Dead (Marina Yaru)

AIP next picked up an Italo-French omnibus film called *Histoires extraordinaires* which featured three Poe stories, each one helmed by a different European director: Roger Vadim directed 'Metzengerstein', starring Jane and Peter Fonda, Louis Malle helmed 'William Wilson', starring Alain Delon and Brigitte Bardot, and Federico Fellini wrote and directed 'Toby Dammit', adapted from 'Never Bet the Devil Your Head' and starring Terence Stamp.

For American distribution, AIP retitled the film *Spirits of the Dead* and added a narration by Vincent Price, once more tying it spuriously to the ongoing Poe series. Arkoff and Nicholson had offered the producers $200,000 for the rights, but they were turned down initially because Arkoff wanted to excise footage from the Fellini sequence. With no other buyers at the table after a year, Arkoff had made the same offer and it was accepted.

With the British film industry increasingly in trouble towards the end of the 1960s, Amicus Productions, the makers of portmanteau horror such as *Dr Terror's House of Horrors* (1965) and *Torture Garden* (1968), was in the same position as Tigon and Hammer in that co-production was now seen as the only way forward. Amicus boss Milton Subotsky had a project based on *The Disorientated Man,* a novel by the pseudonymous Peter Saxon, which he felt would make a good film if an appropriate production partner could be found for it. As it happened, he received a phone call from 'Deke' Heyward, who asked if he had anything that might suit Vincent Price, whom AIP was now contracted to keep gainfully employed. Subotsky sent Heyward a script and a deal was struck, with *The Oblong Box* team of Hessler and Wicking as director and writer. Heyward came up with the idea of reteaming Price with Lee also (they had appeared together in *The Oblong Box*), and bringing along Peter Cushing as well: the screen's three current 'Titans of Terror'.

The film, now titled *Scream and Scream Again*, was shot at Shepperton in May 1969 and on its release in the spring of 1970, it was another huge success for both Amicus and AIP. It also received excellent reviews, even being compared by the *Los*

Scream and Scream Again (Vincent Price, Alfred Marks, Clifford Earl)

Angeles Times to Roman Polanski's *Rosemary's Baby* (1968). A wierd mixture of sci-fi and horror, with everything from pop band Amen Corner, MI6, vampires, car chases, foreign intrigue and an army of human robots thrown into its rag-bag of ingredients, *Scream and Scream Again* has surprisingly attained cult status over the years, even though its three 'Titans' barely shared a scene together and the real stars of the film were Alfred Marks as a police inspector and the sinister-looking Michael Gothard as a superhuman robot vampire! Saxon's novel was about an invasion from space; Wicking's screenplay ditched the aliens and substituted foreign agents with a plan to take over the world by replacing heads of state with robotic clones, similar in principle to the 'Red scare' dramas of *Invasion of the Body Snatchers* and its like. This was conveyed in a multiplicity of plot-strands, which had many reviewers (and Milton Subotsky himself) scratching their heads, but the marquee promise of Price, Lee and Cushing on the same bill was enough to bring the faithful out in droves, and the film fared far better than its muddled narrative naturally deserved.

AIP then teamed with Tigon again for *The Haunted House of Horror* (US: *Horror House*, 1970), starring former *Beach Party* fixture Frankie Avalon. Tony Tenser had pitched a screenplay called *The Dark* to the company, written by a promising newcomer named Michael Armstrong. As Tenser biographer John Hamilton explained in his book, *Beasts in the Cellar*, '*The Dark* seemed to be custom-made for AIP–a group of horny teenagers conduct a séance in an abandoned house, and discover that one of them is a psychotic killer. Armstrong's original script, written eight years earlier when he was still a teenager himself, was more concerned with the explicit heterosexual and homosexual tensions within the group, rather than the violence inherent in the story, but the American drive-in giants considered the idea to be an easy sell.'

Arkoff and Nicholson approved the script and the project was off and running. At a press conference with Tenser, Heyward praised the screenplay as 'having all the terror of *Psycho* and yet with a young feel.' Armstrong found Tenser easy to work with but AIP not nearly so accommodating, initially insisting that the film should be top-lined by Boris Karloff. Ultimately, Karloff was deemed too ill to work and his place was taken by former British matinee idol Dennis Price. Price's career had been on the skids for some time, when his private life (homosexuality and bankruptcies) had eclipsed his work, after which he had drifted into alcoholism and a failed suicide attempt. He was now fair game for anyone who cared to offer him a cameo role, and the ever-frugal Hammer had already sought him out.

The Dark involved a group of 'teenagers', gathered in an old mansion, who are being murdered one by one, but which one is the killer? In some ways, the story set the template for the teen 'slasher' films that proliferated in the 1980s but, in 1970, it seemed more like a belated attempt to cash-in on the sixties' teen scene that was already fading into social history.

AIP wanted an American lead, either Fabian or Frankie Avalon, both of whom were under contract. Armstrong had his sights set on David Bowie, but he jumped at the chance to direct his own script and reluctantly went for Avalon as 'the lesser of two evils'. AIP also wanted the script rewritten, and Heyward added material, as well as promoting the inexperienced Julian Barnes to the difficult role of the murderer in place of Robin Stewart.

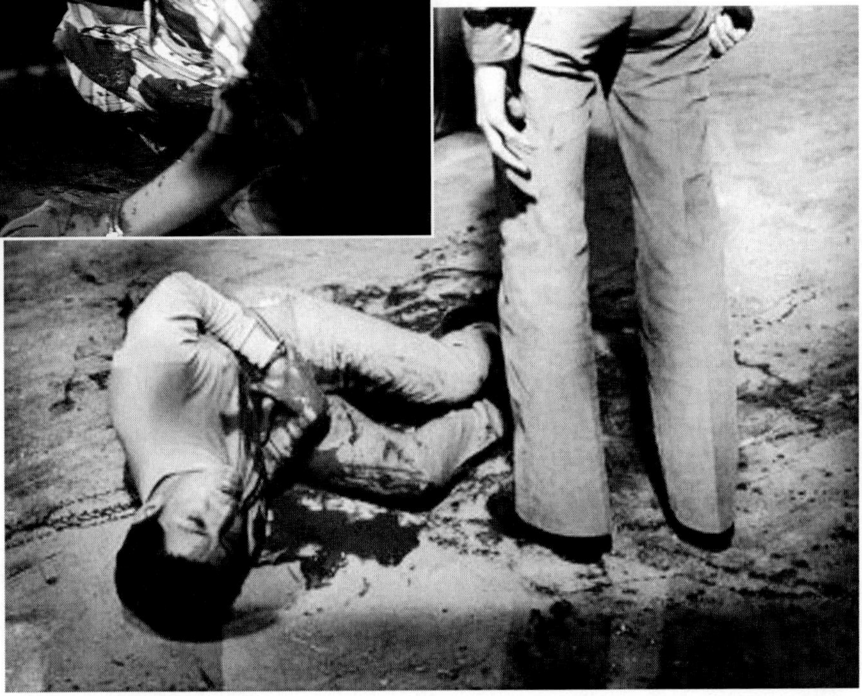

The Haunted House of Horror (Frankie Avalon, Julian Barnes [INSET] Mark Wynter)

Heyward and Armstrong continued to butt heads, and it was suggested to Tenser that a new director be found for the film. Gerry Levy, who had just directed *The Body Stealers* for Tigon, was put on notice.

When Arkoff and Nicholson arrived in London to view the film, Armstrong was invited to attend along with Tenser, Heyward and Danny Skouras, AIP's European Director of Sales. The print that was shown had been assembled by Levy and editor Peter Pitt, and Armstrong was outraged: 'What came on bore no resemblance to my film in any shape or form; you couldn't follow the plot; it was a mess', he recalled. Arkoff and Nicholson were just as unhappy, but for different reasons; new scenes were ordered, but without Armstrong's participation. Writing as Peter Marcus, Levy added a romantic subplot and two more murders, as well as a musical number at the opening. AIP retitled the film *Horror House* for its US release, where it went out on the drive-in circuit with *Scream and Scream Again*, and Michael Armstrong went to Germany to direct an extremely bloody *Witchfinder General* rip-off called *Mark of the Devil* (1970), which was subsequently banned by the British censor.

Meanwhile, AIP's attempts to go 'up-market' were meeting with mixed results at best. They had originally announced *De Sade* in 1967, to be based on an unpublished novel by Louis M Heyward called *Theatre of Horrors*. Among the directors considered were Michael Reeves and Gordon Hessler; Roger Corman had worked on the script with Richard Matheson, but he walked away from the project. AIP then hired Cy Endfield, whose filmography included *Mysterious Island* (1961) and *Zulu* (1964).

An international cast was assembled, with Keir Dullea in the title role (his first since Kubrick's *2001: A Space Odyssey*), voluptuous Austrian actress Senta Berger, John Huston and Lili Palmer, and a co-production deal was struck between AIP and West German company Columbia Film-Verleih. But *De Sade* was doomed from the start: Endfield came down with the 'flu' when the sex scenes in the film became too much for him and Corman was hired to replace him for the remainder of the shoot, although he received no screen credit. He later claimed that AIP did not pay him what he felt that he was owed for *De Sade*, which persuaded him to say a final goodbye to Arkoff and Nicholson and form his own company.

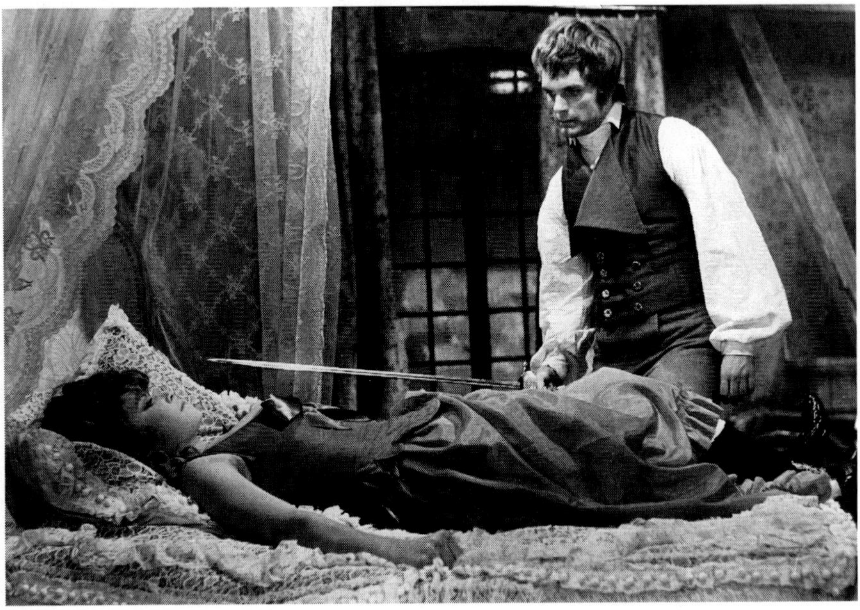

De Sade (Keir Dullea, Senta Berger)

Cry of the Banshee (Patrick Mower, Andrew McCullough)

During these debacles, AIP went the tried-and-tested route of casting Vincent Price in a film ostensibly based on a work by Edgar Allan Poe, *Cry of the Banshee.* Poe never wrote such a tale, but that did not prevent the company from promoting the film with a supposed Poe 'poem', which spurred *Los Angeles Times* journalist John Mahoney to observe, 'A phrase, a verse, is cribbed from Poe, tacked onto the main title and sprinkled into the ads. The tormented poet takes the rap again.'

Cry of the Banshee was originally written by Tim Kelly, but Gordon Hessler was not keen on Kelly's version and he hired Christopher Wicking to perform a rewrite. Wicking introduced Celtic witchcraft into the plot and set it in Elizabethan England: powerful local magistrate Lord Edward Whitman orders the destruction of a coven of witches, thereby becoming a target for their leader, Oona. In response, she summons a 'banshee' to wipe out the lord's family one by one. In the course of the changes, any resemblance between the film's banshee and that of folklore became non-existent; a banshee is a spirit whose cry portends death, and it has nothing to do with witchcraft and even less to do with the shape-shifting 'werewolf' that Patrick Mower becomes at intervals in the course of the story. Not that *Cry of the Banshee* had anything to do with Poe either, but it was sold as a Poe movie and a blatant attempt to cash in on the success of *Witchfinder General*, and it did well enough on both counts to ensure a continuation of the series for a while longer.

On its US release in August 1969, *De Sade* was a critical and commercial flop. A mixture of art-house and exploitation, it was neither fish nor fowl, but its failure did not deter AIP from trying to expand its artistic horizons. Eschewing Gothic horror in favour of Gothic romance, the company was inspired by the success of Franco Zeffirelli's 1968 *Romeo and Juliet* to make a new version of *Wuthering Heights*, and young British director Robert Fuest was chosen to helm the production. Fuest had cut his teeth on episodes of TV's *The Avengers* and he had recently directed a thriller for EMI called *And Soon the Darkness.*

The cast was impressive. Shakesperean actor Timothy Dalton, fresh from his film debut as Phillip II in *The Lion in Winter*–was hired to play Heathcliff, with Anna Calder-Marshall as Catherine Earnshaw. Others in the line-up were Harry Andrews, Rosalie Crutchley, Julian Glover, Hugh Griffith and Ian Ogilvy, and the film was shot on location in Yorkshire, famously the setting of Emily Brönte's novel. All in all, *Wuthering Heights* was one of AIP's largest-scale productions to date.

In an April 1970 *Times* article by Ronald Faux, 'Deke' Heyward was quoted as saying: 'I'm the only American here. For the first time in thirty years Hollywood said to me, "No big names, no huge publicity, just a good film that stands on its merits". This is very encouraging except now we stand naked in judgement. It has to be really good with two to three million dollars invested. The last version, with Laurence Olivier as Heathcliff and Merle Oberon as Cathy, portrayed him as a regular nice guy and her as sweetness and light. That was not the truth... Heathcliff was a bastard and Cathy a real bitch and that's how they'll be in this film.' It is doubtful if Emily Brönte would have agreed with him!

In an unpublished 1994 interview with author Tony Earnshaw, Fuest recalled *Wuthering Heights* as a happy film. 'I owe that film to Bryan Forbes [then Head of Production at Elstree Studios]. Bryan put in a good word for me with two Americans, Sam Arkoff and Jim Nicholson. I'd just finished *And Soon the Darkness* and brought it in on time, and they offered me this. The script wasn't right, but I think the book is impossible to film.' Impossible or no, his version of *Wuthering Heights* passed the two-hour mark. AIP was not interested in epic films and cut forty minutes out of it. 'Arkoff and Nicholson hadn't read the book but they'd read the comic!' Fuest said. 'They have comic strips in America and they'd read the comic strip version. Comic Classics, they call them. And it made a lot of money.'

Despite Fuest's claim that it made 'a lot of money', the film's box-office was below par. The critics compared it unfavourably to the famous 1939 version and a proposed

Wuthering Heights (Timothy Dalton)

The Vampire Lovers (Ingrid Pitt, Pippa Steel)

sequel, *Return to Wuthering Heights,* was never made, nor were the adaptations of other classic novels that AIP had hoped to produce, including *The House of Seven Gables, A Tale of Two Cities* and *Camille.* Fuest told Earnshaw, 'I think *Wuthering Heights* has some good things in it, but the script (by Patrick Tilley) wasn't right and I wasn't right. But I loved it and I still think there's some nice things in it.' John Coquillon's cinematography and a haunting score by Michel Legrand are plusses, and the film is one of AIP's finer achievements, but it was always going to be a struggle to compete with the David O Selznick-produced Laurence Olivier-Merle Oberon classic, and AIP's executive board should perhaps have realised that.

In late 1969, the inevitable teaming of AIP and Hammer occurred when production commenced on *Vampire Lovers,* the fourth screen adaptation of J Sheridan Le Fanu's seminal 1871 novella, *Carmilla.* In 1932, Carl Dreyer had based *Vampyr* on the story and Roger Vadim had modernised it in *Blood and Roses* (*Et mourir de plaisir*, 1960), but the most faithful version to date had been Camillo Mastrocinque's *Terror in the Crypt* (*La cripta e l'incubo,* 1964), starring Christopher Lee. The relaxation of censorship had now made it possible to deal with the lesbianism that was implicit in the novella, and the Fantale Films' team of producers Harry Fine, Michael Style and screenwriter Tudor Gates had brought the project to Hammer.

Hammer's managing director Sir James Carreras gained the interest of AIP and the resulting film, directed by Roy Ward Baker, was the first R-rated horror in the US, despite the fact that AIP trimmed some of the plentiful gore from its domestic

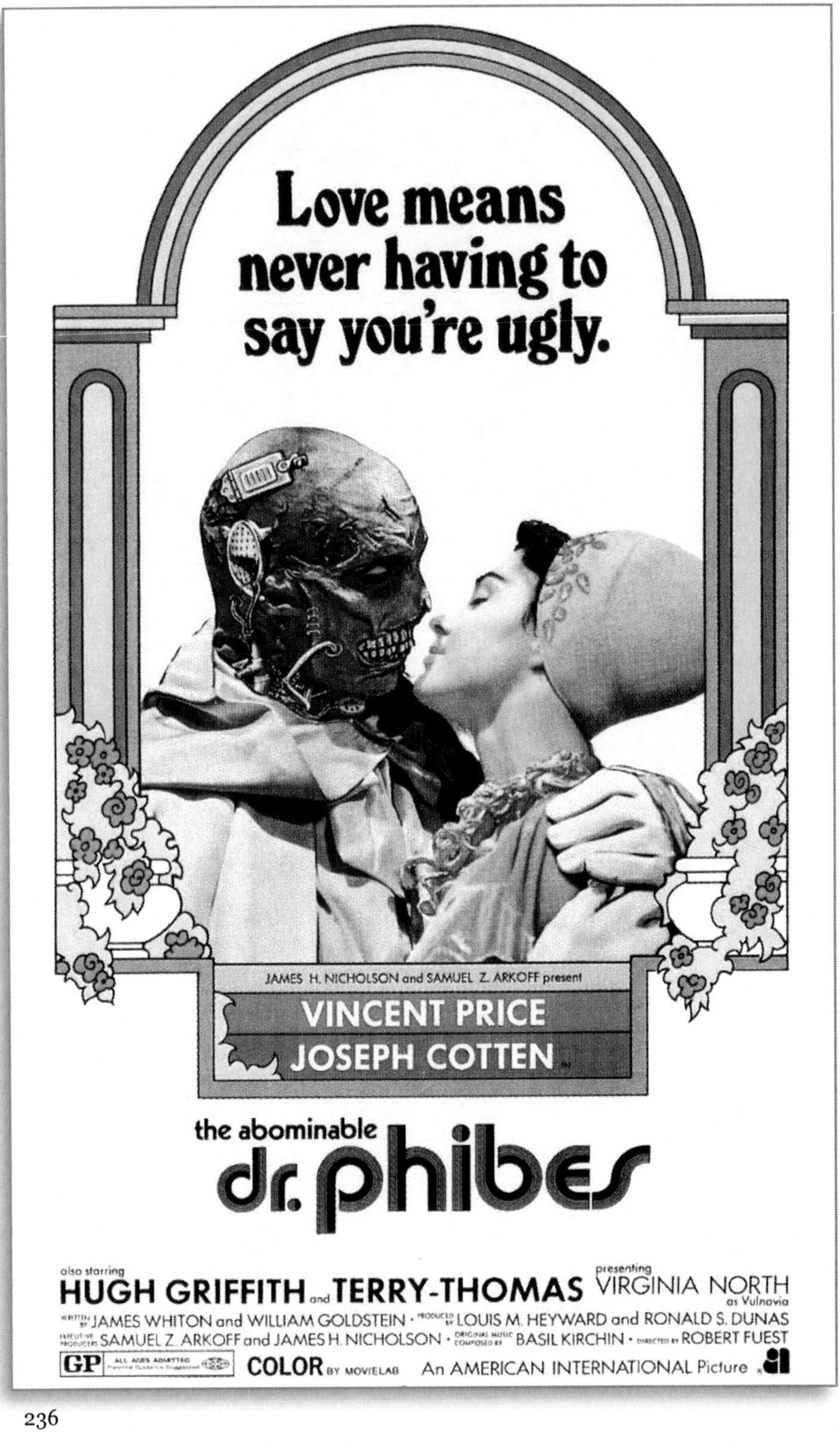
Love means
never having to
say you're ugly.
JAMES H. NICHOLSON and SAMUEL Z. ARKOFF present
VINCENT PRICE
JOSEPH COTTEN
the abominable
dr. phibes
also starring
HUGH GRIFFITH and TERRY-THOMAS
presenting
VIRGINIA NORTH
as Vulnavia
JAMES WHITON and WILLIAM GOLDSTEIN
LOUIS M. HEYWARD and RONALD S. DUNAS
SAMUEL Z. ARKOFF and JAMES H. NICHOLSON
BASIL KIRCHIN
ROBERT FUEST
GP
COLOR BY MOVIELAB
An AMERICAN INTERNATIONAL Picture

version; female nudity still meant an automatic R-rating in America and stars Ingrid Pitt and Madeleine Smith provided an ample quota. With reliable box-office draw Peter Cushing in the line-up, *The Vampire Lovers* did good business on both sides of the pond but AIP took fright at the licentiousness of the 'new' Hammer and decided that further co-production was not a commercial proposition. American money was moving out of the UK, in any event, which was to leave Hammer and Tigon (among many other companies) financially high and dry, but American International itself would continue to produce in Britain for some time yet.

Despite *Wuthering Heights*'s tepid box office, Arkoff and Nicholson were pleased with Fuest's work on it. A script called *The Curses of Dr Phibe* had recently crossed their desks, penned by novice screenwriters James Whiton and William Goldstein. It was deemed to be a perfect project for Vincent Price and AIP decided to film it in London on an enlarged budget of $500,000. Louis Heyward was brought on board as producer and Fuest was hired to direct; he immediately rewrote the script, which then became *The Abominable Dr Phibes*.

The story concerned Anton Phibes, scientist, musician, doctor and scholar, who has been horribly disfigured in the car accident that also claimed the life of his wife Victoria when the doctors who operated upon her subsequently failed to save her. Years later, Phibes takes his revenge on the nine in the form of the plagues of Egypt that Moses brought down on the head of the Pharaoh. One is stung to death by bees, another is bitten by bats, a third by locusts, and so on.

Joining Price was Hollywood veteran Joseph Cotten, and the film benefited from a strong supporting cast, including Hugh Griffith, Terry Thomas and John Cater. Model-turned-actress Virginia North was cast as Vulnavia, Phibes's mysterious female acolyte, after being spotted in a play called *Council of Love*: 'I played the daughter of the Devil. I'd go around and do terrible things. The people who made the movie saw me in the play and decided I was what they wanted. You might say I was ready made

The Abominable Dr Phibes (Joseph Cotten, Vincent Price)

for the role,' she told the Associated Press. A second model-turned-actress had the unenviable task of playing Phibes's dead wife; Caroline Munro had to do little more than lie prone in an ornate coffin throughout the film, but it led her to bigger things, including a long stint as the British TV commercials face of Lamb's Navy Rum.

As Phibes, Price had to appear mute and talk through a speaker in his neck, his lines being read aloud by a crew-member to give Cotten his cues. Cotten complained that he had to *know* all his lines while Price merely had to dub his in later. 'Yes, but I still know them, Joe,' Price riposted.

Having learned his craft on the surreal fantasy of ABC-TV's *The Avengers*, Fuest had seen the satirical possibilities in Whiton and Goldstein's script and decided to play that up when it came to shooting *The Abominable Dr Phibes*. The story was set in the 1920s and Fuest (and set designer Brian Eatwell) embellished the ambience of the film with art deco interiors and a robot band–'Dr Phibes' Clockwork Wizards'–to keep the doctor and Vulnavia entertained between murders. This tongue-in-cheek approach was extended to the police investigation of them, in which two of the most bumbling cops since Keystone attempt to solve the riddle posed by the 'abominable' Dr Phibes. In an interview with *Bizarre*, Fuest told editor Sam Irvin that Arkoff and Nicholson had no idea that he was making a funny film. 'Had they known, I think they might have stopped me,' he said. As it transpired, he had nothing to worry about: Arkoff and Nicholson liked *The Abominable Dr Phibes*. 'It was so freshly different from anything that Vincent Price had made at AIP since the first of the Corman films,' Fuest remarked.

Marketed (erroneously) as Price's 100th film, *The Abominable Dr Phibes* was released in May 1971 and originally advertised with the tagline, 'Love means never having to say you're ugly', a parody of the famous slogan from *Love Story*, which had played earlier that year. It initially had trouble finding an audience until a new campaign made it clear that it was a horror film. According to Fuest, it then ran for six months in Paris at one cinema alone.

The Abominable Dr Phibes became one of AIP's biggest hits, and it immediately

Dr Phibes Rises Again (Valli Kemp, Vincent Price)

required a sequel. As Fuest recalled for Irvin, 'I wrote the script to the second one and sent it to AIP for approval. They had one of their writers change a few things, and the sequence of events was rearranged.' The writer in question was Robert Blees, who had penned the likes of *The Black Scorpion* (1957) and *Screaming Mimi* (1958), and their joint efforts gave the new film an Egyptian motif, partly to coincide with the upcoming British Museum exhibition of artefacts from the tomb of Tutankhamen: Phibes awakens from the state of suspended animation into which he placed himself at the close of *The Abominable Dr Phibes* and sets out to find the pharaoh's tomb under which flows the River of Life that will restore his dead wife to him. But he has a rival in his quest in the form of Beiderbeck, who is also seeking eternal life–not to mention pursuit by the same bumbling policemen.

Phibes II (as it was called during shooting) went into production in December 1971, but its road to the screen was rockier than that of its predecessor.

Roberty Quarry, who played Beiderbeck, was an actor who had bounced around Hollywood since the 1940s, never achieving a great deal of success. In 1970, director Bob Kelljan had cast him in the lead role of *Count Yorga, Vampire*, which became a 'sleeper' hit and inspired a sequel, *The Return of Count Yorga* (1971), again starring Quarry. Made on a tiny budget of $64,000, the original film had been conceived as a softcore offering, but Quarry had convinced its producers to turn it into a straight horror thriller instead. The alternative version, cut to a GP rating in the US, made a huge profit as an indie pickup for AIP. But having become a horror 'star' at the age of 45 from playing Yorga had created some insecurities in the actor, and he and Price did not get along at all well.

Cinefantastique published a report by Chris Knight and Peter Nicholson from the Elstree set. At the time, Quarry was effusive about his co-star: 'He's lovely. He's a terrific, marvelous guy... Some people think that we are at odds about something, but it's just a way of showing affection. We have a good time... It's got better as we've gone along.' There was more to what was going on between Price and Quarry than 'affection', however: AIP was grooming Quarry to be its next horror star. Vincent

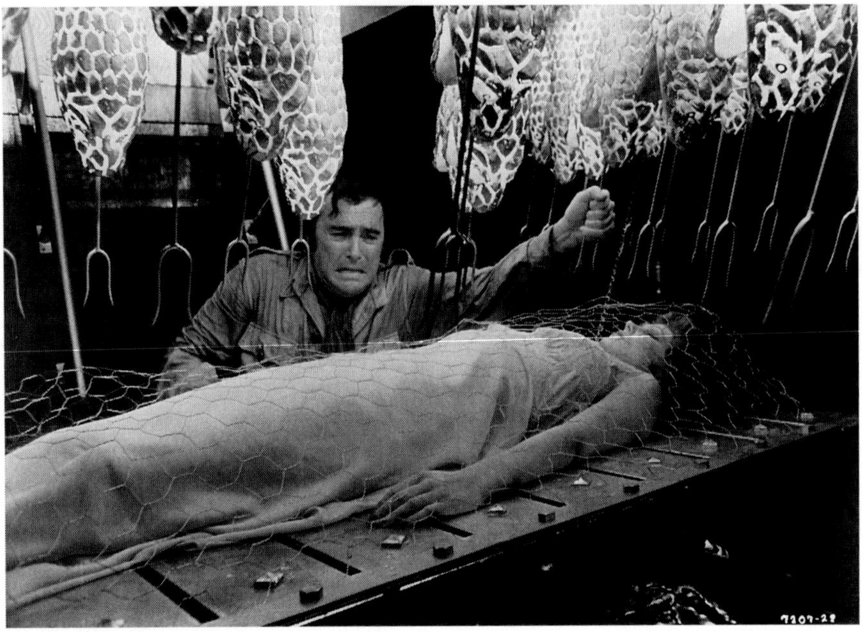

Price was nearing the end of his contract with the company, and Quarry was well aware that he was the king in waiting.

According to Price's daughter Victoria, Quarry said that the animosity between he and Price stemmed from an offhand remark. 'Shortly after shooting began, they had a big cocktail reception. An English publicist came up to Vincent and asked, "How do you feel about Mr Quarry coming in as your replacement at AIP?" Vincent told me what happened. He wasn't happy about it. So I went to the producer and told him what happened. Well, it was too late. The damage had been done. The publicity made it sound as if I were out to dethrone the king. That made a rift between us. I never saw Vincent socially after that incident.'

There were budgetary problems as well, and new lines were given to the cast on almost a daily basis as the script was revised to patch over scenes that were cut on grounds of cost. The original script had called for set pieces which were beyond AIP's financial reach, such as scenes in a pyramid that was intended to have several levels primed with traps.

When what was finally called *Dr Phibes Rises Again* was ready for release, AIP's ad campaign pulled out all the hyperbolic stops: 'Flesh crawls! Blood curdles! Phibes lives!', 'They haven't built the COFFIN that can hold HIM'... The colourful deaths in the film included a man clawed to death by an eagle and devoured; another stung to death by scorpions, and Beiderbeck ageing like Dorian Gray at the climax. (The gore was toned down for the American PG-rated version.)

Dr Phibes Rises Again was also intended to sire a sequel. A third film, proposed by original co-creator James Whiton, was to be called *The Brides of Phibes*. Like Phibes himself, it never saw the light of day. James Nicholson was soon to relinquish his co-chairmanship of AIP, turning it over to partner Sam Arkoff, who had little interest in horror. *Dr Phibes Rises Again* did not make nearly as much as its predecessor and AIP would head instead in a different and even more exploitative direction.

Neither Hammer, Tigon, Amicus or, indeed, American International had any real idea of how to proceed at the turn of the 1970s. Audience taste was changing rapidly,

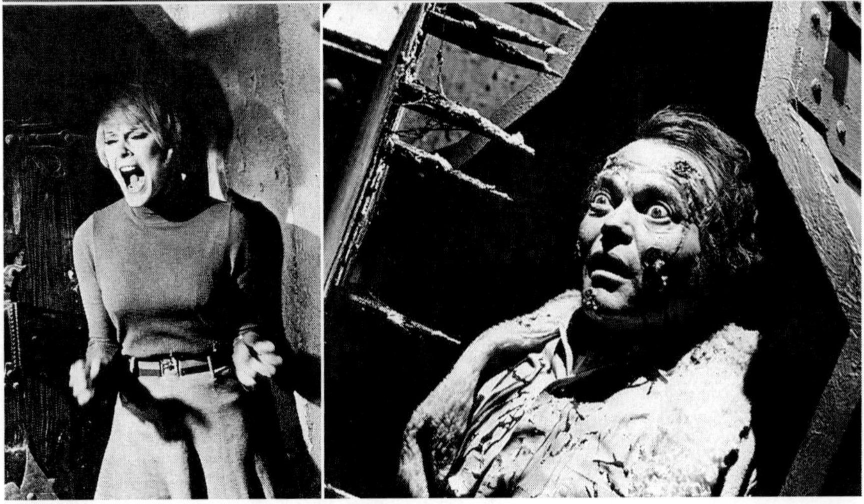

Baron Blood / **BELOW:** *Elke Sommer, Luciano Pigozzi*

and the lifting of censorship restrictions had driven a coach-and-horse through the one market upon which all their livelihoods had come to depend. When nearly anything was now permissable on the screen, where did film companies which had specialised in 'adult' material go next? The answer was backwards, which in AIP's case meant co-financing a Mario Bava Gothic called *Gli orrori del castello di Norimberga* (US: *Baron Blood*, 1972) with Joseph Cotten, on the rebound from his appearance in *The Abominable Dr Phibes,* after the lead had been turned down by both Vincent Price and Ray Milland.

A deliberate attempt to evoke Bava's Gothics of the 1960s, *Baron Blood* was shot at a real castle in Austria and co-starred German actress Elke Sommer. The plot, concocted by Vincent Fotre and William Bairn, concerns a student who is looking into his family's history. He finds that one of his ancestors was a cruel and sadistic baron, who was cursed to a violent death by a witch whom he had executed. The student is foolish enough to recite a spell that brings about the baron's return from the grave, and the torture and murders begin anew...

Baron Blood was not well received–Roger Ebert's *Chicago Sun-Times*' review being typical: 'Sometimes you can enjoy horror movies because they're so bad, but *Baron Blood* isn't bad enough. And Joseph Cotten makes an unconvincing evil count, mainly because he seems so nice most of the time... The publicity for the movie warns against the possibility of 'apoplectic strokes, cerebral hemorrhages, cardiac seizures, or fainting spells', but they're just trying to make themselves look good. The only first aid they really need is hot coffee for the patrons who doze off.'

AIP no longer appeared to understand its audience. Despite the success of *The Vampire Lovers*, it had excised much of the gore from Bava's original cut of *Baron Blood* in order to achieve a PG rating in the States, oblivious to the fact that horror fans were demanding ever more graphic material after the 1969 release of George Romero's cult-'sleeper' *Night of the Living Dead*.

Meanwhile, AIP's British arm was slowly winding down. In 1971, the company had produced a curious psychological thriller called *Who Slew Auntie Roo?*, written by Jimmy Sangster and Robert Blees and directed by *Queen of Blood*'s Curtis Harrington. It featured Shelley Winters and a slew of British character players, including the venerable Ralph Richardson, and it was in the vein of Robert Aldrich's classic *Whatever Happened to Baby Jane?* (1963). But the concept of a modern-day retelling of the fairy tale of Hansel and Gretel was not the most attractive proposition for a genre which was about to be changed out of all recognition by *The Exorcist*. Harrington directed this odd little film with the same sense of mischief that he had brought to *Games* (1967), a tricksy thriller in the vein of Henri-Georges Clouzot's *Les Diaboliques* (1955), but *Who Slew Auntie Roo?* arrived too late in the *grande-dame guignol* cycle to make any impact with either critics or audiences.

Who Slew Auntie Roo? (Michael Gothard, Mark Lester / RIGHT: Shelley Winters)

IF STARK TERROR WERE ECSTASY
...living
here
would be
sheer
bliss!
MADHOUSE
Samuel Z. Arkoff presents
Color prints by Movielab
'MADHOUSE' Starring VINCENT PRICE · PETER CUSHING · ROBERT QUARRY
Screenplay by GREG MORRISON and KEN LEVISON · Based on the novel 'Devilday' by Angus Hall · Produced by MILTON SUBOTSKY and MAX ROSENBERG
Directed by JAMES CLARK · Original music composed and conducted by DOUGLAS GAMLEY
An AMERICAN INTERNATIONAL-AMICUS Co-Production · An AMERICAN INTERNATIONAL Release
PG
PARENTAL GUIDANCE SUGGESTED

Madhouse (Robert Quarry, Peter Cushing, Vincent Price)

With the British film industry entering one of its worst-ever slumps, the final film in Vincent Price's tortuous contract was *Madhouse,* co-produced with Amicus and again starring Price and Quarry. A readily-available Peter Cushing was added to the mix, and AIP's long-promised adaptation of Angus Hall's novel *Devilday* reached the screen in a cut-price version in which horror movie star Paul Toombes (Price) returns to his famous role of 'Dr Death' after years in a mental institution following the murder of his wife only to find the 'Dr Death' murders of which he was accused starting up around him once more.

With the requisite British rent-a-cast of supporting players, *Madhouse* should have been better than it was, but former editor Jim Clark's direction was uncertain and the screenplay by Ken Levison and Greg Morrison abandoned the book's satanic theme and went instead for slasher-mystery. By the time the film was released in 1974, *Madhouse* appeared quaint against director William Friedkin's blasphemous fright-fest. Horror films made by small British and American companies could no longer compete in the global marketplace, which the box office receipts for *Madhouse* subsequently confirmed.

AIP continued its relationship with Amicus for two more non-horrors based on novels by Edgar Rice Burroughs: *The Land That Time Forgot* (1975) and *At the Earth's Core* (1976), both starring *The Virginian*'s Doug McClure and the latter featuring Peter Cushing and Caroline Munro. The Burroughs films were science-fantasy, and successful as such, with *The Land That Time Forgot* becoming one of the biggest hits of the year at the British box office. But *At the Earth's Core* was also the final Amicus film. The company had been torn apart by changes in the business and in-fighting between its owners, Milton Subotsky and Max J Rosenberg, and Rosenburg alone produced the last Burroughs' film to be released by AIP, *The People That Time Forgot*. An era was drawing to a close.

Louis 'Deke' Heyward's final film for AIP was *Murders in the Rue Morgue* (1971), a

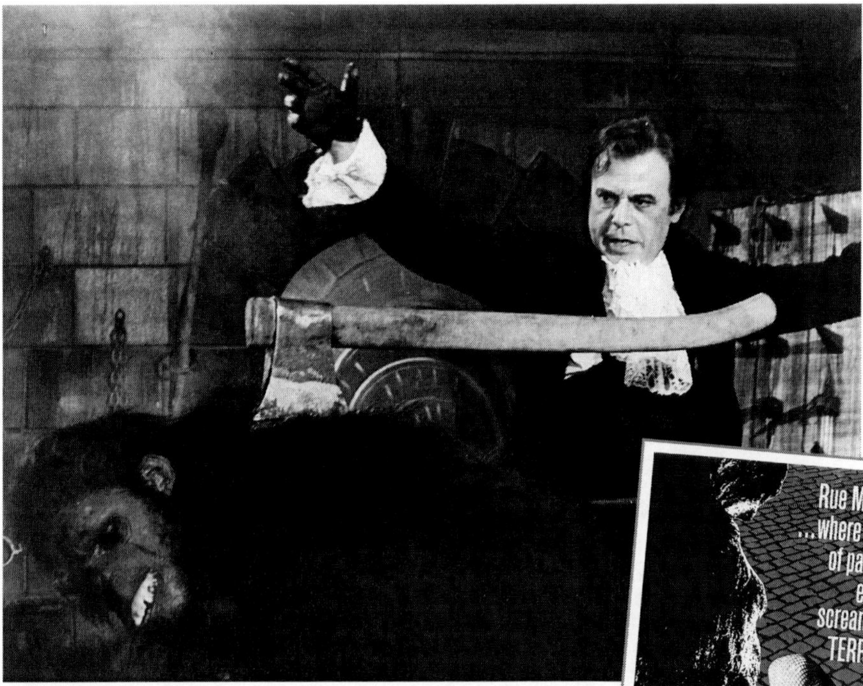

Murders in the Rue Morgue (Herbert Lom)

Price-less Poe adaptation featuring Jason Robards and shot in Spain. Hessler and Wicking were up to their usual tricks of muddying a simple revenge yarn with a complex narrative structure and a welter of psycho-babble, and AIP re-edited the whole film, making it even more incomprehensible in the process. An intriguing premise was buried beneath a hack-job that no one but the most avid devotee of art-house horror could make any sense out of, and the Poe series which had begun so spectacularly for AIP some eleven years earlier came to a confused and ignominious end.

After the failure of *Murders in the Rue Morgue*, 'Deke' Heyward resigned from his post as head of AIP's London office and returned to Hollywood, where he produced a television game show called *Tic Tac Dough* and cartoons for Hanna-Barbera. The closest that he came to making another horror film was a role as executive on US TV's *KISS Meets the Phantom of the Park* (1978).

American International closed its British division and re-sited production closer to home. The later 1970s brought major change to the company, and difficult challenges in a brave new world of American films, when big-budget blockbusters like *Jaws* (1975) and *Star Wars* (1977) saw Hollywood's 'Big 5' studios conspire to beat low-budget indie filmmakers at their own game.

Foxy Brown (Pam Grier) / INSET: The changing face of American International through the 1960s and '70s

8 BLAXPLOITATION

EXPLOITATION MEETS RACIAL EQUALITY

When James H Nicholson left AIP, the company was profoundly changed. Nicholson had been the creative force, whereas Sam Arkoff was more interested in the financial side of things. According to the trade publications of the time, Nicholson left because he wanted to make his own independent productions; AIP had become, to his way of thinking, a victim of its own success–growing far beyond his wildest dreams–and there was little scope for him to make his own, more 'personal' films.

The truth was more complex. In 1964, Nicholson and his wife Sylvia had filed for divorce. In the view of the press, Sylvia was the innocent spouse and 'victim' of Nicholson's philandering with starlet Susan Hart. The divorce settlement essentially took Nicholson's power at AIP away from him. The AIP stock was divided piecemeal: Nicholson and Sylvia each received 172,500 of the company's shares, which left Arkoff as the principal shareholder. Arkoff was made Chairman of the Board, and his name now appeared above Nicholson's in the credits of their films. Staff were hired and fired and projects greenlit without Nicholson's approval. Nicholson finally decided to leave and let Sam Arkoff run everything himself, which he pretty much was already doing anyway.

Nicholson left AIP in 1972 and went over to 20th Century-Fox, which offered him a six-picture deal. Only one film was made–the well-received *The Legend of Hell House* (1973) based on a novel by Nicholson's old friend Richard Matheson and directed by John Hough. Before it was even released, Jim Nicholson was dead. He had suffered a seizure while dining in a restaurant; the waitress had urged his wife to get him to a hospital, fast. Not long after, he died of a malignant brain tumour, leaving second wife, Susan Hart, a widow. He was 56 years old.

***The Legend of Hell House* (Pamela Franklin) / LEFT: James H Nicholson**

Years later, Arkoff told Mark Thomas McGee: 'Once Jim left, it changed AIP. And I didn't really realise it for years. Jim and I used to have lunch at least four days a week. And we'd spend a couple of hours a day, generally, together, planning this and that, so on and so forth. We were equals... he could have come back and made pictures for us any time he wanted to. Actually, he was offered a deal at Fox which was probably a little better than I could have afforded, but he could have come back.'

AIP was not the same company after Nicholson's departure. Arkoff did not have the same love for horror and sci-fi as his partner and he felt that horror, in particular, was *passé* by 1972. It was during this time that Arkoff began to look for the next Big Thing in exploitation–and he found it in a movie called *Shaft*, starring black actor Richard Roundtree in the role of a private eye in Harlem. *Shaft*, with its best-selling soundtrack by Isaac Hayes, was one of only three profitable films for M-G-M that year, grossing $13 million on a budget of $500,000.

Variety credited *Shaft* and director Melvin Van Peebles's *Sweet Sweetback's Baadasssss Song* as the first of the so-called 'blaxploitation' films, in which predominately black casts featured in genre films which previously had been the province of white actors and filmmakers. The films also made use of soul and funk soundtracks and were initially designed to appeal mainly to urban black audiences. But that appeal soon broadened to white audiences as well. (The term 'blaxploitation' was coined by former film publicist Junius Griffin, head of the Los Angeles branch of the National Association for the Advancement of Coloured People [NAACP].)

Since the 1950s, AIP had been at the vanguard of every new trend, and Arkoff wanted in on this new black action. AIP's first blaxploitation film was *Slaughter* (1972), which was made on a budget of $750,000 and featured one-time football star Jim Brown in the role of an ex-Green

***Slaughter* (Stella Stevens, Jim Brown)**

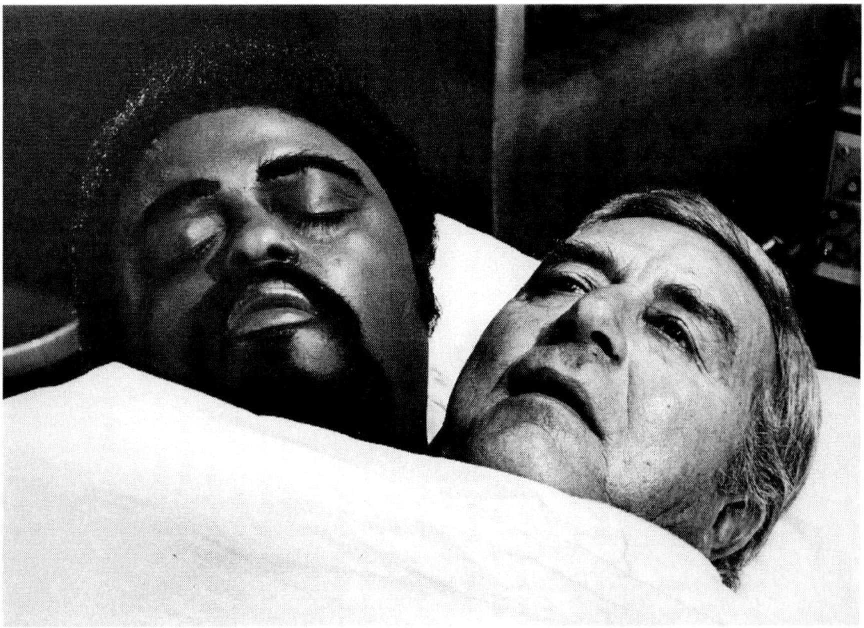

The Thing With Two Heads (Roosevelt Grier, Ray Milland)

Beret who avenges the killing of his family by the Mafia and is then leaned on by the Treasury Department to hunt down and capture an escaped mobster in Mexico. In addition to Brown, the film starred A-lister Stella Stevens, a veteran of the likes of *The Nutty Professor* (1963), *The Silencers* (1966) and *The Ballad of Cable Hogue* (1970), and the villain was played by Rip Torn, who made his feature debut for Elia Kazan in *Baby Doll* (1956). Directed by Jack Starrett, who had helmed *The Born Losers* for AIP, *Slaughter* was filmed mostly in Mexico City. In an interview for *Hollywood Reporter*'s May 2 issue, producer Monroe Sachson revealed that the location of the story had to be changed to a non-Mexican setting, as the Mexican censorship board objected to 'any reference to their country if it shows it in any bad light.' This was despite the fact that the film was co-produced by the Mexican company Estudios Churubusco, which put up one third of the film's budget, with the rest of the money coming from Sachson and AIP.

Thanks to Starrett's flair for action scenes and pro-footballer Brown's popularity with audiences, *Slaughter* was a hit for AIP and began its own cycle of blaxploitation movies. The theme song, written and performed by singer-songwriter Billy Preston, also scored and gave the film its own original sound to compete with that of Hayes's track for *Shaft*. Although Brown had already appeared in several Hollywood films, starting with the western *Rio Conchos* (1964), *Slaughter* was his first starring vehicle. He went on to become one of the biggest actors in the blaxploitation field, appearing with the equally well-liked Fred Williamson in *Three the Hard Way* (1974) and the Italian-American western *Take a Hard Ride* (1975).

In some respects, AIP had already tested the waters of blaxploitation with its comedy-horror film *The Thing With Two Heads* (1972), in which the head of a white bigot (Ray Milland, who was also in the ecological horror thriller *Frogs* for AIP the same year) is transplanted onto the body of a black man (Roosevelt Grier), causing no end of conflict between the 'heads'. That movie was also a success, but for its next blaxploitation offering, AIP took inspiration from the Yorga franchise.

Vampire films were still box office in the early seventies, so Arkoff commissioned

Blacula (William Marshall)

the first 'black vampire film', *Blacula,* in early 1972. The outrageous concept (not to mention title) ensured that AIP would have another hit on its hands. Written by Raymond Koenig and Joan Torres, *Blacula* featured a cast and crew who had extensive backgrounds in both film and television: director William Crain had helmed episodes of TV series *The Mod Squad*, and in support were Vonetta McGee (*Hammer,* 1972), Denise Nicholas *(In the Heat of the Night,* 1968), soap opera veteran Thalmus Rasulala and ubiquitous character actor Elisha Cook Jr, who had appeared in everything from John Huston's *The Maltese Falcon* (1941) to William Castle's *House on Haunted Hill* (1958).

The character of Blacula himself (who is referred to as such only once in the film) was played by the distinguished African-American actor William Marshall, the first black actor to portray a vampire in cinema. A veteran of both stage and television, Marshall, with his commanding voice and imposing stature, proved ideal for the role of Mamuwalde, an African prince who is bitten by Count Dracula (Charles Macaulay) and transformed into a vampire. In the original script, Marshall's character was called Andrew Brown but Marshall worked with the producers to ensure that he would be given a more racially-dignified background; the name was changed to Mamuwalde, the *Roots*-orientated association being designed to appeal to black audiences. He was yet another oppressed victim of 'The Man', but 'The Man' in this case was Count Dracula!

Blacula was produced between January and March, and though Arkoff felt the horror cycle had pretty much run its course, he nevertheless banked on the fact that urban audiences would go for a black-themed horror film–and he was right.

Prior to the release of *Blacula,* AIP's marketing department put out pre-release posters which made reference to slavery. The company also held special promotional screenings of the film in New York, in which anyone wearing a long, flowing cape would be granted free admission.

Blacula (William Marshall, Denise Nicholas)

Released in August 1972, *Blacula* was an immediate hit and it began a whole cycle of black-themed horror films, including *Blackenstein* (1973), a black version of *The Exorcist* entitled *Abby* (1974), a voodoo thriller called *Sugar Hill* (also 1974) starring Robert Quarry, and *Dr Black, Mr Hyde* (1975). The plot of *Blacula* parallels that of Hammer's own update, *Dracula AD 1972:* a centuries-old African prince, who is now a vampire, finds himself in modern-day Los Angeles, much as Christopher Lee's Count Dracula found himself in contemporary London that same year. The rest of the scenario is much as expected, but with different cultural references.

Viewed today, *Blacula* is hopelessly dated, from its stereotypical gay antiques dealer who inadvertently releases Blacula from his centuries-old sleep, to the 'jive' dialogue and the hairstyles and costumes. The only thing that holds it together is Marshall himself, dominating the screen whenever he appears, which is not often enough. Crain's direction is flat, but the film retains a certain charm despite itself. The underlying theme of oppression of the black race (Mamuwalde visits Dracula in Transylvania to seek his help in ending the slave trade) is never developed, as the plot has little more on its mind than titillating its audience. But on that simple level, it succeeds reasonably well.

AIP's next effort starring a black lead was an important one for the company, and the genre. *Black Mama White Mama* (1973) was essentially an unofficial remake of Stanley Kramer's *The Defiant Ones* (1958), which had starred Tony Curtis and Sidney Poitier as two escaped prisoners–one white, one black–who are shackled together and must cooperate with each other to survive. *Black Mama White Mama* took this concept and made it more exploitive: this time, the escapees were *women*.

Margaret Markov, a film and TV actress who had a supporting role in the Liza Minnelli drama *The Sterile Cuckoo* (1969), played the white half of the pair. But it was the 'Black Mama' who would become a star of blaxploitation films, and her name was Pam Grier.

Born in North Carolina, Grier was the child of a Tech Sergeant in the US Air Force which meant that she was moved around a lot, including time spent in England. In 1967, when she was 18, Grier relocated to Los Angeles where she was hired by AIP as a receptionist. Her looks immediately attracted attention and she was asked by an agent if she had thought about becoming an actress. As a result, she was introduced to Roger Corman and director Jack Hill at New World Pictures, who were casting for another 'women in prison' movie to be shot in the Philippines, called *The Big Doll House* (1971). Up to that point, her only appearance in a film had been as an extra in Russ Meyer's X-rated extravaganza *Beyond the Valley of the Dolls* (1970), but she went to the audition and was given the role.

As she wrote in her autobiography, *Foxy: My Life in Three Acts,* Grier took her first starring role very seriously: 'I had no concept of A, B or C movies. A movie was a movie and I intended to deliver an A performance, no matter what anybody else did. I analysed each of my lines, why I was saying certain things, and I kept my acting goals in mind. I even sang the theme song for the film when they discovered I had a good singing voice.'

***Black Mama White Mama* (Pam Grier, Margaret Markov)**

Grier's work ethic saw to it that she would be remembered long after her co-stars–more interested in partying–were forgotten. She immediately signed for a second film for New World, *Women in Cages* (1971). She recalled, '...I played a similar role to the first–an American woman in prison in a foreign country with a sadistic female guard. For this role, my wardrobe was pretty similar to what I wore in the first movie–a long T-shirt, a bra and a pair of underpants. They sure weren't losing any money on costumes.' (Grier's statuesque form–5'8" tall, with vital statistics of 40-28-40–ensured that producers were constantly thinking up ways for her to undress in their films.)

Black Mama White Mama, directed by Eddie Romero and co-produced by one-time AIP 'teen' star John Ashley, was the company at its most exploitive. Granted, film censorship had practically conceded defeat by this time, especially

CHICKS IN CHAINS
-where they come from
this is...
FUN!
BLACK
MAMA
WHITE
MAMA
our associates, ltd. presents
an american international release
"BLACK MAMA, WHITE MAMA" · starring margaret markov · pam grier
R
RESTRICTED

in America's big cities, where hardcore porn films like *Deep Throat* were being shown openly in public cinemas, but *Black Mama White Mama* went further along the road of sexploitation than AIP had ever dared before, earning what came to be called a 'hard R' rating. Nudity, sex scenes, masturbation, a woman tortured with electric wires taped to her breasts, and other eye-opening situations were included in the scenario, co-written by Jonathan Demme, who would go on to direct *The Silence of the Lambs* (1991). Needless to say, Grier stripped to her waist on several occasions.

After starring in several movies for Corman and *Black Mama White Mama* for AIP, Grier got her breakthrough role in blaxploitation thriller *Coffy* (1973) for AIP's new head of production, Larry Gordon. She wrote: 'I was hired for a role where I finally made some real money. It was the part of a woman named Coffy in a movie of the same name, which had originally been written for a white woman. She had turned it down, however, because she was not willing to do her own stunts, since stunt work can be so dangerous.

'Very few actresses were willing or capable of performing stunts. I didn't blame them, but this was where I got singled out. Unafraid, I was a natural adventurer and stunt person as I rode horses and motorcycles and jumped off of buildings into nets. If you needed a woman of colour to handle a gun, do a wheelie on a chopper or fall off a cliff into a rice paddy, I was the one to call. Push me out of a plane, throw me into a fire, I was ready. It all excited me, and I loved the challenge.'

And so it was that Pam Grier became the first female action star in the movies, black or white. There had never been a woman of either race who had top-lined an action film, performed her own stunts and could act into the bargain; Grier suddenly became one of AIP's–and the blaxploitation genre's–biggest stars.

Coffy (Pam Grier)

Coffy is a violent 'revenger', again directed by Jack Hill, which starts with Grier blowing a man's head off with a shotgun–and that comes before the opening credits. Coffy is a nurse who becomes a vigilante when drug dealers turn her sister into a junkie who has to be placed in rehab, and Grier is memorable as the avenging angel who takes to the streets with any weapon that she can find to bring the dealers to (her own brand of rough) justice.

Hill also made sure to show Grier stepping out of her clothes at every opportunity, and she had no problem with that, as she related in her autobiography: 'When it came time for me to show up in a bra and panties for my role in *Coffy*, I was willing to do that too. My stay in Europe had opened me up, but there was a debate about what to do when I had a Janet Jackson-style wardrobe malfunction. A strap

on my black and white polka-dot dress broke, and I was so into the scene that I was unaware that I had bared my nipple. Since it had occurred on its own, not planned, I was all for leaving it in. Why would people be afraid of a nipple?'

Grier's commanding performance in the film made her an icon. When *Coffy* was released in June 1973, it was an instant sensation on the drive-in circuit, ultimately earning over $4 million. *Chicago Sun-Times*' critic Roger Ebert lavished praise on it: '*Coffy* is a marriage between a soft-core skin flick and a blaxploitation movie, with a couple of new twists: 1) it's against drugs and 2) it has a girl for a hero. She is a young actress of beautiful face and astonishing form... but she also has a kind of physical life to her that is sometimes missing in beautiful actresses. She doesn't seem to be posing or doing the fashion-model bit; she gets into an action role and does it right. And she has great cleavage, too.'

Before *Coffy* had even been released, Grier had segued neatly into *Scream Blacula Scream*, the sequel to *Blacula,* again starring William Marshall in the title role. In this almost-instant follow-up, the vampire Mamuwalde, aka Blacula, is revived by African voodoo and returns to love and kill again. Grier plays Lisa, the object of his affections and, as directed by Bob Kelljan (who had helmed both *Count Yorga* films), *Scream Blacula Scream* evidenced a more assured approach to its subject than the original film had shown. Released a mere two weeks after *Coffy, Scream Blacula Scream* assured Grier maximum exposure (of the screen variety; the film was rated PG in the States although it gained the usual X certificate [with cuts] in the UK) and kept audiences aware of her, even though it made less than its predecessor.

Writing in *The New York Times*, Roger Greenspun was lukewarm: 'The director, Bob Kelljan, has at least the shadow of an idea—that the vampire's curse really is a curse, all pain and no pleasure, and is as miserable for the vampire as for his victim. In William Marshall (Mamuwalde) and Pam Grier (Lisa) he has two good performers—powerful, ironic, potentially rather complicated. But he hasn't enough for them to do.

Scream Blacula Scream

It is as if the movie had completed filming without their ever having developed the shooting script. But I'll bet there will be another chance for Blacula.' In that, he was mistaken; there were no more Blacula sequels.

Despite the voluptuous presence of Grier, AIP did not ignore the more *macho* aspects of blaxploitation, and their next effort in the genre was a sequel to *Slaughter* called *Slaughter's Big Rip-Off* (1973), the title itself a rip-off of the sequel to *Shaft*–*Shaft's Big Score*–which had returned Richard Roundtree to the role. *Slaughter's Big Rip-Off* did the same for Jim Brown and was directed, surprisingly perhaps, by Gordon Douglas, who had helmed the classic sci-fi movie *Them!* for Warner Bros in 1954. More recently, Douglas had directed Frank Sinatra in the gritty crime drama *The Detective* and he attempted to bring the same approach to *Slaughter's Big Rip-Off*. Unfortunately, it did not quite come off and aside from the genuinely startling car stunt and a scene in which Brown pushes Don Stroud's head through a car window, scalping him in the process, the film was a mostly routine actioner, not helped by some odd casting choices. Even the James Brown score was forgettable, and *Slaughter's Big Rip-Off* failed to generate further sequels.

Meanwhile, AIP made use of the talents of Fred Williamson, another ex-football player who had taken up an acting career in films such as Robert Altman's *MASH* and Otto Preminger's *Tell Me That You Love Me, Junie Moon*. AIP handed him the lead role in *Black Caesar* (1973), a remake of the 1931 Edward G Robinson starrer *Little Caesar*. The film was written and directed by Larry Cohen, who had conceived *Black Caesar* with singer and actor Sammy Davis Jr in mind, but after the phenomenal success of *Shaft*, he had retooled the script for Williamson.

Cohen had previously directed a feature called *Bone* (1972), starring African-American actor Yaphet Kotto, and he would become better known through his quirky horror film, *It's Alive* (1974). His sure directorial hand is evident in *Black Caesar*'s brisk running time of 87 minutes. Williamson played Tommy Gibbs, a child of the ghetto, whose goal is to be an underworld kingpin. Full of anger at the racism that he sees in all stratas of society, he decides that power is the only thing that will quell his frustration. After enacting a high-profile 'hit', he is accepted into a Mob family, whereupon his arrogance leads him into a gang war.

Williamson proved himself to be a more powerful actor than Brown ever was, and he dominates the film. Cohen punctuates the drama with bouts of violence, in much the same way as Francis Ford Coppola did in *The Godfather* the previous year and, as a result, *Black Caesar* transcended the limitations of the blaxploitation genre with its authentic sense of time and place and above-average performances.

Although *The New York Times*'s review mostly dismissed the film as 'black bad guys against white bad guys', its critic gave full marks to Williamson nonetheless, noting, 'Mr Williamson, who led the slave revolt in the recent *The Legend of Nigger*

Slaughter's Big Rip-Off / BELOW: *Black Caesar*

Charley, this time is equally imposing, tough and unflappable–if not as dignified–as the "Black Caesar", who seems to be subject to some of the shocks as well as the fate of the original Caesar.' *Black Caesar* was well-enough received to spawn a sequel, again directed by Cohen, called *Hell Up in Harlem* (1973).

Hell Up in Harlem

Sugar Hill was another blaxploitation/horror hybrid–an odd little film shot on location in Houston, Texas. Directed by Paul Maslansky, who had produced both of Michael Reeves's first features (*Castle of the Living Dead* and *Revenge of the Blood Beast*), as well as the British cult-item *Death Line* (aka *Raw Meat*); *Sugar Hill* is his only directorial credit to date.

***Sugar Hill* (Marki Bey)**

The film was a simple revenge fantasy in which Diana 'Sugar' Hill (Marki Bey), with the help of 'Lord of the Dead' Baron Samedi (Don Pedro Colley) and his army of zombies, uses voodoo to avenge herself on the gangsters responsible for her boyfriend's death. The zombies themselves are the corpses of slaves brought to America from Guinea, which gives the plot its blaxploitation twist, but they are also over-the-top creations, complete with bulging eyeballs and costumes festooned in grave dirt and cobwebs. Unlike the zombies of George Romero's revisionist *Night of the Living Dead,* these undead were throwbacks to the original walking dead-men of classics such as *White Zombie* (1932) and *I Walked With a Zombie* (1943), not the cannibalistic monsters of modern myth.

Bey acquits herself well in a role which

could easily have been written for Pam Grier, although she has neither Grier's physical prowess nor her acting chops, taking brutal revenge upon the mobsters, one by one. The head gangster (Robert Quarry) is saved for last, of course, and meets his maker when all the zombies converge upon him. This was Quarry's final role for AIP–one that he was contracted to do against his wishes (after which he disappeared back into the relative obscurity from which *Count Yorga, Vampire* had rescued him)–but he makes the most of a token character, camping it up with an acid tongue and an ersatz Southern accent.

Colley's portrayal of Baron Samedi was clearly inspired by Geoffrey Holder's fey turn in the previous year's James Bond outing, *Live and Let Die*. The baron pops up in various guises throughout the film, including that of a bartender in a nightclub: 'Perhaps a drink on the house, sir. My particular special–a drink that I'm famous for: the Zombie!'

In the years since, *Sugar Hill* has gained something of a cult following among horror and blaxploitation fans for its refusal to take itself seriously, and it remains one of AIP's more agreeable blaxploitation offerings.

Meanwhile, Grier herself continued her ascent up the short but spectacular ladder of blaxploitation fame with *Foxy Brown*, as she recalled in her autobiography: '*Foxy Brown* (was) an action/adventure film about a sexy black woman who seeks revenge when her government agent boyfriend is shot down by gangsters. Jack Hill, my old friend, was the director, and I understood the role since Foxy Brown was a fighter and so was I. While my role in *Coffy* had reminded me of my mother, a nurse who

stood up for herself, Foxy Brown was my aunt Mennon, who had a bad temper and was quick to pick a fight.'

Even by the standards of the genre, *Foxy Brown* is a brutal film. Grier plays the title character, described by her screen brother (Antonio Fargas) as 'a whole lot of woman'. We never quite learn what Foxy's background is, but when her boyfriend is murdered by mobsters, she takes on the role of a high-class hooker so that she can infiltrate their 'family' and take revenge. *Foxy Brown* was originally conceived as a sequel to *Coffy* but AIP decided that it would rather feature an original character than have Coffy return. There was no time to do a script rewrite, so it is never established what Foxy actually does for a living.

What she did for a killing was plain to see, however. During the course of the film, Foxy immolates a couple of gangsters who have drugged and raped her, shoots several people and pilots a plane on a runway at one of the mobsters, cutting him to pieces with its propeller. For the *pièce de résistance,* she orchestrates the castration of the gang-leader and presents his severed member to his girlfriend in a pickle jar. In the process, *Foxy Brown* earned itself a 'hard R' rating thanks to Hill pulling out all the stops in terms of violence, sex and foul language, and Grier dominates the film as a veritable angel of death.

Foxy Brown

Grier's three-picture deal with AIP culminated in *Sheba, Baby* (1975), in which she played a Chicago private detective who returns to her home in Louisville to help her father battle the Mob. By this time, however, the blaxploitation field was running out of steam, a victim of its own success and the sheer repetition of its plot lines.

The genre was also controversial; some said that it was a trend born of 'black power', while others held that it merely reinforced white stereotyping of blacks as pimps, hookers, drug-dealers and thugs. The NAACP, Southern Christian Leadership Conference and National Urban League joined forces to form the Coalition Against Blaxploitation to bring about an end to the genre.

The Coalition asked AIP's vice president, Richard Zimbert, if any of the profits from its blaxploitation films were being put into black banks. It also wanted to know if any African-Americans had been hired to work behind the camera, as most of the blaxploitation movies from mainstream studios had white producers and directors. Zimbert responded, 'We've got black publicists. We've got black people all throughout the country. We advertise in black media. *Blacula* had an all black cast, a black director.' Someone–whether from the Coalition or not is unknown–was less than placated by Zimbert's explanation and his car was torched; fortunately, he was not in it at the time. Junius Griffin, the head of the Coalition, assured him, 'I disavow it and will not condone it. You cannot preach against violence and actually partake in it yourself.'

Despite the controversy, blaxploitation was a spent force by 1976. Grier made one more film for AIP, *Friday Foster* (1975), before moving on to other things. It was the mixture as before: sex, violence, foul language... though with a better than average supporting cast of Carl Weathers, Eartha Kitt, Paul Benjamin and Yaphet Kotto. But AIP was flogging a dead horse.

Grier gave full marks to AIP for advancing her career, as she told Mark Thomas McGee: 'Sam (Arkoff) gave me my biggest break. People always ask if I had to go the casting couch route with him and I say with Sam Arkoff there is no such thing as a casting couch.'

For all its 1970s trendiness, the blaxploitation genre was at heart an old-style school of filmmaking: the studios, AIP included, were merely making conventional gangster and horror films dressed in blackface. The movies were rough around the edges but, in essence, they were throwbacks to a studio system in which stars were made and the public was given what it wanted. In retrospect, it seems more as though the (mostly) white producers, writers and directors were still exploiting the very people whom they were supposed to be empowering. Blaxploitation was, ultimately, Hollywood hypocrisy at its most blatant.

9

LOSING TOUCH

THROUGH MAINSTREAM TO MERGER

On November 29, 1974, an article appeared in the *Hollywood Reporter* in which Sam Arkoff claimed, 'American International is on the threshold of the highest level of motion picture production and distribution in its history... We will make available to exhibitors an average of one film a week, year round. Timing of a release is also a critical matter. If producers and exhibitors will remain as flexible as possible we are able to properly polish our product before offering it to the public. And we can slant our publicity, advertising and promotion to peak at the most advantageous moment.'

At the time, AIP was moving in the direction of attempting to compete with the majors, something that Arkoff had wanted to do since at least the late sixties. And some headway was being made; in addition to its higher-profile blaxploitation films, which all the majors had emulated, AIP had released such cutting-edge offerings as Brian De Palma's *Sisters* (1973), which had gained both critical acclaim and box office success, with De Palma being hailed as 'the new Hitchcock'.

Known as *Blood Sisters* in the UK, De Palma's film was 'cutting-edge' in more ways than one. Its shocking gore reached a new level for American horror films, and its sub-text and dark themes were genuinely disturbing. De Palma was a student of Hitchcock, and *Sisters* owes more to The Master than any non-Hitchcock film made up to that time. The screenplay was written by De Palma and Louisa Rose, and he even persuaded Hitchcock composer Bernard Herrmann to write the score.

De Palma, a former physics student-turned-filmmaker, had already made several movies–*The Wedding Party* with a young Robert De Niro (shot in 1963 but unreleased until 1969), *Greetings* (1968), *Hi, Mom!* (1970, again with De Niro), and a comedy

Sisters (Margot Kidder)

called *Get to Know Your Rabbit* (1972)–when he came across an item on Siamese twins Masha and Dasha Krivoshlyapova, who were literally inseparable and underwent years of cruel experiments in Russian institutions. From this, the germ of an idea was born and De Palma combined it with elements from *Psycho* and *Rear Window* to create *Sisters,* which upped the ante in violence to a level far beyond where Hitchcock had dared to go. The film also employed modish cinematic techniques like POV and split-screen to increase tension.

The story deals with the brutal murder of a salesman, which is witnessed by a journalist from a neighbouring apartment. The police do not believe that the crime ever took place because they cannot find a body. With the help of a private detective, the journalist attempts to solve the case, with all the clues pointing to Margot Kidder as one of (possibly) two sisters.

With a story construct akin to that of *Psycho* (the character who appears to be the protagonist is killed in the first act) and a theme of voyeurism similar to that in *Rear Window, Sisters* was a heady brew. One character is stabbed repeatedly, including in the mouth, and the 'evil' sister castrates her guardian after a hallucinatory sequence

***Sisters* (William Finley, Margot Kidder)**

to rival those in Roman Polanski's *Repulsion* (1965). Embellished with Herrmann's unsettling score, *Sisters* remains one of De Palma's most assured films and it received the kind of reviews that AIP previously could only have dreamed of. In the *Chicago Sun Times,* Roger Ebert wrote: 'The movie begins with events so commonplace they're almost trivial, and the horror of the situation is revealed only gradually... De Palma directs with a nice feeling for the incongruous.' In *The New York Times,* Vincent Canby opined, 'The performances are fine, especially Miss Kidder's as the loony twin whom we first meet when she's doing a walk-on on a popular television quiz show called *Peeping Toms* which, like so many of Mr De Palma's comic fancies, is just terrible enough to become a reality. An intelligent horror film is very rare these days...'

Sisters put Brian De Palma firmly on the map, and AIP also discovered the likes of John Milius (who helmed *Dillinger* for the company) and Martin Scorsese, who cut his directorial teeth on another tale of the Great Depression, *Boxcar Bertha.*

In 1974, the company picked up another indie in *Macon County Line,* an action movie set in the American South which was made for $225,000. In terms of cost to gross, it became the most profitable film of 1974, bringing in $18.8 million in the US and over $30 million worldwide.

Macon County Line was one of several Southern-set movies that purported to be based on actual events, along with Charles B Pierce's *The Legend of Boggy Creek* (1972) and Tobe Hooper's *The Texas Chain Saw Massacre* (1974). In the case of *Macon County Line,* producer Max Baer Jr and director Richard Compton admitted that the entire script was fictional but the film was such a success that Arkoff became executive producer on the follow-up, *Return to Macon County* (1975), starring Nick Nolte and Don Johnson (prior to his TV success in *Miami Vice*).

It seemed as though all was going swimmingly for AIP, but the film business was changing rapidly in the mid-1970s. Steven Spielberg's *Jaws* was released in the summer of 1975 and became a phenomenon which had the same impact on action filmmaking as *The Exorcist* did on horror two years before. The major studios were now making the same kinds of genre movies as AIP, and the company had to pour more and more money into its productions to compete. Arkoff remained optimistic: 'We have come of age and we are in the position to take on all comers!' he announced in 1975. As if to nail the point home, AIP released *Walking Tall Part 2*, the sequel to Cinerama's sleeper hit of 1973. Bo Svenson stood in for the original's Joe Don Baker as Sheriff Buford Pusser, but *Walking Tall Part 2* still provided a hit for AIP.

Arkoff figured that there was more money to be had in them thar Southern-fried actioners and in 1976, AIP released *Bobbie Jo and the Outlaw,* starring future TV *Wonder Woman* Lynda Carter, heavily promoting the fact that she appeared nude in the film–the only time that she ever did so. Co-starring was preacher-turned-actor Marjoe Gortner. Directed by Mark L Lester, *Bobbie Jo and the Outlaw* did very well on the drive-in circuit.

Gortner starred again for AIP in *The Food of the Gods* (1976), a loose adaptation of the novel by HG Wells. The surprising thing about the film was that it was written, directed and produced by Bert I Gordon, who had not made a film for AIP since 1958 when he felt that he was not being paid what he was owed. With an interesting cast including Pamela Franklin, Ralph Meeker, Ida Lupino and Belinda Belaski, *The Food of the Gods* manages to waste their talents in a hackneyed 'nature strikes back' tale along the lines of AIP's *Frogs* (1972), a bizarre tale of a nature-hating patriarch (Ray Milland) who gets his comeuppance in the form of a revolt by lizards, snakes and, yes, frogs. It is often considered to be one of the worst horror films of all time, although Milland (in his last film for the company) brings a certain gravitas.

Despite its many deficiencies, *The Food of the Gods* became the company's most

The Food of the Gods

successful release of the year and Gordon was put on notice to provide a follow-up, which he did with *Empire of the Ants.* AIP also released a comedy western called *The Great Scout & Cathouse Thursday* (1976), with Lee Marvin, Oliver Reed and Robert Culp, and directed by Don Taylor, but it found little success.

In the summer of 1976, AIP picked up the British production *I Don't Want to be Born,* retitling it *The Devil Within Her* to capitalise on the current trend for 'Devil' movies in the wake of Richard Donner's hugely successful *The Omen.* Despite a game cast including Joan Collins and Donald Pleasence, audiences thought it risible and it died a quick death. The company soldiered on that summer with *A Small Town in Texas,* another 'redneck' movie directed by Jack Starrett. Again, a drive-in hit, but AIP's attempts to compete with the majors were bringing mixed results at best.

Arkoff put more money into *Futureworld* (1976), a sequel to M-G-M's successful

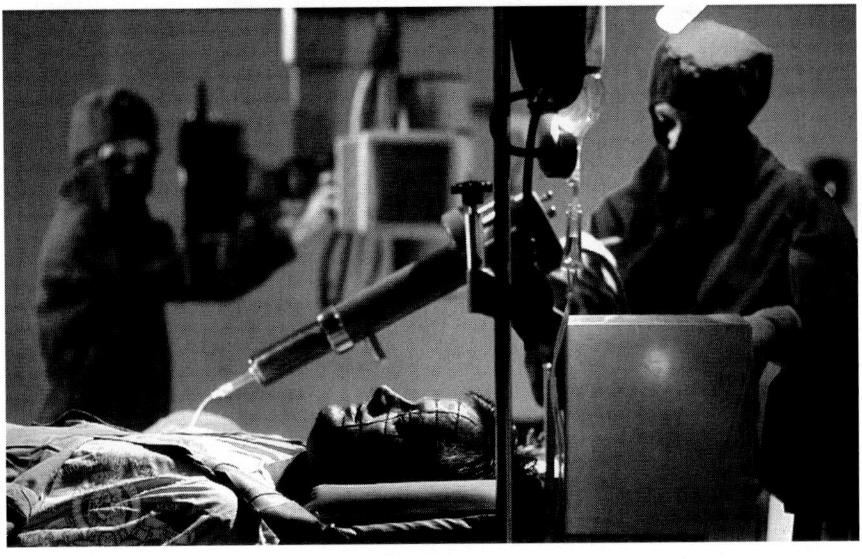

Futureworld

Shout at the Devil

Westworld (1973), which had starred Yul Brynner. *Futureworld* starred Peter Fonda and Blythe Danner (with a cameo by Brynner) but it was nowhere near as good as the original and a review in *The New York Times* quoted a line from the movie: 'This is about as exciting as a visit to the water works.' The sequel had been developed by M-G-M but it had opted to make *Logan's Run* (1976) instead and put *Futureworld* into 'turnaround', whereupon it was picked up by AIP. It did have the distinction of being the first feature film to utilise computer-generated imagery for an animation sequence, however.

In 1976, AIP co-financed *Shout at the Devil,* a pre-First World War adventure directed by Peter Hunt *(On Her Majesty's Secret Service,* 1969) and starring Lee Marvin and Roger Moore. According to producer Michael Klinger, $3.5m of its $10m budget was provided by AIP–a huge sum for the studio–and the film was shot on location in Malta and South Africa. But *Shout at the Devil* made little impact. Critic Roger Ebert called it a 'big, dumb, silly movie that's impossible to dislike,' though audiences did not appear to agree with him.

A more successful movie in 1976 was Charles B Pierce's *The Town That Dreaded Sundown,* a thriller based on a series of murders committed in Texarkana in 1946. Starring Ben Johnson and Andrew Prine, the film was stolidly directed but the claim that it was true sold it to the public and it became a substantial hit for AIP, despite a number of lawsuits against the makers that followed its release. Much 'fact' was in fact fiction, but the scenario at least dared to follow the real-life case in not revealing the identity of the 'Phantom killer', who was never caught.

AIP dipped into sexploitation with a film called *Chatterbox* (aka *Virginia the Talking Vagina,* 1977). The *Los Angeles Times's* review was typical: 'The film's vulgar premise smacks of smirking adolescents... the movie is a male masturbatory fantasy.' The 'porno chic' which had begun with *Deep Throat* in the early seventies was now starting to wane, and *Chatterbox* found itself out of both time and favour.

'CB' (Citizens' Band) radio was a big craze in the US at this time, which led AIP to make a road movie called *Breaker! Breaker!* (1977), starring martial arts expert Chuck Norris in his first leading role. Norris played a trucker in search of his brother, who has disappeared in a Texas town run by a corrupt judge. *Breaker! Breaker!* fitted nicely into AIP's 'redneck' stream and also cleaned up at the drive-ins.

Empire of the Ants

Arkoff still felt that mainstream production was the future for AIP and following Bert Gordon's *Empire of the Ants* (1977)–another predictable giant monsters-on-the-loose tale based loosely on a story by HG Wells and starring Joan Collins and Robert Lansing–he decided to go for broke with a big-budget Wells adaptation, *The Island of Dr Moreau*. The all-star cast featured Burt Lancaster, Michael York, Nigel Davenport, Barbara Carrera and Richard Basehart and shooting took place on the US Virgin Islands, *The Island of Dr Moreau* was the second time that filmmakers had adapted Wells's novel (if one discounts Eddie Romero's unofficial take, *Terror Is a Man*, in 1959), the first having been Erle C Kenton's *Island of Lost Souls* (1932), with Charles Laughton and Richard Arlen; the earlier pre-Code version accentuated the horror in Wells's tale of an obsessed vivisectionist who conducts experiments on a remote Pacific island in an attempt to turn animals into humans.

AIP's version was directed by Don Taylor, a former actor (and husband of Hazel Court) who had helmed *Escape From the Planet of the Apes* (1971), the third in the successful sci-fi franchise. *The Island of Dr Moreau* was routinely directed, but the performances of Lancaster (as Moreau) and York as the shipwrecked survivor were earnest and Al Ramrus and John H Shaner's script tried its best to wring a mature moral debate out of Wells's 'essay in youthful blasphemy'. *The Island of Dr Moreau* was a minor hit at the box office, but 1977 was the summer of George Lucas's *Star Wars* and nothing could compete on that level of ballyhoo. Arkoff saw the writing on the wall: now that sci-fi had gone mainstream, he would have to make even bigger films in order to keep his company's head above water.

Ironically, Roger Corman's New World Pictures were making the kinds of films that one might have expected AIP to produce at the time. Horrors such as *God Told Me To* (1976), written and directed by Larry Cohen (who had cut his teeth at AIP on *Black Caesar*), and New World's pickup of David Cronenberg's *Rabid* (1977), with porn legend Marilyn Chambers, were precisely the sort of exploitation fare that AIP had specialised in. But Corman serviced his market more assiduously than Arkoff, and he made and released films that fitted it to a 't'. He was also aware that the

The Little Girl Who Lives Down the Lane (Jodie Foster) / ABOVE: *The Island of Dr Moreau* (Burt Lancaster)

majors were now in the sci-fi and horror fields and by the end of the seventies, he had produced his own *Star Wars* knock-off, *Battle Beyond the Stars*, an outer space remake of Akira Kurosawa's *The Seven Samurai*, starring George Peppard and Richard Thomas.

AIP was in competition not only with the majors but with Corman himself, a monster of a movie mogul whom the company had helped to create. In 1977, AIP picked up *The Little Girl Who Lives Down the Lane,* a Canadian-French production directed by Nicolas Gessner, starring Jodie Foster and Martin Sheen. It was a well-received if somewhat controversial thriller, with Foster as a 13-year-old alone in a small Canadian town and leading a mysterious and dangerous double life. The film was her first starring role after her critically-acclaimed performance in Martin Scorsese's *Taxi Driver* (1976) as a child hooker. The theme of *The Little Girl Who Lives Down the Lane* was similarly paedophilic, with Foster involved with an older man in the story; her real-life sister Connie provided the requisite nude scene.

Despite the controversy, the film won two awards at the American Academy of Science Fiction, Fantasy and Horror Films, for Best Film and Best Actress (Foster), although Janet Maslin, in *The New York Times*, thought it ' a mild-mannered horror movie for people who don't much enjoy being scared' and *Variety* considered it to be '..far-fetched nonsense with little to appease shriek freaks'.

Arkoff's pronounced disdain for 'artsy-fartsy' films notwithstanding, a second critically-acclaimed film was picked up by AIP in 1977–*Rolling Thunder,* starring William Devane and Tommy Lee Jones. Written by Paul Schrader, who had also penned *Taxi Driver, Rolling Thunder* was a powerful drama about a Vietnam 'vet' who returns to his hometown, where he is given a hero's welcome. Some thugs decide to steal the town's gifts to him, murdering his wife and son in the process, and the vet enlists an old army buddy to take his revenge on the killers.

Devane is excellent in the lead role, with Jones also first-rate as his buddy. The film had originally been produced and scheduled for release by 20th Century Fox but a preview in San Jose proved disastrous when the audience turned violent. Producer Larry Gordon recalled: 'The lobby looked like Guadalcanal–which, by the way, is a salesman's dream!' Unfortunately, Fox did not see it that way and demanded cuts. Gordon refused and took the film to AIP, which was only too happy to distribute such a 'hot potato'. *Rolling Thunder* was praised by media critic Gene Siskel, who listed it as one of his ten best films of 1977. (It is also a favourite of director Quentin Tarantino, who named his subsidiary company Rolling Thunder Pictures.)

But good reviews do not pay the bills and AIP continued its line of 'redneck' movies with *Walking Tall: Final Chapter*, again featuring Bo Svenson and directed by Jack Starrett. There was no critical acclaim for this one, however, with Vincent Canby in *The New York Times* referring to it as 'a thin, tired movie even when the screen is awash in blood.' Nevertheless it perfomed well, which was more to Arkoff's taste.

***Rolling Thunder* (William Devane)**

The Incredible Melting Man

The Incredible Melting Man also did well, with production funding provided by Max J Rosenberg, who had been one half of Amicus Productions. The familiar story saw astronaut Alex Rebar transform into a murderous, melting monster after returning from outer space. Times had changed since the fifties and the accent was more on gore than sci-fi (with some gratuitous nudity thrown in for good measure) thanks to Rick Baker's gruesome makeup effects. The film's exploitative theme made it one of AIP's last true 'drive-in' movies.

Larry Cohen returned to AIP the same year with *The Private Files of J Edgar Hoover*, starring Hollywood veteran Broderick Crawford in the title role of the FBI boss. Another attempt at mainstream fare which brought more critical kudos, but it did not exactly set the box office on fire.

The People That Time Forgot was AIP's last British co-production, but Arkoff continued to import foreign films like *El ultimo mondo cannibale* (US: *Cannibal World,* 1977), directed by Ruggero Deodato, and *Holocaust 2000* (1977), a British-Italian co-production starring Kirk Douglas. The latter was a clone of 20th Century Fox's *The Omen* (1976), with Simon Ward as the Antichrist who plans to use his father's nuclear power project to bring about the end of the world. Also known as *The Chosen, Holocaust 2000* was lost in the glut of occult thrillers following in the wake of *The Exorcist* and *The Omen*.

AIP pressed on with *Jennifer,* a blatant rip-off of Brian De Palma's *Carrie,* the social misfit in this instance taking revenge on her schoolmates through her ability to control snakes. With a supporting cast that included Nina Foch, John Gavin and Jeff Corey, *Jennifer* was routinely directed by Bruce Mack.

AIP continued to turn out low-budget movies that appealed to 'urban' audiences, like *Youngblood* (1978), the tale of an African-American teenager who falls in with a Los Angeles street gang. *Here Come the Tigers* (1978), on the other hand, was a rare family film directed by Sean S Cunningham, whose real claim to fame would be the infamous 'slasher' *Friday the 13th* the following year. Lensed by, of all people, Wes Craven, whose directorial efforts had included the even more infamous *The Last House on the Left* (1972), *Here Come the Tigers* was a miscalculation for AIP, as audiences in the late seventies were more interested in Steven Spielberg's *Close Encounters of the Third Kind* (1977) than they were in a family movie about a kids' baseball team.

High-Ballin' was another trucker movie, this time a Canadian import that AIP picked up in part because of its cast, which included Peter Fonda. Shot in and around Toronto, *High-Ballin'* premiered in the city in May 1978 but was not seen in the US until August, when it was given only a limited release before being sold to US television. Either way, it was poorly received, with Clyde Gilmour's review in the *Toronto Star* being typical: 'A popcorn movie, intended to be half-watched while your mind is toying with other matters.' Arkoff tried to go mainstream again with *Matilda*, an ill-conceived comedy about a boxing kangaroo. It featured name actors Elliott Gould, Harry Guardino and Robert Mitchum and it was made for $5.2m, but to no avail. If the thinking was to recreate the success of *Rocky*, then it was sadly mistaken.

AIP also picked up the Spanish horror film *¿Quien puede matar a un niño?* (US: *Who Can Kill a Child?*) about an English couple (Lewis Fiander and Prunella Ransome) who find themselves on an island inhabited by homicidal children. While it did not cause much of a stir at the time, the film, directed by Narciso Ibáñez Serrador, has become a cult item since. In a review on *The New York Times*'s website, Robert Firsching opined, 'Unlike most Spanish shockers, this is not an unintentionally funny melodrama or a sexually-charged exploitation film. It is a serious-minded horror film with a message, based on Juan Jose Plans's novel.'

Mean Dog Blues was another 'prison' picture picked up by AIP, but low-budget action films were becoming increasingly high-risk as the majors got in on the action and poured money into genre movies. AIP attempted to compete by releasing *The Norseman*, a Viking saga with Lee Majors, which went nowhere. More successful was *Force 10 from Navarone*, a sequel to 1961's *The Guns of Navarone* and based on the novel by Alistair MacLean. The leading roles were played by Robert Shaw and Edward

Who Can Kill a Child?

Force 10 From Navarone (Harrison Ford, Robert Shaw)

Fox, and it was directed by Guy Hamilton *(Goldfinger,* 1964); co-starring in it were Harrison Ford and Barbara Bach. *Force 10 from Navarone* was one of AIP's most high-profile films of the era and it was screened at Camp David as the Thanksgiving movie for US President Jimmy Carter. Released in December 1978, to mixed reviews but good box office, the film benefited commercially from the presence of Ford, who had been one of the breakout stars of *Star Wars,* and by a second teaming of Bach and Richard Kiel, who had featured in the third biggest film of 1977, the James Bond adventure *The Spy Who Loved Me*. Hamilton's flair for action gave the sequel some weight, and a brief topless scene for Bach did not exactly hurt business either.

Filmed in Yugoslavia and at Shepperton Studios, *Force 10 from Navarone* was expensive to produce; it cost $5m and grossed $7.2m in the US. Gone were the days of double features, when AIP could turn out two movies for the price of one and make their $200,000 investment back almost overnight.

After releasing *The Evictors*, a Charles B Pierce thriller starring Vic Morrow and Michael Parks, AIP went back to the mainstream with *Love at First Bite*, a horror-comedy intended to cash in on the success of the Broadway revival of *Dracula* with Frank Langella, which would also be turned into a film. The most amusing aspect of *Love at First Bite was* the casting of George Hamilton as Dracula; the man with the world's most famous tan playing a vampire who can never be touched by sunlight is irony itself–but within what was essentially a one-joke movie.

Released in April 1979, *Love at First Bite* was the first of a 'new wave' of vampire films. It was also the most financially successful, thanks in large part to a good cast: Hamilton as the count, Susan St James (from TV's *McMillan and Wife*) as model Cindy Sondheim and the object of his affections, Richard Benjamin as psychiatrist Jeffrey Rosenberg, comedian Dick Shawn as a NYPD detective, and Arte Johnson of *Rowan and Martin's Laugh-In* fame as Renfield.

The plot is promising: Dracula languishes in his castle, mooning over pictures of Sondheim in fashion mags. He and Renfield take off for Manhattan in search of her, so that he can make her his 'bride'. Sondheim's boyfriend is a descendant of Van Helsing, the vampire's arch-enemy, and when he sees the tell-tale marks on Sondheim's neck, he tries to convince the authorities that Dracula is loose...

Love at First Bite was no *Young Frankenstein*, Mel Brooks's hilarious homage to Universal's horror series, but it was a considerable improvement on *Vampira* (US: *Old Dracula*), a painfully unfunny British import that AIP had picked up in 1974. Though not by much; the screenplay by Robert Kaufman never really develops its

***Love at First Bite* (George Hamilton)**

Love at First Bite (*Susan Saint James, George Hamilton*)

premise and Stan Dragoti's direction is graceless; cheap jokes are the order of the day, poking fun at various racial, ethnic and sexual groups. Hamilton does an effective Lugosi impression, but story and direction work against him at every turn, especially when he has to utter banal lines like, 'I don't drink wine and I don't smoke shit.'

It is difficult to argue with success, however, and *Love at First Bite* was a big hit for AIP; good thing too, as the budget was $3 million. It ended up grossing over $43m and ranked number thirteen on the list of top grossing films of 1979.

Even more money was poured into the next big AIP project, an adaptation of Jay Anson's 1977 paranormal non-fiction, *The Amityville Horror*. Anson had based the book on the experiences of the Lutz family, who had moved into a new home in Amityville, New York, in the early 1970s but quickly fled after they were terrified by supposed supernatural events; the house had been the scene of a mass murder some years before and it was thought to be infested by 'demonic' entities.

Arkoff snapped up the rights, sensing another *Exorcist* phenomenon, as the book had become a best-selling sensation. James Brolin was cast as George Lutz, the family patriarch, and the role of Kathy Lutz was given to Margot Kidder, who had become an international star as the result of playing Lois Lane in Richard Donner's *Superman* (1978) but had previously featured for AIP in Brian De Palma's *Sisters*. Rod Steiger was cast as Father Delaney, the exorcising priest in the saga. (Steiger was a specialist in playing offbeat, often psychotic characters and he had won an Oscar in 1967 for his role as a Southern police chief in *In the Heat of the Night*.)

The director chosen for this high-profile project was Stuart Rosenberg, who had made *Cool Hand Luke* (1967) and a number of comedies, including *The April Fools* with Jack Lemmon (1967), but he had never tackled a horror film.

Although Anson submitted a screenplay to AIP, it was rejected in favour of one written by Canadian Sandor Stern, who streamlined things more to Arkoff's liking. Retaining the basic story–in which newlyweds George and Kathy Lutz move into a house in which a teenager had murdered his family and experience strange events which eventually drive them away, *The Amityville Horror* was originally intended

The Amityville Horror

The Amityville Horror (Margot Kidder, James Brolin)

to have been filmed at the 'scene of the crime', the actual house where the haunting allegedly occurred, at Amityville, Long Island. But the townsfolk wanted to dissuade tourists from overrunning their community and denied AIP permission. Instead, the company found a similar-looking Dutch colonial house in Toms River, New Jersey, at which to shoot the exteriors. A third-floor facade was added, as were the iconic 'evil eye' windows so important to the subsequent publicity, and the interiors were filmed at M-G-M Studios in Culver City, California.

On its US release in July of 1979, *The Amityville Horror* was almost as much of a sensation as the novel had been. It had plenty of competition; *Newsweek* was calling it 'Hollywood's Scary Summer', and the cover of its June issue had featured Sigourney Weaver menaced by the title creature of *Alien*. Also in release that summer were John Badham's *Dracula,* with Frank Langella recreating his surprise Broadway hit; George A Romero's *Dawn of the Dead* and Don Coscarelli's sleeper success *Phantasm,* which would spawn several sequels. The current revival in popularity of horror films had really started the previous year with John Carpenter's *Halloween,* which was still playing in many US cinemas.

The Amityville Horror exemplified the trend, despite some scathing reviews. In the *Chicago Sun Times,* Roger Ebert wrote of a 'dreary and terminally depressing series of glum things that happen to the residents of the Ocean Boulevard house... We watch two hours of people being frightened and dismayed, and we ask ourselves... what for?', while in *The New York Times,* Janet Maslin was acerbic: 'So many horror movie clichés have been assembled under the roof of a single haunted house that the effect is sometimes mind-bogglingly messy. There is apparently little to which the director, Stuart Rosenberg, will not resort...'

Maslin ended her review by plugging a tribute to AIP in New York, however: '*The Amityville Horror* opens today at the Cinerama and other theatres. It was also screened at the Museum of Modern Art on Tuesday, to introduce the museum's tribute to the movies made by American International Pictures. The AIP festival will include *The*

Amityville Horror, but it's too lifeless to be on a par with the fast, funny, deliberately slapdash movies that have made AIP a B-movie bastion. This one is a B-minus.' The museun's tribute included such classics as *Panic in Year Zero* and *X-The Man With the X-Ray Eyes.* It was to prove an opportune moment for a celebration of the company's achievements; it would not be around for much longer.

The reviews did little to keep audiences from *The Amityville Horror;* the film made over $86 million in the US alone. One might be forgiven for thinking that AIP had finally joined the Hollywood 'big boys' but, behind the scenes, all was not well. Arkoff was actively considering a merger of the company. As early as October 1978, he had announced, 'We've been the Woolworths of the movie business but Woolworths is being out-priced.'

At the time, Arkoff had commenced in negotiations with Filmways Inc, a company formed by Martin Ransohoff and Edwin Kasper in 1952, which had produced everything from game shows to sitcoms such as *Green Acres, The Beverly Hillbillies* and *Mister Ed* for US television. In the 1960s, it had moved into feature films with the likes of *The Fearless Vampire Killers, Eye of the Devil* and *What's the Matter with Helen?* On March 26, 1979, *Boxoffice* Magazine carried the headline, 'AIP, Filmways Agree to Merger.' In its June 4 edition was a rejoinder: 'Arkoff to Keep Title Despite AI's Merger.' The accompanying article read, in part: 'Samuel Z Arkoff will retain his role of president and chief executive when the pending merger of American International into Filmways takes place... He will reportedly earn an annual salary of $225,000 with cost-of-living increases to be included. Arkoff's five-year contract includes a clause that will allow him to terminate the contract after two years.'

AIP continued to produce and distribute films under its own banner for a few months more. *California Dreaming* was a teen comedy-drama released in 1979 and starring Glynnis O'Connor and Dennis Christopher. It went nowhere. Neither did *Seven* (1979), an action adventure directed by Andy Sidaris and starring William Smith and Barbara Leigh. *Something Short of Paradise,* another rom-com, was also short of successful, despite a cast that included Susan Sarandon.

Meteor (*Natalie Wood / ABOVE: Sean Connery, Karl Malden*)

AIP had pinned more of its hopes (and a $16m budget) on Ronald Neame's *Meteor,* released in October and starring Sean Connery, Natalie Wood, Karl Malden and Henry Fonda, and co-produced with the Shaw Brothers of Hong Kong. But it was a disaster movie in many more ways than one.

The screenplay by Stanley Mann and Edmund H North concerned a collision between a comet and an asteroid named Orpheus. A huge chunk of Orpheus breaks off as a result and heads in the general direction of Earth; if it hits, it will mean the end of human life on the planet. To stop the meteor, NASA wants to use a nuclear weapons satellite called Hercules (just to continue with the Greek analogies) but soon finds that it cannot succeed without help, and the USSR joins forces with the US to save the world...

Meteor is probably more believable now than it was in 1979. Neame had helmed the very successful Irwin Allen sea-borne disaster *The Poseidon Adventure* (1972), and *Meteor* is only marginally sillier. The actors chew the scenery (especially Martin Landau as an unhinged army general) and the effects are nowhere near as good as those in the concurrent James Bond adventure *Moonraker*. But *Meteor* now seems oddly prescient: the first building hit by meteor-splinters in New York City happens to be the World Trade Centre, which is a resonant sight to see at this remove, in light of events on 9/11.

As had been the case with *The Amityville Horror,* the reviews for *Meteor* were not kind. In *The New York Times,* Janet Maslin wrote: 'The menace of the title looks like a big hunk of week-old bread... The chief American scientist is played by Sean Connery, who, of course, sounds like a Scotsman... The suspense is sludgy and the character development nil; even the inadvertent comedy is spotty.' *Variety* concurred: 'Meteor really combines several disasters in one continuous cinematic bummer,' it assessed. 'There's an avalanche, an earthquake, a tidal wave and a giant mud bath. All in all, special effects wizards Glen Robinson and Robert Staples, along with stunt co-ordinator Roger Greed, got a good workout.' The film failed to live up to its box office expectations and it would be one of the last under the AIP banner.

CHOMPS was an ill-conceived attempt to bring a family science-fiction comedy to an audience which could not have cared less. Directed by Don Chaffey *(Jason and the Argonauts,* 1963), *CHOMPS* was the oddball tale of a young man who creates a robot dog that has superior strength, x-ray eyes, and that can detect when a crime is being committed. However, the usual greedy businessman tries to use the invention for his own nefarious purposes.

The cast included Wesley Eure, Valerie Bertinelli and Conrad Bain (the last two of whom were familiar to US TV viewers at the time) and the film was co-produced by Hanna-Barbera, the animation house known for characters like *Tom and Jerry* and *Huckleberry Hound.* Joseph Barbera was a friend of Arkoff's and had approached him about AIP collaborating with Hanna-Barbera on live-action films. Arkoff was enthused about the idea and they provisonally agreed to do nine films. The idea for the first was Barbera's, but his concept was to have a robotic Doberman as the lead character. Arkoff's son Louis felt that the dog should be non-threatening in the style of *Benji* (1974), a family comedy which had been so successful that it had inspired several sequels. Barbera said later that he thought the change had contributed to the film's lacklustre performance. On its release, audiences stayed away in droves. There were no more collaborations between AIP and Hanna-Barbera after CHOMPS.

In November 1979, AIP picked up a Spanish-American action film called *Jaguar Lives!* starring Joe Lewis, Christopher Lee, Donald Pleasence and Barbara Bach. The all-star cast also included Capucine, Joseph Wiseman, Woody Strode and John Huston! It was an attempt to cash in on the once-popular kung-fu craze, but the movie was a day late and a dollar short. It bombed.

CHOMPS (Wesley Eure)

Mad Max (Mel Gibson)

AIP's final foreign import was none other than the original *Mad Max,* the Australian dystopian sci-fi movie directed by George Miller that was to make an international star of Mel Gibson. As it had been a huge success in Oz, AIP snapped up the US rights while Warner Bros handled the rest of the international marketplace. Miller's tale of a post-apocalyptic world in which an Aussie cop (Gibson), out for revenge against those who had murdered his family, fights to the death with a brutal gang of motorcyclists, captured the imagination of audiences the world over.

The American release was problematic, however. At the time, few Australian films had been seen in the States, other than a couple of 'art house' productions directed by Peter Weir: *Picnic at Hanging Rock* (1975) and *The Last Wave* (1977). American viewers had very little experience of Australian accents and while AIP thought the film an outstanding action piece, it was afraid that the audience would fail to understand the

The Visitor (Glenn Ford) / ABOVE: *Defiance* (Jan-Michael Vincent)

dialogue, so it overdubbed all of the actors with American accents. This might seem faintly ridiculous now, but such was the thinking in the 1970s.

Surprisingly, *Mad Max* did not take off immediately in the US market. When AIP released its version on February 15, 1980, it received mixed reviews. In *The New York Times*, Tom Buckley opined, '*Mad Max* is ugly and incoherent, and aimed, probably accurately, at the most uncritical of moviegoers. It's worth noting that much of the rudimentary dialogue in this Australian film has been dubbed from "shrine" (sic?), the thick dialect of the subcontinent, into country-and-western English. You can tell because the lip movement and sound are often slightly out of synchronisation.' *Mad Max* became a cult film in the US only after being shown on Home Box Office, one of the first cable channels to screen uncut movies. By then it was too late for AIP.

How to Beat the High Cost of Living (Jane Curtin, Susan Saint James, Jessica Lange)

AIP's next release was *Defiance*, another actioner, this time starring Jan-Michael Vincent and Art Carney. It was less successful, both with critics and with audiences. *The Visitor* was an Italian-American sci-fi/horror starring John Huston, Shelley Winters and Glenn Ford and was essentially a rip-off of other, better movies about young girls with telekinetic powers. Directed, under a pseudonym, by Giulio Paradisi, *The Visitor* borrowed from a variety of Hollywood blockbusters, including *Close Encounters, The Omen* and *The Exorcist*, but it was too weird for the patrons of 1980.

Nothing Personal (1980) was another flop, with Suzanne Somers from TV sitcom *Three's Company* out of her depth against Donald Sutherland in a rom-com about a professor who objects to the killing of baby seals; Somers aids him in his attempts to have the killings halted. Ecologically-minded it may have been, but it worked as neither comedy nor socially-conscious drama. AIP's penultimate film was *Gorp*, a comedy with Dennis Quaid and Rosanna Arquette. An attempt to cash in on the success of *National Lampoon's Animal House* (1978), *Gorp* was set at a Jewish summer camp in upstate New York and put the accent on drugs, sex and the rude antics of a group of waiters. It was yet another financial failure.

The final film to bear the AIP name was *How to Beat the High Cost of Living. R*eleased in July 1980, it was a star-studded comedy of modern living which should have connected with audiences more than it did. Produced on a budget of $4.75m, it grossed $7.5m in the US, but not nearly enough to drag AIP out of the red.

Dressed to Kill (Angie Dickinson)

Arkoff's name is on Brian De Palma's *Dressed to Kill* (1980) as producer, along with Fred Caruso and George Litto, which was appropriate considering that *Sisters*, De Palma's breakthrough movie, had been released by AIP. *Dressed to Kill* was released under the Filmways banner, however. AIP, now totally absorbed into Filmways, was finally no more.

In his autobiography *Flying Through Hollywood by the Seat of My Pants,* Arkoff wrote, '*Dressed to Kill* was a picture I was proud of, a truly brilliant film, full of unexpected plot twists and more thrills and heart-stopping moments than the roller coaster at Coney Island.' Proud he may have been, but Arkoff resigned from Filmways in December 1980 and sold his stock in the company. 'The merger was the biggest mistake of my life,' he confessed in his autobiography. 'But I figure that everyone is entitled to one major mistake and this was definitely mine. (Richard) Bloch and Filmways had bought AIP because of what we had accomplished over the last quarter century; then they promptly tried to change us.'

Arkoff walked away with $4.3 million, a tidy sum. 'It's not my style to sell at a loss,' he told Mark Thomas McGee. He did not rest on his laurels for long. In 1982, he established a new company, Arkoff International Pictures, to produce along the lines of the original AIP. The new 'AIP' only produced a handful of films, however, including Larry Cohen's *Q: The Winged Serpent* (1982), *The Final Terror* (1983), *Up the Creek* (1984) and *Hell Hole* (1985). The business had changed dramatically and Arkoff found himself to be something of a dinosaur in the brave new world of ancillary markets, such as home video.

The drive-in market had essentially collapsed. Roger Corman knew this and had started to make films for straight-to-video release, which had really taken off in the early 1980s. Unlike Arkoff and Nicholson, Corman never tried to produce A-class movies, always keeping his investments at manageable levels. With his New World Pictures, and his later Concorde and New Horizons companies, he continued to make low-budget genre films for whatever new markets were to come along: video, DVD, Blu-ray, the SyFy Channel in the US, and currently streaming video.

On September 17, 2001, *Daily Variety* published Arkoff's obituary, with the headline, 'Arkoff Made Art of B-Movies'. Written by Richard Natale, the piece began, 'Sam Arkoff, the gruff, outspoken producer and co-founder of American International Pictures, and the creator of hundreds of action exploitation films in the 1950s and 1960s, has died. He was 83.

'At the company's height, AIP's B-grade movies filled a niche bill fodder for the nation's drive-in and sub-run theaters. Arkoff was prescient in tapping the post-war youth market, attracting them with horror, action and sexual innuendo–which would later filter up the major studios.'

The obituary did not mention James H Nicholson by name. Gary A Smith claimed that in later years, Arkoff took all of the credit for AIP's success. 'It's almost as if Jim Nicholson never existed at all,' he wrote.

Regardless of who deserves the credit–and it is generally accepted that Nicholson was the creative force while Arkoff was the money man–American International Pictures changed the film industry and the whole nature of production. The company pioneered movies aimed at teenagers which, for better or worse, is now the standard in Hollywood. AIP's list of 'discoveries'–Francis Ford Coppola, Martin Scorsese, Brian De Palma, Jack Nicholson, Pam Grier *et al*–is extensive enough to warrant a book by itself.

AIP set trends which can be seen in films to this day. It was among the first to put the titles and credits at the *end* of a film, rather than at the beginning. It was among the first to promote *female* action stars, such as Grier. And it was among the first, along with Hammer Films in the UK, to add sex to its horrors, releasing its only Hammer co-production, *The Vampire Lovers*, with an R-rating in the US.

Q-The Winged Serpent (David Carradine)

By 1979, both companies had ceased to exist. As producer Aida Young once said in respect of Hammer, 'There was a time, and then there wasn't a time.' The same held true for AIP.

But what a time it was. And what a wonderful legacy of crazy, quirky, creepy, 'artsy-fartsy' or just plain *fun* movies that almost a quarter of a century of American International Pictures has left us.

The TWIN TERROR SHOW
EVERY MAN its PRISONER... EVERY WOMAN its SLAVE!
IT CONQUERED THE WORLD
TWO NEW SCIENCE-
SHOCKERS ON O
PROGRAMME
SEE. WORLD CONQUERED
HORRIBLE BEAST FR
BEYOND THE STAR
SEE. BEAUTY BECOME
MONSTER FROM T
UNKNOWN!
SEE. THE HIDEOUS
"FLYING FINGERS
SEE. TERRIFYING
SHE CREATURE WHO
LURES MEN - WITH
HER UNEARTHLY
BEAUTY!
SEE.
THE WORLD
GRIPPED BY
TERROR...
PANIC...
DEATH!
X CERTIFICATE
PETER GRAVES · BEVERLY GARLAND · LEE VAN CLEEF
ANGLO AMALGAMATED FILM D
HAMMER HOUSE. 113/117. WARDOUR ST

HAT TOPS THEM ALL!

Anglo's
NEW AMERICAN
'Exploitation Special"
SENSATION!

DON'T MISS THESE TRADE SHOW DATES

"IT CONQUERED THE WORLD"
THURS., SEPT. 27
at 2.30 p.m.
HAMMER THEATRE
WARDOUR ST., W1

"THE SHE CREATURE"
FRI., SEPT. 28
at 10.30 a.m.
HAMMER THEATRE
WARDOUR ST., W1

PICTURES WITH A PURPOSE—
BOX-OFFICE RESULTS!

RIBUTORS LIMITED
LONDON, W.1.

AMERICAN INTERNATIONAL PICTURES
PRODUCTION FILMOGRAPHY

...AS AMERICAN RELEASING CORPORATION 1955

The Fast and the Furious/*Prod:Roger Corman/Dir:John Ireland, Edward Sampson/Scr:Roger Corman, Jean Howell, Jerome Odlum/*Stars:John Ireland, Dorothy Malone, Bruce Carlisle

Five Guns West/*Prod:Roger Corman/Dir:Roger Corman/Scr:R Wright Campbell/*Stars:John Lund, Dorothy Malone, Mike Connors

The Beast with a Million Eyes/*Prod:David Kramarsky/Dir:David Kramarsky, Lou Place, Roger Corman/Scr:Tom Filer/*Stars:Paul Birch, Lorna Thayer, Dona Cole

Apache Woman/*Prod:Roger Corman, Alex Gordon/Dir:Roger Corman/Scr:Lou Rusoff/*Stars:Lloyd Bridges, Joan Taylor, Lance Fuller

Day the World Ended/*Prod:Roger Corman, Alex Gordon/Dir:Roger Corman/Scr:Lou Rusoff/*Stars:Richard Denning, Lori Nelson, Adele Jergens

The Phantom From 10,000 Leagues/*Prod:Dan and Jack Milner/Dir:Dan Milner/Scr:Lou Rusoff/*Stars:Kent Taylor, Cathy Downs, Michael Whalen

1956

The Oklahoma Woman/*Prod:Roger Corman/Dir:Roger Corman/Scr:Lou Rusoff/*Stars:Peggie Castle, Richard Denning, Cathy Downs

Gunslinger/*Prod:Roger Corman/Dir:Roger Corman/Scr:Charles B Griffith, Mark Hanna/*Stars:Beverly Garland, John Ireland, Allison Hayes

...AS AMERICAN INTERNATIONAL PICTURES

It Conquered the World/*Prod:Roger Corman/Dir:Roger Corman/Scr:Lou Rusoff, Charles B Griffith/*Stars:Peter Graves, Lee Van Cleef, Beverly Garland

Girls in Prison/*Prod:Alex Gordon/Dir:Edward L Cahn/Scr:Lou Rusoff/*Stars:Richard Denning, Joan Taylor, Mae Marsh

Hot Rod Girl/*Prod:Norman T Herman/Dir:Leslie H Martinson/Scr:John McGreevy/*Stars:Lori Nelson, Chuck Connors, John Smith

The She-Creature/*Prod:Alex Gordon/Dir:Edward L Cahn/Scr:Lou Rusoff/*Stars:Chester Morris, Marla English, Tom Conway

Flesh and the Spur/*Prod:Alex Gordon/Dir:Edward L Cahn/Scr:Charles B Griffith, Mark Hanna, Lou Rusoff, Edward L Cahn/*Stars:Marla English, John Agar, Touch Connors

Runaway Daughters/*Prod:Alex Gordon/Dir:Edward L Cahn/Scr:Lou Rusoff/*Stars:Marla English, John Litel, Anna Stein

Shake, Rattle & Rock!/*Prod:Alex Gordon, James H Nicholson/Dir:Edward L Cahn/Scr:Lou Rusoff/*Stars:Touch Connors, Lisa Gaye, Sterling Holloway

1957

The Astounding She-Monster/*Prod:Ronald V Ashcroft/Dir:Ronald V Ashcroft/Scr:Frank Hall/*Stars:Robert Clarke, Kenne Duncan, Shriley Kirkpatrick

Naked Paradise/*Prod:Roger Corman/Dir:Roger Corman/Scr:Charles B Griffith, Robert Wright Campbell/*Stars:Richard Denning, Beverly Garland, Lisa Montell

Voodoo Woman/*Prod:Alex Gordon/Dir:Edward L Cahn/Scr:Russ Bender, V I Voss/*Stars:Marla English, Tom Conway, Mike Connors

Dragstrip Girl/*Prod:Samuel Z Arkoff, Alex Gordon/Dir:Edward L Cahn/Scr:Lou Rusoff/*Stars:Fay Spain, Steven Terrell, John Ashley

Rock All Night/*Prod:Roger Corman/Dir:Roger Corman/Scr:Charles B Griffith/*Stars:Dick Miller, AbbyDalton, Russell Johnson

The Undead/*Prod:Roger Corman/Dir:Roger Corman/Scr:Charles B Griffith, Mark Hanna/*Stars:Pamela Duncan, Richard Garland, Allison Hayes

I Was a Teenage Werewolf/*Prod:Herman Cohen/Dir:Gene Fowler Jr/Scr:Herman Cohen, Aben Kandel/*Stars:Michael Landon, Whit Bissell, Yvonne Lime

Invasion of the Saucer Men/*Prod:Robert J Gurney Jr, James H Nicholson/Dir:Edward L Cahn/Scr:Robert J Gurney Jr, Al Martin/*Stars:Steven Terrell, Gloria Castillo, Frank Gorshin

Reform School Girl/*Prod:Samuel Z Arkoff/Dir:Edward Bernds/Scr:Edward Bernds/*Stars:Gloria Castillo, Ross Ford, Edward Byrnes

The Tommy Steele Story/*Prod:Herbert Smith/Dir:Gerard Bryant/Scr:Norman Hudis/*Stars:Tommy Steele, Chas McDevitt, Nancy Whiskey

The White Huntress (UK:Golden Ivory)/*Prod:Robert J Gurney Jr, James H Nicholson/Dir:George Breakston/Scr:Robert J Gurney Jr, Al Martin/*Stars:Robert Urquhart, John Bentley, Susan Stephen

Motorcyle Gang/*Prod:Samuel Z Arkoff, Alex Gordon/Dir:Edward L Cahn/Scr:Lou Rusoff*/ Stars:Anne Neyland, Steven Terrell, John Ashley

The Amazing Colossal Man/*Prod:Bert I Gordon, Samuel Z Arkoff, James H Nicholson/Dir:Bert I Gordon/Scr:Mark Hanna, Bert I Gordon, George Worthing Yates*/Stars:Glenn Langan, Cathy Downs, William Hudson

Sorority Girl/*Prod:Roger Corman/Dir:Roger Corman/Scr:Leo Lieberman, Ed Waters*/Stars:Susan Cabot, Barboura Morris, Dick Miller

I Was a Teenage Frankenstein (UK: Teenage Frankenstein)/*Prod:Herman Cohen/Dir:Herbert L Sttock/Scr:Kenneth Langtry*/Stars:Whit Bissell, Phyllis Coates, Gary Conway

Blood of Dracula (UK: Blood Is My Heritage)/ *Prod:Herman Cohen/Dir:Herbert L Strock/ Scr:Ralph Thornton*/Stars:Sandra Harrison, Louise Lewis, Gail Ganley

The Saga of the Viking Women and Their Voyage to the Waters of the Great Sea Serpent/*Prod:Roger Corman/Dir:Roger Corman/ Scr:Lawrence L Goldman*/Stars:Abby Dalton, Susan Cabot, Bradford Jackson

1958

The Screaming Skull/*Prod:John Kneubuhl, T Frank Woods, John Coots/Dir:Alex Nicol/Scr:John Kneubuhl*/ Stars:John Hudson, Peggy Webber, Russ Conway

Terror From the Year 5,000 (UK: Cage of Doom)/*Prod:Robert J Gurney Jr, Samuel Z Arkoff, James H Nicholson, Gene Searchinger/Dir:Robert J Gurney Jr/Scr:Robert J Gurney Jr, Henry Slesar*/ Stars:Ward Costello, Joyce Holden, Salome Jens

Jet Attack/*Prod:Alex Gordon/Dir:Edward L Cahn/ Scr:Orville H Hampton*/Stars:John Agar, Audrey Totter, Gregory Walcott

Suicide Battalion/*Prod:Samuel Z Arkoff, Lou Rusoff/Dir:Edward L Cahn/Scr:Lou Rusoff*/ Stars:Mike Connors, John Ashley, Jewell Lain

The Cool and the Crazy/*Prod:Elmer C Rhoden Jr/Dir:William Witney/Scr:Richard C Sarafian*/ Stars:Scott Marlowe, Richard Bakalyan, Gigi Perreau

Daddy-O/*Prod:Elmer C Rhoden Jr/Dir:Lou Place/ Scr:David Moessinger*/Stars:Dick Contino, Sandra Giles, Bruno VeSota

Dragstrip Riot (UK: The Reckless Age)/ *Prod:O Dale Ireland/Dir:David Bradley/Scr:George Hodgins*/Stars:Gary Clarke, Fay Wray, Connie Stevens

Attack of the Puppet People (UK: Six Inches Tall)/*Prod:Bert I Gordon/Dir:Bert I Gordon/ Scr:Bert I Gordon, George Worthing Yates*/Stars:June Kenney, John Agar, John Hoyt

The Bonnie Parker Story/*Prod:Samuel Z Arkoff, James H Nicholson, Stan Shepetner/Dir:William Witney/Scr:Stan Shepetner*/Stars:Dorothy Provine, Jack Hogan, Richard Bakalyan

Machine-Gun Kelly/*Prod:Roger Corman/ Dir:Roger Corman/Scr:Robert Wright Campbell*/ Stars:Charles Bronson, Susan Cabot, Morey Amsterdam

High School Hellcats/*Prod:Charles 'Buddy' Rogers/Dir:Edward L Bernds/Scr:Mark Lowell, Jan Lowell*/Stars:Yvonne Lime, Brett Halsey,Jana Lund

Hot Rod Gang/*Prod:Lou Rusoff/Dir:Lew Landers/ Scr:Lou Rusoff*/Stars:John Ashley, Jody Fair, Steve Drexel

How to Make a Monster/*Prod:Herman Cohen, James H Nicholson/Dir:Herbert L Strock/ Scr:Herman Cohen, Abel Kandel*/Stars:Robert H Harris, Gary Conway, Gary Clarke

War of the Colossal Beast (UK: The Terror Strikes)/*Prod:Bert I Gordon/Dir:Bert I Gordon/ Scr:George Worthing Yates*/Stars:Sally Fraser, Dean Parkin, Roger Pace

Hell Squad/*Prod:Burt Topper/Dir:Burt Topper/ Scr:Burt Topper*/Stars:Wally Campo, Brandon Carroll, Fred Gavin

Tank Battalion/*Prod:Richard Bernstein/ Dir:Sherman A Rose/Scr:Richard Bernstein, George Waters*/Stars:Don Kelly, Leslie Parrish, Edward G Robinson Jr

Teenage Caveman (UK: Out of the Darkness)/ *Prod:Roger Corman/Dir:Roger Corman/Scr:R Wright Campbell*/Stars: Robert Vaughn, Darah Marshall, Leslie Bradley

Night of the Blood Beast/*Prod:Gene Corman, Roger Corman/Dir:Bernard L Kowalski/Scr:Martin Varno*/Stars:Michael Emmet, Angela Greene, Ed Nelson

She Gods of Shark Reef/*Prod:Ludwig H Gerber/ Dir:Roger Corman/Scr:Robert Hill, Victor Stoloff*/ Stars:Bill Cord, Don Durant, Lisa Montell

The Brain Eaters/*Prod:Ed Nelson/Dir:Bruno VeSota/Scr:Gordon Urquhart*/Stars:Ed Nelson, Joanna Lee, Leonard Nimoy

Earth Vs the Spider/*Prod:Bert I Gordon/Dir:Bert I Gordon/Scr:Laszlo Gorog, George Worthing Yates*/ Stars:Ed Kemmer, June Kenney, Eugene Persson

Submarine Seahawk/*Prod:Alex Gordon, Orville H Hampton/Dir:Spencer Gordon Bennett/Scr:Lou Rusoff*/Stars:John Bentley, Brett Halsey, Wayne Heffley

1959

Paratroop Command/*Prod:Samuel Z Arkoff, James H Nicholson, Stanley Shepetner/Dir:William Witney/Scr:Stanley Shepetner*/Stars:Richard Bakalyan, Ken Lynch, Jack Hogan

Operation Dames/*Prod:Stanley Kallis/Dir:Louis Clyde Stoumen/Scr:Edward J Lasko*/Stars:Eve Meyer, Chuck Henderson, Don Devlin

Roadracers/*Stanley Kallis/Dir:Arthur Swerdloff/ Scr:Stanley Kallis, Ed Lasko*/Stars:Joel Lawrence, Marian Collier, Skip Ward

Tank Commandos/*Prod:Burt Topper/Dir:Burt Topper/Scr:Burt Topper*/Stars:Donato Ferretta, Robert Barron, Maggie Lawrence

The Headless Ghost/*Prod:Herman Cohen/Dir:Peter Graham Scott/Scr:Kenneth Langtry, Herman Cohen/* Stars:Richard Lyon, Liliane Sottane, David Rose

Horrors of the Black Museum/*Prod: Herman Cohen/Dir: Arthur Crabtree/Scr: Herman Cohen*/Stars: Michael Gough, June Cunningham, Graham Curnow

Diary of a High School Bride/*Prod:Burt Topper/ Dir:Burt Topper/Scr:Burt Topper, Roberta Lowell, Jan Englund*/Stars:Anita Sands, Ron Foster, Chris Robinson

Ghost of Dragstrip Hollow/*Prod:Lou Rusoff/ Dir:William J Hole Jr/Scr:Lou Rusoff*/Stars:Jody Fair, Russ Bender, Henry McCann

A Bucket of Blood/*Prod:Roger Corman/Dir:Roger Corman/Scr:Charles B Griffith*/Stars:Dick Miller, Barboura Morris, Antony Carbone

Attack of the Giant Leeches/*Prod:Gene Corman, Roger Corman/Dir:Bernard L Kowalski/Scr:Leo Gordon*/Stars:Ken Clark, Yvette Vickers, Jan Shepard

The Angry Red Planet/*Prod:Sidney Pink, Norman Maurer/Dir:Ib Melchior/Scr:Sidney W Pink, Ib Melchior*/Stars:Gerald Mohr, Naura Hayden, Jack Kruschen

1960

House of Usher (UK: The Fall of the House of Usher)/*Prod:Roger Corman/Dir:Roger Corman/ Scr:Richard Matheson*/Stars:Vincent Price, Mark Damon, Myrna Fahey

The Jailbreakers/*Prod:Alexander Grasshoff/ Dir:Alexander Grasshoff/Scr:Alexander Grasshoff/* Stars:Robert Hutton, Mary Castle, Michael O'Connell

Why Must I Die?/*Prod:Richard Bernstein/Dir:Roy Del Ruth/Scr:Richard Bernstein, Herbert G Luft, George Waters*/Stars:Terry Moore, Debra Paget, Bert Freed

The Amazing Transparent Man/*Prod:Lester D Guthrie, Robert L Madden, John Miller/Dir:Edgar G Ulmer/Scr:Jack Lewis*/Stars:Marguerite Chapman, Douglas Kennedy, James Griffith

Beyond the Time Barrier/*Prod:Robert Clarke/ Dir:Edgar G Ulmer/Scr:Arthur C Pierce*/Stars:Robert Clarke, Darlene Tompkins, Vladimir Sokoloff

The Hand/*Prod:Bill Luckwell/Dir:Henry Cass/ Scr:Ray Cooney, Tony Hilton*/Stars:Derek Bond, Reed De Rouen, Bryan Coleman

Konga/*Prod:Herman Cohen, Nathan Cohen, Stuart Levy/Dir:John Lamont/Scr:Herman Cohen, Aben Kandel*/Stars:Michael Gough, Margo Johns, Jess Conrad

1961

Master of the World/*Prod:Samuel Z Arkoff, Anthony Carras, James H Nicholson/Dir: William Witney/Scr:Richard Matheson*/Stars:Vincent Price, Charles Bronson, Henry Hull

Pit and the Pendulum/*Prod: Roger Corman/ Dir:Roger Corman/Scr:Richard Matheson/* Stars:Vincent Price, Barbara Steele, John Kerr

Reptilicus/*Prod:Samuel Z Arkoff, Sidney Pink, Johann Zalabery/Dir:Sidney Pink/Scr:Ib Melchior, Sid Pink/* Stars:Bent Mejding, Asbjørn Andersen, Povl Wøldike

Samson and the 7 Miracles of the World/ *Prod:Salvatore Billitteri, Luigi Carpentieri, Ermanno Donati/Dir:Riccardo Freda/Scr:Oreste Biancolli, Duccio Tessari*/Stars:Gordon Scott, Yôko Tani, Hélène Chanel

1962

Battle Beyond the Sun/*Prod:Roger Corman (US version)/Dir:Mikhail Karzhukov, Aleksandr Kozyr, Francis Ford Coppola/Scr:Mikhail Karzhukov, Evgeniy Pomeshchikov, Aleksey Sazonov*/Stars:Aleksandr Shvorin, Ivan Pereverzev, Linda Barrett

The Premature Burial/*Prod:Roger Corman/ Dir:Roger Corman/Scr:Charles Beaumont, Ray Russell*/Stars:Ray Milland, Hazel Court, Alan Napier

Journey to the Seventh Planet/*Prod:Sidney Pink/Dir:Sidney Pink/Scr:Sidney Pink, Ib Melchior/* Stars:John Agar, Carl Ottosen, Greta Thyssen

Night of the Eagle (US: Burn, Witch, Burn!)/ *Prod:Julian Wintle, Leslie Parkyn/Dir:Sidney Hayers/Scr:Charles Beaumont, Richard Matheson, George Baxt*/Stars: Peter Wyngarde, Janet Blair, Margaret Johnston

Tales of Terror/*Prod:Samuel Z Arkoff, Roger Corman, James H Nicholson/Dir:Roger Corman/ Scr:Richard Matheson*/Stars:Vincent Price, Peter Lorre, Basil Rathbone

Panic in Year Zero!/*Prod:Arnold Houghland, Lou Rusoff/Dir:Ray Milland/Scr:John Morton, Jay Simms*/Stars:Ray Milland, Jean Hagen, Frankie Avalon

1963

Operation Bikini/*Prod:Samuel Z Arkoff, James H Nicholson, Lou Rusoff/Dir:Anthony Carras/Scr:John Tomerlin*/Stars:Tab Hunter, Frankie Avalon, Scott Brady

Free, White and 21/*Prod:Larry Buchanan/ Dir:Larry Buchanan/Scr:Larry Buchanan, Harold Hoffman, Cliff Pope*/Stars:Frederick O'Neal, Annalena Lund, George Edgley

Beach Party/*Prod:James H Nicholson, Lou Rusoff/ Dir: William Asher/Scr:Lou Rusoff*/Stars:Robert Cummings, Dorothy Malone, Frankie Avalon

The Haunted Palace/*Prod:Roger Corman/ Dir:Roger Corman/Scr:Charles Beaumont*/ Stars:Vincent Price, Debra Paget, Lon Chaney Jr

The Comedy of Terrors/*Prod:Samuel Z Arkoff, James H Nicholson/Dir:Jacques Tourneur/Scr:Richard Matheson*/Stars: Vincent Price, Peter Lorre, Boris Karloff

Black Sabbath/*Prod:SavatoreVillitteri, Paolo Mercuri/Dir:Mario Bava/Scr:Mario Bava, Alberto Bevilacqua, Marcello Fondato*/Stars:Michele Mercier, Lidia Alfonsi, Boris Karloff

Evil Eye/*Prod:Massimo De Rita/Dir:Mario Bava/ Scr:Mario Bava, Enzo Corbucci, Ennio De Concini, Eliana De Sabata, Mino Guerrini, Franco Prosperi*/ Stars:Leticia Roman, John Saxon, Valentina Cortese

1964

X: The Man With X-Ray Eyes/*Prod:Roger Corman/ Dir:Roger Corman/Scr:Robert Dillon, Ray Russell*/ Stars:Ray Milland, Diana van der Vlis, Harold J Stone

The Masque of the Red Death/*Prod:Roger Corman, George Willoughby/Dir:Roger Corman/ Scr:Charles Beaumont, R Wright Campbell*/ Stars:Vincent Price, Jane Asher, Hazel Court

Pyro...The Thing Without a Face (UK: Wheel of Fire)/*Prod:Richard C Meyer, Sidney W Pink/Dir:Julio Coll, Luis Garcia/Scr:Sidney W Pink, Luis de los Arcos*/ Stars:Barry Sullivan, Martha Hyer, Sherry Moreland

Under Age/*Prod:Harold Hoffman/Dir:Larry Buchanan/Scr:Larry Buchanan, Harold Hoffman*/ Stars:Annabelle Weenick, Judy Adler, Roland Royter

Bikini Beach/*Prod:Samuel Z Arkoff, James H Nicholson/Dir: William Asher/Scr: William Asher, Leo Townsend, Robert Dillon*/Stars:Frankie Avalon, Annette Funicello, Martha Hyer

Diary of a Bachelor/*Prod:Sandy Howard/ Dir:Sandy Howard/Scr:Ken Barnett*/Stars:Joe Silver, Dagne Crane, Denise Lor

Pajama Party/*Prod:Samuel Z Arkoff, James H Nicholson/Dir:Don Weis/Scr:Louis M Heyward*/ Stars:Tommy Kirk, Annette Funicello, Elsa Lanchester

The Tomb of Ligeia/*Prod:Pat Green/Dir:Roger Corman/Scr:Robert Towne*/Stars:Vincent Price, Elizabeth Shepherd, John Westbrook

Muscle Beach Party/*Prod:Robert Dillon, James H Nicholson/Dir: William Asher/Scr: William Asher, Robert Dillon*/Stars:Frankie Avalon, Annette Funicello, Luciana Paluzzi

1965

Space Probe Taurus/*Prod:Leonard Katzman, Burt Topper/Dir:Leonard Katzman/Scr:Leonard Katzman*/Stars:Francine York, James Brown, Baynes Barron

Portrait in Terror/*Prod:Jay Roades/Dir:Michael Road/Scr: Vic Webber*/Stars:William Campbell, Anna Pavane, Patrick Magee

How to Stuff a Wild Bikini/*Prod:Samuel Z Arkoff, James H Nicholson/Dir: William Asher/Scr: William Asher, Leo Townsend*/Stars:Annette Funicello, Dwayne Hickman, Brian Donlevy

Planet of the Vampires/*Prod:Fulvio Lucisano/ Dir:Mario Bava/Scr:Mario Bava, Alberto Bevilacqua, Callisto Cosulich, Louis M Heyward, Ib Melchior, Antonio Roman, Rafael J Salvia*/Stars:Barry Sullivan, Norma Bengell, Angel Aranda

Monster of Terror (US: Die, Monster, Die!)/ *Prod:Pat Green/Dir:Daniel Haller/Scr:Jerry Sohl*/ Stars:Boris Karloff, Nick Adams, Freda Jackson

Dr Goldfoot and the Bikini Machine/ *Prod:Samuel Z Arkoff, James H Nicholson/ Dir:Norman Taurog/Scr:Elwood Ullman, Robert Kaufman*/Stars:Vincent Price, Frankie Avalon, Dwayne Hickman

The Big TNT Show/*Prod:Phil Spector/Dir:Larry Peerce*/Stars:Joan Baez, The Byrds, David Crosby

Nashville Rebel/*Prod:Fred A Niles/Dir:Jay Sheridan/Scr:Ira Kerns, Jay Sheridan*/Stars:Waylon Jennings, Mary Frann, Archie Campbell

The Ghost in the Invisible Bikini/*Prod:Samuel Z Arkoff, James H Nicholson/Dir:Don Weis/Scr:Louis M Heyward, Elwood Ullman*/Stars:Tommy Kirk, Deborah Walley, Aron Kincaid

1966

Fireball 500/*Prod:Samuel Z Arkoff, James H Nicholson/Dir: William Asher/Scr: William Asher, Leo Townsend*/Stars:Frankie Avalon, Annette Funicello, Fabian

The Wild Angels/*Prod:Roger Corman/Dir:Roger Corman/Scr:Charles B Griffith*/Stars:Peter Fonda, Nancy Sinatra, Bruce Dern

Dr Goldfoot and the Girl Bombs/*Prod:Louis M Heyward, Fulvio Lucisano/Dir:Mario Bava/ Scr:Giuseppe Moccia, Franco Castellano, Louis M Heyward, Robert Kaufman*/Stars:Vincent Price, Fabian, Franco Franchi

Tarzan and the Valley of Gold/*Prod:Sy Weintraub/ Dir:Robert Day/Scr:Clair Huffaker*/Stars:Mike Henry, David Opatoshu, Nancy Kovack

1967

Thunder Alley/*Prod:Burt Topper/Dir:Richard Rush/Scr:Sy Salkowtiz*/Stars:Annette Funicello, Fabian, Diane McBain

Devil's Angels/*Prod:Roger Corman/Dir:Daniel Haller/Scr:Charles Griffith*/Stars:John Cassavetes, Beverly Adams, Mimsy Farmer

The Trip/*Prod:Roger Corman/Dir:Roger Corman/ Scr:Jack Nicholson*/Stars:Peter Fonda, Susan Strasberg, Bruce Dern

Sadismo/*Prod:Salvatore Bilitteri/Scr:Philip Marx*/ Stars:Terry Telli, Burt Topper,Norman Papson

The Glory Stompers/*Prod:John Lawrence/ Dir:Anthony M Lanza/Scr:James Gordon White, John Lawrence*/Stars:Dennis Hopper, Jody McCrea, Chris Noel

1968

Maryjane/*Prod:Maury Dexter/Dir:Maury Dexter/ Scr:Dick Gautier, Petrr Marshall*/Stars:Fabian, Diane McBain, Kevin Coughlin

Witchfinder General (US:The Conqueror Worm)/*Prod:Louis M Heyward, Arnold Miller/ Dir:Michael Reeves/Scr:Tom Baker, Michael Reeves*/ Stars: Vincent Price, Ian Ogilvy. Hilary Dwyer

The Mini-Skirt Mob/*Prod:Maury Dexter/ Dir:Maury Dexter/Scr:James Gordon White*/ Stars:Jeremy Slate, Diane McBain, Sherry Jackson

Wild in the Streets/*Prod:Samuel Z Arkoff, James H Nicholson/Dir:Barry Shear/Scr:Robert Thom*/ Stars:Shelley Winters, Christopher Jones, Diane Varsi

The Savage Seven/*Prod:Dick Clark/Dir:Richard Rush/Scr:Michael Fisher*/Stars:Robert Walker Jr, Joanna Frank, John Garwood

Angels from Hell/*Prod:Kurt Neumann/Bruce Kessler/Scr:Jerry Wish*/Stars:Tom Stern, Ted Markland, Jack Starrett

The Young Animals/*Prod:Maury Dexter/ Dir:Maury Dexter/Scr:James Gordon White*/ Stars:Tom Nardini, Patty McCormack, Joanna Frank

Killers Three/*Prod:Dick Clark/Dir:Bruce Kessler/ Scr:Michael Fisher*/Stars:Robert Walker Jr, Diane Varsi, Dick Clark

Curse of the Crimson Altar (US:The Crimson Cult)/*Prod:Louis M Heyward/Dir:Vernon Sewell/ Scr:Mervyn Haisman, Henry Lincoln*/Stars:Boris Karloff, Christopher Lee, Mark Eden

Three in the Attic/*Prod:Richard Wilson/ Dir:Richard Wilson/Scr:Stephen Yafa*/ Stars:Christopher Jones, Yvette Mimieux, Judy Pace

1969

Marquis de Sade's Justine/*Prod:Harry Alan Towers/Dir:Jesus Franco/Scr:Peter Welbeck*/ Stars:Klaus Kinski, Romina Power, Maria Rohm

Hell's Belles/*Prod:Maury Dexter/Dir:Maury Dexter/Scr:R G McMullen, James Gordon White*/ Stars:Jeremy Slate, AdamRoarke, Jocelyn Lane

The Devil's 8/*Prod:Burt Topper/Dir:Burt Topper/ Scr: Willard Huyck, John Milius, James Gordon White*/Stars:Christopher George, Fabian, Tom Nardini

The Oblong Box/*Prod:Gordon Hessler/Dir:Gordon Hessler/Scr:Lawrence Huntington*/Stars:Vincent Price, Christopher Lee, Rupert Davies

Chastity/*Prod:Sonny Bono/Dir:Alessio de Paola/ Scr:Sonny Bono*/Stars:Cher, Barbara London, Steve Whittaker

The Haunted House of Horror (US:Horror House)/*Prod:Tony Tenser/Dir:Michael Armstrong/ Scr:Michael Armstrong, Gerry Levy*/Stars:Frankie Avalon, Jill Haworth, Dennis Price

De Sade/*Prod:Samuel Z Arkoff, James H Nicholson/ Dir:Cy Endfield/Scr:Richard Matheson, Peter Berg*/ Stars:Keir Dullea, Senta Berger, Lilli Palmer

Hells Angels' 69/*Prod:Tom Stern/Dir:Lee Madden/ Scr:Don Tait*/Stars:Tom Stern, Jeremy Slate, Conny Van Dyke

1970

Scream and Scream Again/*Prod:Max J Rosenberg, Milton Subotsky/Dir:Gordon Hessler/ Scr:Christopher Wicking*/Stars:Vincent Price, Peter Cushing, Christopher Lee

The Dunwich Horror/*Prod:Roger Corman, Jack Bohrer/Dir:Daniel Haller/Scr:Curtis Hanson, Henry Rosenbaum, Ronald Silkosky*/Stars:Sandra Dee, Dean Stockwell, Ed Begley

Bloody Mama/*Prod:Roger Corman/Dir:Roger Corman/Scr:Robert Thom*/Stars:Shelley Winters, Pat Hingle, Don Stroud

A Bullet for Pretty Boy/*Prod:Larry Buchanan/ Dir:Larry Buchanan/Scr:Henry Rosenbaum*/ Stars:Fabian, Jocelyn Lane, Astrid Warner

Cry of the Banshee/*Prod:Samuel Z Arkoff/ Dir:Gordon Hessler/Scr:Tim Kelly, Christopher Wicking*/Stars:Vincent Price, Essy Persson, Hilary Dwyer

Up in the Cellar/*Prod:Samuel Z Arkoff, James H Nicholson/Dir:Theodore J Flicker/Scr:Theodore J Flicker*/Stars:Wes Stern, Joan Collins, Larry Hagman

The Vampire Lovers/*Prod:Harry Fine, Michael Style/Dir:Roy Ward Baker/Scr:Tudor Gates*/ Stars:Ingrid Pitt, George Cole, Peter Cushing

Angel Unchained/*Prod:Lee Madden/Dir:Lee Madden/Scr:Jeffrey Alladin Fiskin*/Stars:Don Stroud, Luke Askew, Larry Bishop

Wuthering Heights/*Prod:Samuel Z Arkoff, James H Nicholson/Dir:Robert Fuest/Scr:Patrick Tilley*/ Stars:Anna Calder-Marshall, Timothy Dalton, Harry Andrews

1971

The Hard Ride/*Prod:Charles Hanawalt/Dir:Burt Topper/Scr:Burt Topper*/Stars:Robert Fuller, Sherry Bain, Tony Russel

The Abominable Dr Phibes/*Prod:Ronald S Dunas, Louis M Heyward/Dir:Robert Fuest/Scr:James Whiton, William Goldstein*/Stars:Vincent Price,Joseph Cotten, Hugh Griffith

Chrome and Hot Leather/*Prod:Wes Bishop/ Dir:Lee Frost/Scr:Michael Allen Haynes, David Neibel, Don Tait*/Stars:William Smith, Tony Young, Michael Haynes

Murders in the Rue Morgue/*Prod:Louis M Heyward/Dir:Gordon Hessler/Scr:Christopher Wicking, Henry Slesar*/Stars:Jason Robards, Herbert Lom, Chrstine Kaufmann

Bunny O'Hare/*Prod:Norman T Herman, Gerd Oswald/Dir:Gerd Oswald/Scr:Stanley Z Cherry, Coslough Johnson*/Stars:Bette Davis, Ernest Borgnine, Jack Cassidy

Together/*Prod:Sean S Cunningham, Stephen Minasian/Dir:Sean S Cunningham/Scr:Sean S Cunningham*/Stars:Marilyn Chambers, Maureen Cousins, Jade Hagen

1972

Frogs/*Prod:George Edwards, Peter Thomas/ Dir:George McCowan/Scr:Robert Hutchinson, Robert Blees*/Stars:Ray Milland, Sam Elliott, Joan Van Ark

Boxcar Bertha/*Prod:Roger Corman/Dir:Martin Scorsese/Scr:Joyce H Corrington, John W Corrington*/ Stars:Barbara Hershey, David Carradine, Barry Primus

Dr Phibes Rises Again/*Prod:Louis M Heyward/ Dir:Robert Fuest/Scr:Robert Fuest, Robert Blees*/ Stars:Vincent Price, Robert Quarry, Peter Cushing

Slaughter/*Prod:Monroe Sachson/Dir:Jack Starrett/ Scr:Mark Hanna, Don Williams*/Stars:Jim Brown, Stella Stevens, Rip Torn

Blacula/*Prod:Joseph T Naar, Norman T Herman/ Dir:William Crain/Scr:Joan Torres, Raymond Koenig*/Stars:William Marshall, Vonetta McGee, Denis Nicholas

The Unholy Rollers/*Prod:Roger Corman/ Dir:Vernon Zimmerman/Scr:Howard R Cohen*/ Stars:Claudia Jennings, Louis Quinn, Betty Anne Rees

1973

Black Mama White Mama/*Prod:John Ashley, Eddie Romero/Dir:Eddie Romero/Scr:H R Christian*/ Stars:Pam Grier, Margaret Markov, Sid Haig

Black Caesar/*Prod:Larry Cohen, Benjamin Fisz, Kenneth Rive/Dir:Larry Cohen/Scr:Larry Cohen*/ Stars:Fred Williamson, Gloria Hendry, Art Lund

Sisters/*Prod:Edward R Pressman/Dir:Brian De Palma/Scr:Brian De Palma, Louisa Rose*/ Stars:Margot Kidder, Jennifer Salt, Charles Durning

Coffy/*Prod:Robert A Papazian/Dir:Jack Hill/ Scr:Jack Hill*/Stars:Pam Grier, Booker Bradshaw, Robert DoQui

Scream Blacula Scream/*Prod:Joseph T Naar/ Dir:Bob Kelljan/Scr:Joan Torres, Raymond Koenig, Maurice Jules*/Stars:William Marshall, Don Mitchell, Pam Grier

Dillinger/*Prod:Buzz Feitshans/Dir:John Milius/ Scr:John Milius*/Stars:Warren Oates, Ben Johnson, Michelle Phillips

Slaughter's Big Rip-Off/*Prod:Monroe Sachson/ Dir:Gordon Douglas/Scr:Charles Johnson*/Stars:Jim Brown, Ed McMahon, Don Stroud

Hell Up in Harlem/*Prod:Larry Cohen/Dir:Larry Cohen/Scr:Larry Cohen*/Stars:Fred Williamson, Julius Harris, Gloria Hendry

1974

Bamboo Gods and Iron Men/*Prod:Cirio H Santiago/Dir:Cesar Gallardo/Scr:Kenneth Metcalfe, Joseph Zucchero*/Stars:James Iglehart, Shirley Washington, Chiquito

The Bat People/*Prod:Lou Shaw/Dir:Jerry Jameson/Scr:Lou Shaw*/Stars:Stewart Moss, Marianne McAndrew, Michael Pataki

Sugar Hill/*Prod:Elliot Schick/Dir:Paul Maslansky/ Scr:Tim Kelly*/Stars:Marki Bey, Robert Quarry, Don Pedro Colley

Foxy Brown/*Prod:Buzz Feitshans/Dir:Jack Hill/ Scr:Jack Hill*/Stars:Pam Grier, Antonio Fargas, Peter Brown

Truck Turner/*Prod:Paul Heller, Fred Weintraub/ Dir:Jonathan Kaplan/Scr:Oscar Williams, Michael Allin*/Stars:Isaac Hayes, Yaphet Kotto, Alan Weeks

The Nine Lives of Fritz the Cat/*Prod:Steve Krantz/Dir:Robert Taylor/Scr:Fred Halliday, Eric Monte, Robert Taylor*/Stars:Skip Hinnant, Reva Rose, Bob Holt

Savage Sisters/*Prod:John Ashley, Eddie Romero/ Dir:Eddie Romero/Scr:Harry Corner, H Franco Moon*/ Stars:Gloria Hendry, Cheri Caffaro, Rosanna Ortiz

Act of Vengeance/*Prod:Buzz Feitshans/Dir:Bob Kelljan/Scr:Betty Conklin, H R Christian*/Stars:Jo Ann Harris, Peter Brown, Jennifer Lee

Abby/*Prod: William Girdler, Mike Henry, Gordon Cornell Layne, David Sheldon/Dir: William Girdler/ Scr:G Cornell Layne*/Stars:William Marshall, Terry Carter, Austin Stoker

1975

Sheba, Baby/*Prod:David Sheldon/Dir: William Girdler/Scr: William Girdler, David Sheldon*/ Stars:Pam Grier, Austin Stoker, D'Urville Martin

The Wild Party/*Prod:Ismail Merchant/Dir:James Ivory/Scr: Walter Marks*/Stars:James Coco, Raquel Welch, Perry King

The Land That Time Forgot/*Prod:John Dark, Max J Rosenberg, Milton Subotsky, Samuel Z Arkoff/ Dir:Kevin Connor/Scr:James Cawthorn, Michael Moorcock*/Stars:Doug McClure, John McEnery, Susan Penhaligon

Cornbread, Earl and Me/*Prod:Joseph Manduke/ Dir:Joseph Manduke/Scr:Leonard Lamensdorf*/ Stars:Moses Gunn, Rosalind Cash, Bernie Casey

Murph the Surf/*Prod:Chuck Courtney/Dir:Marvin Chomsky/Scr:E Arthur Kean*/Stars:Robert Conrad, Don Stroud, Donna Mills

Cooley High/*Prod:Steve Krantz/Dir:Michael Schultz/Scr:Eric Monte*/Stars:Glynn Turman, Lawrence Hilton-Jacobs, Garrett Morris

Hennessy/*Prod:Peter Snell/Dir:Don Sharp/Scr:John Gay*/Stars: Rod Steiger, Lee Remick, Richard Johnson

Return to Macon County/*Prod:Elliot Schick/ Dir:Richard Compton/Scr:Richard Compton*/ Stars:Nick Nolte, Don Johnson, Robin Mattson

Sixpack Annie/*Prod:John C Broderick/Dir:Fred G Thorne/Scr:Norman Winski, David Kidd, Will David*/ Stars:Lindsay Bloom, Jana Bellan, Joe Higgins

Friday Foster/*Prod:Arthur Marks/Dir:Arthur Marks/Scr:Orville Hampton*/Stars:Pam Grier, Yaphet Kott, Godfrey Cambridge

1976

The Food of the Gods/*Prod:Bert I Gordon/ Dir:Bert I Gordon/Scr:Bert I Gordon*/Stars:Marjoe Gortner, Pamela Franklin, Ralph Meeker

A Small Town in Texas/*Prod:Joe Solomon/ Dir:Jack Starrett/Scr: William Norton*/Stars:Timothy Bottoms, Susan George, Bo Hopkins

Squirm/*Prod:George Manasse/Dir:Jeff Lieberman/ Scr:Jeff Lieberman*/Stars:Don Scardino, Patricia Pearcy, R A Dow

At the Earth's Core/*Prod:John Dark, Max J Rosenberg, Milton Subotsky/Dir:Kevin Connor/ Scr:Milton Subotsky*/Stars:Doug McClure, Peter Cushing, Caroline Munro

Futureworld/*Prod:James T Aubrey, Paul N Lazarus III/Dir:Richard T Heffron/Scr:Mayo Simon, George Schenck*/Stars:Peter Fonda, Blythe Danner, Arthur Hill

JD's Revenge/*Prod:Arthur Marks/Dir:Arthur Marks/Scr:Jaison Starkes*/Stars:Glynn Turman, Louis Gossett Jr, Joan Pringle

A Matter of Time/*Prod:J Edmund Grainger, Jack H Skirball/Dir: Vincente Minnelli/Scr:John Gay*/ Stars:Liza Minnelli, Ingrid Bergman, Charles Boyer

The Town That Dreaded Sundown/*Prod:Charles B Pierce/Dir:Charles B Pierce/Scr:Earl E Smith*/ Stars:Ben Johnson, Andrew Prine, Dawn Wells

1977

Tentacles/*Prod:Enzo Doria/Dir:Ovidio G Assonitis/ Scr:Jerome Max, Tito Carpi, Steve Carabatsos*/ Stars:John Huston, Shelley Winters, Bo Hopkins

The People That Time Forgot/*Prod:John Dark, Max Rosenberg/Dir:Kevin Connor/Scr:Patrick Tilley*/ Stars:Patrick Wayne, Doug McClure, Sarah Douglas

The Island of Dr Moreau/*Prod:Skip Steloff, John Temple-Smith/Dir:Don Taylor/Scr:Al Ramrus, Richard Alan Simmons*/Stars:Burt Lancaster, Michael York, Nigel Davenport

Rolling Thunder/*Prod:Lawrence Gordon, Norman T Herman/Dir:John Flynn/Scr:Pal Scrader, Heywood Gould*/Stars:William Devane, Tommy Lee Jones, Linda Haynes

The Incredible Melting Man/*Prod:Samuel W Gelfman/Dir: William Sachs/Scr: William Sachs*/ Stars:Alex Rebar, Burr DeBening, Myron Healey

1978

Jennifer/*Prod:Steve Krantz/Dir:Bruce Mack/ Scr:Kay Cousins Johnson*/Stars:Lisa Pelikan, Bert Convy, Nina Foch

High-Ballin'/*Prod:Joe Slan/Dir:Peter Carter/ Scr:Paul F Edwards*/Stars:Peter Fonda, Jerry Reed, Helen Shaver

Our Winning Season/*Prod:Joe Roth/Dir:Joseph Ruben/Scr:Nick Niciphor*/Stars:Scot Jacoby, Deborah Benson, Dennis Quaid

Matilda/*Prod:Albert S Ruddy/Dir:Daniel Mann/ Scr:Timothy Galfas, Albert S Ruddy*/Stars:Elliott Gould, Clive Revill, Harry Guardino

Force 10 from Navarone/*Prod:Oliver A Unger/ Dir:Guy Hamilton/Scr:Robin Chapman*/Stars:Robert Shaw, Harrison Ford, Barbara Bach

1979

The Evictors/*Prod:Charles B Pierce/Dir:Charles B Pierce/Scr:Charles B Pierce, Garry Rusoff, Paul Fisk*/ Stars:Vic Morrow, Michael Parks, Jessica Harper

The Amityville Horror/*Prod:Elliot Geisinger, Ronald Saland/Dir:Stuart Rosenberg/Scr:Sandor Stern*/Stars:James Brolin, Margot Kidder, Rod Steiger

Love at First Bite/*Prod:Joel Freeman, Melvin Simon/ Dir:Stan Dragoti/Scr:Robert Kaufman*/Stars:George Hamilton, Susan Saint James, Richard Benjamin

Meteor/*Prod:Arnold Orgolini, Theodore Parvin, Run Run Shaw/Dir:Ronald Neame/Scr:Stanley Mann, Edmund H North*/Stars:Sean Connery, Natalie Wood, Karl Malden

CHOMPS/*Prod:Joseph Barbera/Dir:Don Chaffey/ Scr:Dick Robbins, Duane Poole, Joseph Barbera*/ Stars:Wesley Eure, Valerie Bertinelli, Conrad Bain

1980

Nothing Personal/*Prod:David M Perlmutter/ Dir:George Bloomfield/Scr:Robert Kaufman*/ Stars:Donald Sutherland, Suzanne Somers, Lawrence Dane

Gorp/*Prod:Louis S Arkoff, Jeffrey Konvitz/ Dir:Joseph Ruben/Scr:Jeffrey Konvitz*/Stars:Michael Lembeck, Dennis Quaid, Philip Casnoff

How to Beat the High Co$t of Living/ *Prod:Robert Kaufman, Jerome M Zeitman/ Dir:Robert Scheerer/Scr:Robert Kaufman*/Stars Susan Saint James, Jane Curtin, Jessica Lange

Samuel Z Arkoff 1918-2001

BIBLIOGRAPHY

Arkoff, Sam & Trubo, Richard
Flying Through Hollywood by the Seat of my Pants
Birch Lane, 1992

Anonymous
'Arkoff Made Art of B-Movies'
Daily Variety, September 2001

Corman, Roger (with Jim Jerome)
How I Made a Hundred Movies in Hollywood and Never Lost a Dime
Da Capo Press, 1990

Court, Hazel
Hazel Court Horror Queen: An Autobiography
Tomahawk Press, 2008

Dixon, Wheeler Winston
'Fear and Self-Loathing: Horror and Homophobia in the Films of Herman Cohen'
Senses of Cinema, 2009

Graham, Aaron W
'Little Shop of Genres: An Interview with Charles B Griffith'
Senses of Cinema, 2005

Grier, Pam (with Andrea Cagan)
Foxy,: My Life in Three Acts
Springboard Press, 2010

Hamilton, John
Beasts in the Cellar: The Exploitation Film Career of Tony Tenser
FAB Press, 2005

Humphreys, Justin
'The Kind of Fiend That Wins - the Making of The Abominable Dr Phibes'
Little Shoppe of Horrors #29

Irvin, Sam
'Interview with Robert Fuest'
Bizarre, 1974

McGee, Mark Thomas
Fast and Furious: The Story of American International Pictures
McFarland & Company, 1984
-Faster and Furiouser: The Revised and Fattened Fable of American International Pictures
McFarland & Company, 1995

Meikle, Denis
Merchant of Menace: The Life and Films of Vincent Price (Expanded Edition)
Hemlock Books, 2015

Migliore, Andrew & Strysik, John
The Lurker in the Lobby: A Guide to the Cinema of HP Lovecraft
Night Shade Books, 2006

Nason, Richard W
'HypnoVision Bows'
The New York Times, April 1959

Pirie, David
A Heritage of Horror: The English Gothic Cinema 1946-1972
Fletcher & Son, Ltd, 1973

Rigby, Jonathan
English Gothic: A Century of Horror Cinema
Reynolds & Hearn, 2000

Smith, Gary A
American International Pictures: The Golden Years
Bear Manor Media, 2013

imdb.com

wikipedia.com

Other **HemlockFilm** *titles:*

MIND WARP:
The Fantastic True Story of Roger Corman's New World Pictures
Christopher T Koetting
HITCHCOCK'S BLONDE
John Hamilton
THE HAMMER VAMPIRE*
Bruce G Hallenbeck
HAMMER FANTASY & SCI-FI*
Bruce G Hallenbeck
FRIGHT FILMS: The World's Scariest-Ever Movies
David Tappenden
RETRO SCREAMS: Terror in the New Millennium
Christopher T Koetting
X-CERT: The British Independent Horror Film 1951-1970*
John Hamilton
URBAN TERRORS: New British Horror Cinema 1997-2008
M J Simpson
THE HAMMER FRANKENSTEIN*
Bruce G Hallenbeck
EMPIRE OF THE 'B's:
The Mad Movie World of Charles Band's Empire Pictures*
Dave Jay, Torsten Dewi, Nathan Shumate
THE AMICUS ANTHOLOGY*
Bruce G Hallenbeck
X-CERT2: The British Independent Horror Film 1971-1983*
John Hamilton
MERCHANT OF MENACE: The Life and Films of Vincent Price*
Denis Meikle
***also in hardcover**

Available from all good booksellers or direct from Hemlock Books (*www.hemlockbooks.co.uk*)